NEW YORK INSTITUTE OF FINANCE

STOCKS
BONDS
OPTIONS
FUTURES

SECOND EDITION

STUART R. VEALE

NEW YORK INSTITUTE OF FINANCE

NEW YORK • TORONTO • SYDNEY • TOKYO • SINGAPORE

NEW YORK INSTITUTE OF FINANCE
NYIF and NEW YORK INSTITUTE OF FINANCE are trademarks of
Executive Tax Reports, Inc., used under license by Penguin Putnam Inc.

This publication is designed to provide accurate and authoritative information in regard
to the subject matter covered. It is sold with the understanding that the publisher is not
engaged in rendering legal, accounting, or other professional service. If legal advice or
other expert assistance is required, the services of a competent professional person
should be sought.
—*From the Declaration of Principles jointly adopted by a Committee of the American
Bar Association and a Committee of Publishers and Associations*

Please be aware that the views and opinions expressed are solely those of the author
and do not necessarily reflect those of Prudential Securities. The information in the
book can and will differ from the research provided by our own analysts. No
representation is made that the information presented is accurate or complete.

Library of Congress Cataloging-in-Publication Data

Stocks, bonds, options, futures / [edited by Stuart R. Veale.—2nd ed.]
p.   cm.
Includes index.
ISBN 0-7352-0175-7
1. Investments—United States.   2. Securities—United States.   3. Futures—United
States.   4. Options (Finance)—United States.   5. Commodity exchanges—United
States.   6. Brokers—United States.   I. Veale, Stuart R.   II. New York Institute
of Finance.

HG4921.S7945   2000
332.67'8—dc21   00-021678

Printed in the United States of America

10   9   8   7   6   5   4

DEDICATION

In my 20 years in the investment services industry, one of the most important things I have learned is that you are only as good as the people with whom you work. I am fortunate to have been blessed to work with some of the best. Therefore, it is my pleasure to dedicate this book to:

Charles Potters
Raymond Murphy
Celia Haggerty
Jaime Desmond

Many Thanks!!!

CONTENTS

CHAPTER 20

MUTUAL FUNDS. 285

CHAPTER 21

GLOBAL INVESTING 299

PREFACE

The Investment Services Industry

Few industries have undergone as much change over the last decade as the investment services segment of the financial services industry. Many of the structural and pricing paradigm changes that began in the 1970s and 80s accelerated in the 90s. Most analysts expect the pace of change to accelerate in the first decade of the new millennium.

The segment of the financial services industry that has experienced the greatest amount of change is the full-service brokerage firm. In the 1980s, many full-service firms were trying to transform themselves into "financial supermarkets" that offered one-stop shopping for financial services to both retail and institution clients. These large firms were typically composed of eight major divisions:

- Investment banking—The purpose of the investment banking division is to advise governments, agencies, corporations, and other issuers of securities concerning when and how to raise the capital they need to grow and operate. The investment banking division also advises the firm's clients on mergers, acquisitions, divestitures, restructurings, privatizations, and proxy battles. The result of this work is often new stock or bond offerings that the institutional and retail sales divisions can sell. The investment banking division creates the "product" that feeds the rest of the company.

For its work, this division received advisory fees based on hours dedicated to working with the client and/or a fee tied to the volume of securities that were underwritten. The personnel that work in this division are the brightest graduates of the country's best business schools. They are some of the best-paid professionals in the country with senior investment banking professionals frequently getting paid seven-figure salaries.

- Research—The research division is composed of professionals who analyze the global economy, the political environment, the FX market, the fixed-income market, and the equity market and then advise:
  - The firm's investment banking clients on potential business opportunities.
  - The firm's individual and institutional buy-side clients on which strategies, tactics, and securities are appropriate given their respective investment objectives.
- Capital markets—This division executes the listed securities transactions for the firm's buy-side clients, makes a market in the over-the-counter securities, and invests the firm's capital for its own account.
- Money management—This division is in the business of managing money—either in the form of individual accounts or mutual funds. In addition to having a dedicated sales force, the firm's institutional and retail sales forces often either sell the firm's money management services or provide leads to the division's dedicated sales force.
- Institutional sales—This division advises institutional investors, such as banks, insurance companies, and large pension plans. This advice includes what strategies, tactics, products, and securities will best help the investor achieve his or her objectives.

- Retail sales—This division advises individual investors on how to achieve personal financial goals, sells the firm's various products, and services individual investors.

- Insurance division—This division produces and markets through a dedicated sales force, as well as the firm's retail and institutional sales force, a variety of insurance products, including life insurance and annuities.

- Operations—This division processes all of the paperwork behind the transactions, maintains the client records, and prepares and distributes client statements and trade confirmations to the firm's personnel and clients. Some firms, in addition to handling their own back office, also provide back office services to other firms. By renting out their back offices, they can offset some of their own costs.

In trying to be all things to all people, these firms truly become financial supermarkets. While the scope of their operations expand, they create some problems—namely, a number of conflicts of interest. For example:

- Compensating financial advisors on commission—Retail and institutional financial advisors (sales representatives) historically have been paid on a "commission" basis. They received a percentage (35 to 55 percent) of the commission that the client paid every time the client bought or sold a security. Often, during temporary market downturns, investors tend to panic and want to sell everything in their portfolios. Sometimes, the best advice clients can receive is to not sell, but the financial advisor does not get paid for providing that advice. This creates a conflict of interest for the financial advisor. While the vast majority of financial advisors are honorable and act in the best interest of their clients, the conflict of interest creates doubt.

- Research rankings and investment banking clients—The research department is charged with providing unbiased advice to its buy-side clients. This means that they should recommend selling stocks of companies they believe will underperform in the future. However, this can lead to a conflict with the investment banking department if one of the companies on which they want to put a sell recommendation happens to be a client of the investment banking division.

- Preferences for inhouse money management firms—The clients of financial advisors rely on them to advise them on what is the best mutual fund or money manager to manage their assets. However, the firms that employ the financial advisors have a natural preference for their employees to gather assets for the inhouse funds instead of outside funds. In the past, some firms even used to pay their financial advisors a higher percentage of the commission if they sold an inhouse fund.

Partly as a result of deregulation of brokerage commissions and partly because clients recognized and worried about these conflicts of interest, the financial supermarket concept was not so successful as the firm's managers and shareholders envisioned.

Discount Brokers

Many clients decided that, given the high transaction costs and the inherent conflicts of interest in the financial supermarket pricing paradigm, they would prefer to make their own decisions with regard to security selection and market timing. As a result, discount brokerage firms boomed in the late 1980s and 90s. These firms include Charles Schwab and Co. Inc., and Olde Discount.

As the 1990s progressed, the discount firms tried to find their own niche. Some firms started offering research that they either generated internally or purchased from an outside firm and started offering limited levels of advice. Other firms went the other way and continued to offer minimal services at the lowest price available.

Web-based Brokers

The incredible popularity of the Internet and the World Wide Web created an even more efficient way for investors to buy and sell securities. Trades entered over the Internet required no human intervention at all, so the transactions cost were minimal. A large number of securities dealers who deal almost exclusively over the Web has resulted. The leading firms in this area are Datek, E-Trade, and DLJ Direct.

Just as was the case with the discount firms, each Web firm has tried to distinguish itself from its competitors either by price or by providing online research and analytics. Some of the Web-based brokers that compete on price are offering transactions at "no-cost to the investor." The firm is compensated for executing the investors' transactions by selling the names of the investors to third parties and by selling "advertising space" on its Web site.

In fact, the transaction costs associated with buying and selling securities on the Web were so low that this created a new type of investor called the "day trader." The day trader acts as a dealer and tries to buy and sell securities over a very short time horizon (a few minutes to a few hours). As of this writing, day trading—and the firms that exist primarily to support day traders— have become quite controversial. The Securities and Exchange Commission has expressed its concern that day traders are treating the securities market as a casino.

The Future of the Industry

The pricing pressure from the discounters and Web-based firms, as well as the growing aversion of clients to the old pricing model, has caused most full-service firms to adopt a new paradigm. In this new model, many of the conflicts are eliminated.

Those firms that successfully make this transfer are the firms that will survive and thrive in the next millennium.

ACKNOWLEDGMENTS

In the last 10 years in my capacity as a capital markets instructor, I have had the privilege of working with the professionals at Prudential Securities, PaineWebber, Goldman Sachs, Salomon Smith Barney, J.P. Morgan, American Express Private Bank, Morgan Stanley, The Bank of Boston, National Westminster Bank, Citicorp, ING Barings, Lehman Brothers, First Boston, among many others. . . . The greatest benefit of being a teacher is the privilege of learning from your students. I cannot remember a presentation I gave where a question from, or a discussion with, a member of the audience did not contribute to my own understanding of the topic being presented. Therefore, I feel obligated to acknowledge the contribution of the literally thousands of financial services professionals who have attended my presentations over the last decade for their contribution to my education.

With regard to this edition, the author is especially indebted to Thomas D'Arrigo who performed a major rewrite on the chapters on Operations and Trading. I would also like to thank Celia Haggerty and Jaime Desmond for proofing the rough drafts of this text. Finally, I would like to thank my editor Gloria Fuzia for her patience and expertise.

THE SECURITIES INDUSTRY

The recent banking reform legislation removed the last impediments that prevented securities firms from entering the banking business and banks from entering the securities business. This change has unleashed a torrent of new competition from outside the securities industry to compete with the traditional securities firms. Who would have guessed 10 years ago that Travelers, Citicorp, Salomon Brothers, and Smith Barney would all merge into one financial super market?

This increase in competition has caused almost every department within the major full-service securities firms to change the way it does business. The best way to start our review of the securities industry is with a brief overview of the various departments, their functions, and how their business has changed over the last decade.

Investment Banking Department

The purpose of the investment banking department is to advise governments and corporations on various financing and strategic issues. For example:

1. A rapidly growing privately owned company wants to raise some equity capital in order to expand its operations. The company would

hire an investment bank in order to help it make several decisions regarding how to proceed. Among the issues to be considered are:

- Should it sell its stock to a limited number of accredited investors (referred to as a private placement) or should it sell its stock to the public at large (referred to as a public offering)?
- If the stock is to be sold publicly, should it be sold in large blocks to a few investors or in small blocks to many small investors?
- In which country(s) should the stock be sold?
- At what price should the stock be sold?

The investment bank would then help the firm prepare the necessary documentation for either the private or public offering. The investment bank would also assist with the actual sale of the stocks or bonds.

2. A municipality wants to build a new sewer line and would hire an investment bank to help it decide whether:

- To borrow the money by selling bonds to a limited number of accredited investors or sell the bonds to the public at large.
- To issue fixed rate or floating rate debt.
- To issue short- or long-term debt.

3. A large public company changes its strategy and wants to sell off several of its operating divisions that no longer fit within the company's strategy. The company would retain an investment bank in order to help it value the divisions it wants to sell off and find potential buyers to sell off the unwanted divisions.

Naturally, before a corporation's chief executive officer is going to entrust an investment bank with something as important as the initial public offering of its stock or advice on a potential merger or acquisition, he or she is going to have to be convinced as to the professionalism and expertise of the bankers who will be working on the project. Therefore, investment banks try to staff themselves with the most highly trained professional people they can find. Generally, an MBA degree and 5-plus years of business experience are a prerequisite for even being considered. In addition, most investment banks have multi-year internship programs for their new hires.

The major change in the investment banking business is "globalization." As the economy has become global, companies have also become global. Today, a large U.S. multinational is just as likely to issue bonds denominated in pounds as it is in dollars and is just as likely to make an acquisition in Seoul, Korea, as in Sioux Falls, Iowa. Therefore bankers have to have a global perspective and expertise.

Venture Capital/Private Equity

The venture capital division invests in small private companies in exchange for a partial ownership interest in those companies. Typically, these companies are young, small, and sometimes have little more than "an idea." Every venture capital investor hopes to invest in a small company that grows very rapidly and can eventually be sold to a larger company—or be taken public. Of course, only a small percentage of the companies that are started become huge successes, so venture capital investments tend to be quite risky. Of course, if the money is invested in the right companies, the returns can also be quite spectacular.

The money this division invests in these small companies usually includes the firm's own capital, as well as money it raises from investors. These investments are usually structured as partnerships and are offered only to investors with substantial net worth. The big change in venture capital over the last 10 years is the increase in the availability of money to fund small companies. One of the big advantages of business in the U.S. is that venture capital is readily available.

Sales Divisions

The sales department is the department that markets the firm's products and services to its clientele. In most firms this department is organized into three separate divisions: private client, institutional, and mini-institutional.

PRIVATE CLIENT DIVISION

The private client division advises individuals on how to invest their money in order to achieve their personal financial objectives, such as affording college education for their children and providing a comfortable retirement for themselves. The salespeople who work for this division used to be called stockbrokers but are now referred to as investment advisors, financial advisors, or financial planners. The background of private client salespeople tends to be quite varied; however, the vast majority are college graduates. Before being allowed to sell individual securities to the public, all salespeople must pass a licensing exam (referred to as the Series-7 examination).

Of all the divisions, it is the private client division that has been subjected to the greatest amount of new competition and structural change. The largest structural change has been the unbundling of the five traditional services that the private client division provides to its clients. These services include providing market information, executing securities transactions, providing research, providing investment advice, and providing access to proprietary products.

- Market information—Brokers have traditionally provided their clients with price quotes on securities, financial data on potential investments, and basic market data. Today this data is available for free on the Internet and via any of a number of television programs, including Financial News Network, MSNBC, and CNN, as well as many other programs.

- Transaction executions—Brokers have traditionally acted as the middlemen between their clients and the markets and have executed their client's buy and sell orders for securities. Today, while orders still have to be executed through a brokerage firm, investors can access the firm's transaction capabilities directly via the Internet without having the broker act as middleman.

- Research—Brokers have traditionally provided their clients with access to proprietary fixed income and equity research. Today numerous Web sites allow investors to gather information on potential investment opportunities and exchange information with other investors. While firms still generate research, today they post the research on the Internet, send clients e-mail updates when a new report is published on a stock they own, and grant their best clients access to the very models that the analysts use.

- Investment advice—Brokers have traditionally advised their clients on which investment alternatives were appropriate for them, offered their advise regarding which securities offered the best trade-off between risk and reward, and provided guidance as to which strategies have the highest probability of allowing them to achieve their objectives. This has not, and probably will not, change anytime soon. However, today brokers can use a variety of technology-based tools to assist them in designing portfolios to meet specific client objectives.

- Product access—Brokers have traditionally offered their clients access to proprietary products, such as specialized unit investment trusts and initial public offerings underwritten by their firm's investment banking division. This also will not change anytime soon as securities firms compete to offer their clients better investment products.

The pricing model that most firms used when pricing the services they offered to individuals was a "commission-based model."

Under this pricing model, the firm would charge its clients a commission that was far greater than the actual transaction costs—whenever it executed a transaction for its clients. The "excess" commission was used to offset the costs associated with providing the other "bundled" services it provided.

In the 1980s, discount brokerage firms started unbundling these services by offering bare bones securities transactions without any advice, research, or proprietary products. In the 1990s, Web-based brokerage firms were able to offer even lower transaction costs, because the Internet allowed them to lower the cost of providing transactions. Some firms have even gone so far as to pay clients for doing their trades with them. The advent of discounters and Internet firms has forced full-service firms to unbundle their services.

Today, full-service, discount, and Web-based brokers are all trying to position themselves along a continuum that goes from providing only bare bones transaction execution at the low end to providing transactions and some kind of research support electronically in the middle, to fully customized high-level financial planning and investment services at the high end. Most traditional firms are allowing their clients to choose which services they want and offer a variety of ways to pay for them. For example:

- Many full-service firms offer their clients discounted commissions if they want only access to Web-based trading and research and don't feel they need individualized services of an investment advisor.

- Many firms now offer their clients the opportunity to pay for personalized service for a fee that is set as a percentage of the assets they have with the firm, instead of the number of transactions they do.

- Some firms have even experimented with charging an hourly fee for advice.

The ongoing restructuring of the private client business will undoubtedly continue over the next decade.

INSTITUTIONAL CLIENT DIVISION

The institutional client division advises institutions, such as insurance companies, large banks, and large pension plans. The dividing line that defines an account as a "large institution" is typically those institutions with more than $5 billion in assets to invest. Because they deal with the largest clients, the salespeople who cover institutions are typically the most highly trained professionals within the sales force. Most firms require their institutional salespeople to have MBA degrees as well as very strong analytical and communication skills.

MINI-INSTITUTIONAL DIVISION

The high net worth/mini-institutional division serves the needs of wealthy families, smaller banks, pension plans, and insurance companies. Most firms define mini-institutions as investors with accounts of $25 million to $5 billion.

Trading Department

Once the sales department generates buy and sell orders from its clients, those orders are sent to the trading department. The trading department executes the orders by actually buying and selling the securities either on the floor of an exchange, executing the transaction itself, or with another firm. The trading operations have changed as a result of the creation of a number of electronic trading networks (ETNs). The electronic trading networks are services that bypass brokers and allow buyers and sellers to match orders with each other without using a broker. As such they are direct competitors to the traders.

Research Department

The research department has two functions. The one people are more familiar with is finding attractive investment opportunities. In pursuit of this goal, the research analysts are divided into several categories:

- Economists—Most major firms employ a number of economists who monitor the economy on a global basis. Specifically, some of their most important tasks are to forecast the level of economic activity in different regions of the world, the actions of the Federal Reserve Bank, commodity prices, unemployment rates, wage levels, and the dozens of other factors that affect the prices of securities.

- Equity market strategists—Most major firms employ a key individual who is the firm's chief market strategist. This individual is responsible for making the "macro" calls with regard to the market. These include whether the market as a whole will rise or fall and which sectors of the market will be the best performers.

- Industry analysts—These analysts perform the micro analysis of the companies in a specific industry in order to determine how the industry as a whole will perform and which companies will be the best performers within the industry.

- Fixed income market analysts—These analyze the fixed income market in order to determine whether the fixed income market as a whole will be a superior or inferior performer as well as which fixed income market sectors will be the best performers.

- Credit analysts—These analysts review company financial statements and try to determine whether the credit quality of specific bond issues will improve or deteriorate.

The second, and less obvious, role that research analysts play is to work closely with the investment banking department to suggest possible merger candidates and acquisition candidates for the firm's investment banking clients. This causes a possible conflict of interest because it is hard for analysts to be objective regarding the attractiveness of a company's stock as an investment when the company is a client of the investment banking division.

Technology Department

Few industries are as dependent upon technology as the securities industry. If a security company's systems are down, business comes to a standstill. Each minute of down time can cost a securities firm millions of dollars, so keeping the systems running is essential. A typical trading floor has more computer terminals than the NASA command center. The major types of software applications are:

- Data feeds—Securities firms receive continuous prices on all securities transactions executed on all the major stock, futures, and options exchanges around the world. Also, there are numerous trade matching services that provide continuous bids and offers on securities that must be available to the traders so they can find out where they can buy at the lowest price and sell at the highest price possible for their clients.

- News wires—Securities firms run on information. Each news story, press release, and numbers release can affect the prices of numerous securities. Even a delay of a few seconds can be very expensive, so most firms receive several news feeds from different news services. In addition to the text news wires, many firms also receive numerous video news feeds that place tremendous strains on the firm's communication bandwidth.

- Market analytics—Securities firms rely on a variety of both standardized and proprietary tools to analyze the markets, price securities, and to price derivatives. Some of these analytic tools are found on popular subscription services such as Bloomberg™

and Telerate™, whose tools the various firms develop inhouse and are proprietary.

- Customer data—Securities firms now have to provide clients with access to their accounts 24 hours a day, 7 days a week. The days when clients were happy receiving a monthly or quarterly account statement are over. The markets have simply become more volatile.

As the securities business becomes more competitive, the pace of technological innovation is only going to accelerate. Most firms consider their key technology people to be just as valuable as their key investment bankers, salespeople, and traders.

Operations Department

The old adage is that "the job is not over until the paperwork is done." This is certainty true of securities transactions. Most of the securities firms that fail do not fail because they have trouble attracting enough clients; instead, they fail because the "back office" can't keep up with the business they do.

Currently the industry is undergoing a very major change. Just a few years ago securities firms had five business days to "settle" stock transactions (exchange money for stock certificates). This five-day period, referred to as T+5 (or trade plus five) meant that the firm had five days from the day it bought or sold stock for a customer to get the money or stock certificates from the client, and deliver it to the broker for the client on the other side of the trade. Recently that time has been shortened to three days (T+3) and it will soon be shortened again to just one day (T+1).

This means that all of the securities firms have to change their operations from batch processing to processing in real time. This is a far more complex task than even the Y2K project that the firms completed.

Money Management Department

One of the most important and rapidly growing departments of most securities firms is the money management arm. This arm of the firm offers professional money management services to the firm's clients. It is this division of the firm that runs the firm's mutual funds and manages larger portfolios. At many firms, one of the primary objectives of the salespeople (both private client and institutional) is to gather assets for the money management departments.

Wealth Preservation/Insurance Division

This division used to be called the estate planning division. However, the term "estate planning" reminded clients that they would die some day, so the term was changed to "wealth preservation." The goals are still the same: to protect the investors' families and to minimize the estate taxes.

Retirement Planning Department

This department designs and administers retirement plans for the firm's individual and business clients. Most full-service securities firms offer their clients traditional and the new Roth Individual Retirement Accounts, small business retirement plans, 401(k) savings plans, plans for the employees of nonprofit organizations (403[b] plans), as well as plan services for large union and employer plans.

Trust Company/Bank

Most firms have trust companies as subsidiaries that hold assets for retirement accounts and offer trust services to their clients. Many wealthy families use trust companies to reduce their estate taxes and to

insure that their assets are professionally managed for the benefit of
their families both while they are alive and after their deaths.

Derivatives Department

Derivatives are specialized instruments that are used to solve the specific problems of individuals, governments, and corporations. Some of
the typical client problems that derivatives can address include:

- A U.S. company knows that in seven months it will be receiving a
  payment of £1,000,000 from a British customer. The company is
  concerned that the exchange rate between the pound and dollar
  will change and that in seven months the pounds will buy fewer
  dollars. The company asks a securities firm to create a forward
  contract to protect it from a decline in the value of the pound.
  Forward contracts are discussed in more detail in Chapter 14.

- Two years ago a city borrowed $100,000,000 for five years from its
  bank at a rate of prime+1%. The city originally borrowed at a floating rate because it expected interest rates to decline. However,
  today the city manager becomes worried that interest rates, and
  thus the city's interest expense, will rise. To prevent this, the city
  asks a securities firm to design an interest rate swap that will allow
  it to convert its floating rate liability to a fixed rate liability. Interest
  rate swaps are discussed in more detail in Chapter 16.

- An individual investor buys 10,000 shares of a stock when it is selling for $2 per share. The stock subsequently rises to $40 per share
  and the client wants to protect the gain without selling the stock and
  without spending any money. To solve this problem, the derivatives
  department designs an "option collar," which consists of selling a call
  option on the position and using the proceeds to buy a put option.
  Call and put options are discussed in detail in Chapter 17.

These are just a few of the wide variety of problems that the
derivatives department is called on to address. In the past, derivatives

were listed on exchanges and were homogeneous. Today, many derivatives are custom designed by securities firms to solve the specific problems of specific customers. The best analogy is that derivative departments are creating custom-made suits instead of making their clients buy off the rack.

Because derivatives can be quite complex mathematically, the derivatives departments often employ individuals with advanced degrees in mathematics.

Compliance Department

The compliance department is responsible for making sure that the firm complies with the vast number of regulations imposed on securities firms by the Securities and Exchange Commission, State Securities Laws, the Rules and Regulations of the New York Stock Exchange, the National Association of Securities Dealers, the Chicago Board of Trade, the Commodities and Futures Trading Commission, the American Stock Exchange, and other exchanges on which the company does business.

Recent Industry Performance

Despite the challenges the securities industry has faced over the last decade, overall the industry has done very well. The primary reasons for this have been the demographic changes, strong economy, and political stability that the U.S. has enjoyed over the last decade.

THE DEMOGRAPHICS

The demographic trends could not be better as far as the securities industry is concerned. As the baby boomers enter middle age, they have reached a point where they have reached their maximum earnings potential. Simultaneously, their mandatory expenses have declined so they can both spend more and save more. Further, as the baby boomers reach middle age, their interest in planning for retirement becomes more pronounced—especially given the uncertainty surrounding the survivability of the Social Security and Medicare programs.

ECONOMY

On the economic front, the economy has been strong and has been strengthened by a number of confluent factors:

1. The barriers to international trade have been declining. The North American Free Trade Agreement as well as the decline of trade barriers in Europe and Asia has resulted in a boom in global trade. All parties benefit from global trade.

2. Due to the gridlock in Washington, as well as the decline in defense spending, the U.S. has moved from a period of budget deficits to budget surpluses.

3. Energy prices and commodity prices have remained low.

4. The massive application of technology to solving both manufacturing as well as administrative problems has resulted in dramatic increases in productivity—allowing wages to rise without inflation.

While all of the above factors will continue to fluctuate, everything on the horizon suggests that the next decade will be an excellent one for the securities industry.

COMMON STOCK

When most people think of investing, they think of owning "common stock." In fact, owning common stock has become incredibly popular over the last decade. The increase in popularity of common stock is due partly to:

- The changing demographics in the U.S. In the year 2000, the members of the baby boom generation are both in their prime earning years and thinking ahead to retirement. Therefore, they have both the need and the resources to invest in common stocks.

- The booming economy. The 1990s was one of the best decades economically in the history of the U.S. Not only was the economy expanding, but at the same time, interest rates were declining. This was a very unusual and highly fortuitous combination.

- As a result of the economic expansion, stocks have performed extraordinarily well over the last 10 years. Their superior performance has naturally drawn a lot of investor interest. Many people have heard of at least one common stock success story, such as the price of Dell's common stock rising from $1 to $55 from just July 1995 to February 1999.

Most investors fantasize about finding the next "Dell Computer" stock. However, before examining how investors try to find the next big winner, let's first discuss what common stock is and what it represents.

Each share of common stock usually represents a partial, proportional, ownership interest in a company. If a company has only one share of common stock and an investor owns it, the investor owns the entire company and is entitled to 100 percent of the company's profits. If a company has one million shares of common stock, and an investor owns one of them, the investor owns 1/1,000,000th of the company. As an owner of 1/1,000,000th of the company, the investor has an interest in 1/1,000,000th of the company's profits.

How Much of the Company Do I Own?

Each share of stock normally represents a proportional ownership interest in the company. Thus, the number of shares of the company's stock that exist determines the percentage ownership conveyed by owning a single share of stock. However, determining the number of shares that exists is complicated by several factors.

Creating a company requires the filing of a legal document called the "Articles of Incorporation" with the Secretary of State of a particular state. This process of filing these articles "incorporates" the company. Incorporating means that the company is created as an entity from a legal perspective. The choice of in which state to file the articles is important because the governance of the company will be subject to the laws of the state in which it is incorporated. Some states have bodies of law that are more favorable to corporations' shareholders and managers than others.

Today, many companies elect to incorporate in Delaware or Nevada, regardless of where they choose to base their headquarters and/or in which states they choose to operate, because these states have very favorable corporate rules.

One of the parts of any company's articles of incorporation is a paragraph that specifies the maximum number of shares that a company can create. This is referred to as the number of shares that are "authorized." If the creators of the company are planning on keeping the number of owners limited to one (or a few), then the company might authorize the creation of only 100 shares. If the company is hoping to have thousands of shareholders, it may authorize the creation of 100 million shares. Companies try not to authorize more shares than they expect to need because many states impose taxes on the number of shares a company has authorized. A company can change the number of shares it is authorized to issue at any time by amending its articles of incorporation. Changing the number of authorized shares has no direct affect on share price, unless the shareholders believe that the increase in authorized shares is a prelude to an immediate offering of shares that will dilute the interest of existing shareholders.

Once a company exists and has established its maximum number of authorized shares, the company can issue shares. It can issue shares by gifting them to the company's existing owners, managers, and employees, and/or it can sell them to investors (discussed in Chapter 4). If a company has two million shares authorized, gifts 200,000 to existing owners and employees, and sells 800,000 shares to investors, then the company will have issued one million of its two million authorized shares. Since there are presently only one million shares in existence, each share effectively represents a one millionth partial ownership interest in the company. Typically, the number of shares that have been authorized and remain outstanding determines the percentage of ownership conveyed by the ownership of a share.

There are three actions a company can take that will affect the proportional ownership interest represented by an issued share. For example:

- The company can issue additional shares. Assuming the company has not issued all of the shares it is authorized to issue, the company can simply issue additional shares—either to employees or the public. This will dilute the ownership interest represented by each of the shares. For example, if the company were to issue another 500,000 shares, then the ownership interest represented by each share would be reduced to 1/1,500,000th of the company. Because the issuance of additional shares reduces the ownership interest of the existing shares, the articles of incorporation of most companies requires the existing shareholders to approve the issuance of additional shares—prior to their issuance.

- The company can also "buy back" its own shares after it has issued them. For example, the company can buy back shares from retiring employees in order to provide the employees with retirement funds. Likewise, the company could simply think that its stock is undervalued and buy its own stock back in the open market as an investment. If a company repurchases its own stock and holds it as an asset, it is referred to as "Treasury Stock." Since the shareholders own the company and the company owns the Treasury Stock, the remaining shareholders effectively also own the Treasury Stock. In this case, if the company repurchases 150,000 shares in the open market, the number of shares issued and still outstanding is reduced from 1,500,000 to 1,350,000. Therefore, each share that is issued and still outstanding would represent a 1/1,350,000th-ownership interest in the company.

- The third action a company can take that will affect the ownership interest represented by an issued and outstanding share is for the company to create securities that can potentially dilute the shareholder's interest at some point in the future. Some examples would be:

  ➤ Issuing convertible Bonds—Bonds that, in addition to paying interest, include a provision that allows the bond holder to force the company to exchange the bond for a fixed number of shares of the company's common stock.

  ➤ Issuing convertible Preferreds—Preferred stocks that, in addition to paying dividends, include a provision that allows the shareholder to exchange the preferred stock for a fixed number of shares of the company's common stock.

➤ Issuing employee stock options—Options that potentially allow employees to buy shares of common stock at a specified price.

The issuance of any or all of these securities can potentially force the company to issue additional shares at some point in the future. Since the issuance of these securities can cause a future dilution of the current share's ownership interest, shareholders should be aware of them before they buy the stock. For example, suppose the company issued securities and options that could potentially cause the issuance of 350,000 new shares. This means that while the ownership interest represented by a share of stock is currently 1/1,350,000th of the company, it can potentially be diluted to 1/1,700,000th. Stock valuations need to take any potential dilution into account.

Corporate Governance and Organization

There is an old expression "too many cooks spoil the broth." This is certainly true with corporate governance and management. A large company can have many thousands of shareholders and therefore many thousands of owners. Clearly a company can't be effectively directed and managed by thousands of owners. This is especially true when most of the owners have neither the time, the expertise, nor the interest to directly involve themselves in the day-to-day running of the company.

Instead, just as we elect members of Congress and entrust them to run the country for our benefit, shareholders elect members to a board of directors and entrust them to run the company for the benefit of all the owners. Typically, each share of common stock has equal voting rights and the elections of directors are usually held annually. The shareholders are mailed a ballot form called a proxy statement and are asked to vote for or against the nominees listed on the proxy.

The board of directors usually does not run the company itself, and being a member of a corporate board of directors is usually a part-time job. Instead, the board of directors hires a management team to manage the company. The board periodically assesses the performance of the management team that it hired. If the management team performs well, the directors reward it—if it doesn't, the board will fire the managers and hire new ones.

Ideally, the board of directors is independent from the management team so that its selection and assessment process is unbiased and performed solely with the goal of maximizing shareholder value over the long term. Unfortunately, this is rarely the case. Members of Congress—who are supposed to act solely for the benefit of the citizens they represent—often have conflicts of interest with special interest groups and large contributors. Likewise, board members often have conflicts of interest, as well. Often the board of directors contains lawyers, accountants, and consultants who not only serve on the board but also provide services to the company. In effect, the very same people they are supposed to be supervising hire them. These conflicts of interest are hard to resolve.

Advantages of Common Stock as an Investment

Common stock has several key advantages that make it attractive as an investment vehicle.

- The first is that, unlike bonds, certificates of deposit (CDs), and other investment alternatives, common stock has the potential for delivering very large gains. Annual returns that exceed 100 percent are not only possible, but happen on a regular basis.

- The second advantage is that the potential loss from stock purchased with cash is limited to 100 percent of the initial investment. Initially, this may not seem like much of an advantage. However, to anyone who has lost more than 100 percent of his or her investment in a derivative or leveraged real estate transaction can appreciate that having the maximum loss limited to 100 percent of the amount invested is an advantage.

- Stocks offer limited legal liability. Stockholders who are passive and do not take an active part in running a company are protected against any legal liabilities stemming from the company's actions. For example, suppose an investor bought 100 shares of stock in a publishing company that subsequently lost a huge libel suit. Even if the resulting judgment wiped out the company, the plaintiffs would not be able to sue the shareholders personally. While their shareholder's investment in the company may be wiped out, the investors have no additional liability.

- Liquidity. Most stocks are quite liquid. This means that they can be bought and sold quickly at a fair price. The fair price is known because all prices at which transactions occur are immediately announced and the price information is widely disseminated.

- High historic return. While past performance is no guarantee of future performance, on average, stocks have historically offered a very high return relative to other investment alternatives.

- Dividends and capital gains. Stocks offer two ways for investors to benefit from owning them. First, each share of stock represents a partial ownership in a company, so if the company becomes more valuable, so will the ownership interest represented by the company's stock. The appreciation of a stock's value is referred to as a capital gain and a decline is referred to as a capital loss. In addition, if the company generates more cash than it needs to sustain itself, it may elect to distribute the excess to the company owners. These periodic distributions of profits are called "dividend payments." Companies usually pay dividends only after the business is generating more cash than is needed to support its growth and maintenance.

- Stocks are fun. Many investors like the intellectual challenge of trying to find attractive investment candidates. In addition, many investors enjoy talking about stocks with their friends and neighbors. In effect, many investors consider stocks as a kind of adult sport.

Disadvantages of Common Stock as an Investment

While common stocks have many advantages, they also have some definite disadvantages that investors need to be aware of. These include:

- Last to get paid—Since common stock represents ownership in a business, stockholders, like all owners, are last in line to get paid. A company first has to pay its employees, pay its suppliers, maintain its facilities, and pay its taxes. Only after these expenses are met can any money be distributed to owners.

- Limited ownership rights—While shareholders are owners of a company, shareholders of public companies do not and should not expect to have all the same rights that owners of privately or closely held companies enjoy. For example, shareholders cannot walk into the company's headquarters and demand to review in detail the company's books. Nor will they be told the intricacies of the company's marketing strategies and tactics.

- Limited information—Investors may have to make decisions based on limited information. They may never know everything there is to know about a company. The investment field is not a level playing field. Investors with access to the most comprehensive and current information have a clear advantage over investors who do not.

- High volatility—Stock prices tend to be quite volatile. The prices of even conservative stocks can very quickly decline by 40 percent or more. Many investors are uncomfortable with this relatively high volatility. This volatility often causes investors to panic and sell after a decline, which is often the worst thing an investor can do because it locks in a loss. If the investor still believes in the underlying attractiveness of the stock, the investor should buy more and lower the average cost of the position.

- Irrational behavior—The value of stocks sometimes changes for no apparent reason whatsoever. This can be psychologically frustrating for investors who can't understand why the price of the company's stock doesn't seem to track the company's actual results. Investors must always remember that logic alone is not enough for success when it comes to the stock market.

Types of Common Stocks

While all common stocks share the previous characteristics, the universe of common stocks can be further divided into the following classes:

- Utilities—Utilities are the stocks issued by power and water companies. These companies often have limited competition and enjoy somewhat monopolistic conditions. For example, most homeowners don't have a choice of electric companies from which to buy electricity. As a result of their monopolies, utilities are considered low-risk investments. These companies are also highly regulated with regard to the price they are allowed to charge for their products and the return they are allowed to earn on their capital, and thus they also offer a fairly low reward. Most utilities distribute a relatively high percentage of their earnings in the form of dividends.

- Blue chips—Stocks issued by the country's largest and most prestigious companies are referred to as "blue chips." Due to their already large size and market share, these companies sometimes do not have the potential for massive further internal growth. However, they also are not going to go out of business anytime soon. They are considered to be relatively low risk, low reward, investments. Blue chip companies often do not have to raise any additional capital and usually generate surplus cash. As a result, some of them pay dividends to their shareholders.

- Established growth—These companies are large enough to be well-established and well-known, but are small enough to still have the possibility of substantial future growth. They are often currently profitable, but may need to raise additional capital to

Figure 2-1
A Common Stock Certificate (front).

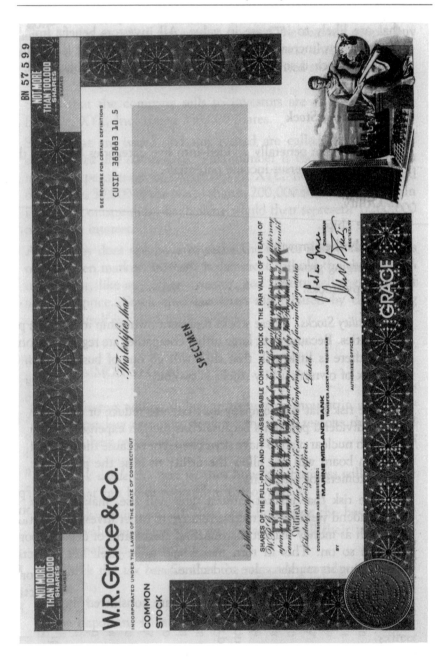

Figure 2-2
A Common Stock Certificate (back).

W. R. GRACE & CO.

A statement of the designations, terms, limitations and relative rights and preferences of the shares of each class authorized to be issued, any variations in relative
rights and preferences between the shares of any series of any class so far as said
rights and preferences shall have been fixed and determined and the authority of
the Board of Directors of the Company to fix and determine any relative rights
and preferences of any subsequent series will be furnished to the holder hereof,
without charge, upon request to the Secretary of the Company or to the Transfer
Agent named on the face hereof.

The following abbreviations, when used in the inscription of ownership on the face of this certificate,
shall be construed as though they were written out in full according to applicable laws or regulations:

JT TEN   —As joint tenants, with right of
                survivorship, and not as tenants
                in common
TEN IN COM—As tenants in common
TEN BY ENT—As tenants by the entireties
Abbreviations in addition to those appearing above may be used.

For value received,_____ hereby sell, assign and transfer unto

PLEASE INSERT SOCIAL SECURITY OR OTHER
IDENTIFYING NUMBER OF ASSIGNEE

(PLEASE PRINT OR TYPEWRITE NAME AND ADDRESS OF ASSIGNEE)

_____ shares
of the capital stock represented by the within Certificate,
and do hereby irrevocably constitute and appoint
_____. Attorney
to transfer the said stock on the books of the within named
Company with full power of substitution in the premises.
Dated_____

Notice The signature to this assignment must correspond with the name
as written upon the face of the certificate in every particular, without
alteration or enlargement or any change whatever.

sustain their future growth. The earnings these companies generate are usually reinvested in further growth and, as a result, they usually do not pay any dividends.

- Emerging growth—These companies are relatively small and have the potential for substantial future growth. They generally will need to raise additional capital to support their growth and pay no dividends. These companies can offer very attractive returns but also have additional risk. Successfully managing rapid growth and its inherent risks is extremely challenging, and many management teams are not up to the task.

- Penny stocks—These companies are the most speculative. They generally trade for less than $5. They represent ownership in companies that may still be in the research and development stage of their first product or companies that have suffered severe setbacks and are barely surviving. These companies are almost always currently losing money. In addition to the high level of business risk they entail, they also tend to be very illiquid. Given the high rate of failure of these companies, most investors are well-advised to avoid them.

Dividend Debate

One of the best ways to start an argument among equity investors is to start a discussion regarding the wisdom of selecting stocks based on whether or not they pay dividends. Some investors refuse to purchase stocks that pay dividends, while others refuse to buy stocks that do not pay dividends. Their respective arguments are as follows:

ANTI-DIVIDEND ARGUMENT

Dividends are a terrible way of rewarding investors because dividends are both taxed twice and taxed immediately. Consider a company that makes a profit of $1 per share and decides to distribute it to its shareholders in the form of a dividend payment. First, if the company is in the 30 percent tax bracket (federal and state combined), then paying taxes at the corporate level of the $1 in profits reduces the cash that's available to investors by $.30. The remaining $.70 is then paid out as a dividend and is immediately taxed again on the individual's tax return. Assuming a combined 40 percent individual tax bracket, another $.28 is lost to taxes. Thus, the investor is left with only $.42 out of the original dollar on an after-tax basis.

Instead, if the company makes a profit of $1 per share, the company should pay its taxes and then either reinvest the remaining $.70 in the business or use it to buy back shares and increase the percentage ownership represented by the remaining shares. In either of these ways, the value of the shares will rise. The rise in share value is not taxed until the shares are sold. In this way, the shareholders receive $.70 worth of benefit instead of $.42 and get to select when they want to pay their personal taxes.

PRO-DIVIDEND ARGUMENT

It is very embarrassing for a company to reduce its dividend payment. Therefore, a company that raises its dividend is making a very strong statement that its future looks bright. Paying dividends also prevents a company from funding less lucrative internal projects or making poor acquisitions. In short, "a bird in hand is worth two in the bush."

Restricting your investments to stocks that pay dividends is a great way to screen for companies that are really successful, because they have the cash to actually pay dividends. Too many companies report earnings that are only "paper earnings." These earnings are more the result of creative accounting than of profitable operations and cannot be used to pay dividends.

Restricting your investments to stocks that have recently raised their dividends is a further screen to select companies that are not only doing well today, but whose management teams expect will do even better in the future.

Stock Splits

As a rule, investors like to purchase shares in multiples of 100-share blocks. A 100-share block is referred to as a "round lot." As a stock's price rises, the price of a round lot can become prohibitive to many investors. For example, while many investors can afford 100 shares of a $15 stock ($1,500), many either cannot afford 100 shares of a $250 stock ($25,000) or would not want to commit that much money to a single stock.

Companies are aware of this and, therefore, when the company's stock price rises above $100 per share, companies sometimes "split the stock." Splitting the stock means that the company issues new shares to its existing shareholders. Since the company issues new shares, each share represents a smaller ownership interest, and is therefore less valuable. For example, if a company's stock was selling for $100 per share and it did a 4-for-1 split—that is, gave each investor three additional shares for every share he or she already owned—each share would be worth $25.

In reality, stock prices often rise when a split is announced since the split allows more investors to invest in the stock at a price they can afford. A stock split generally also improves liquidity.

Price Quotes

Stock prices are quoted in "points" and 16th of a point, where each point is equal to $1. Thus, a price of 100 shares at $48 + 1/16th is equal to:

$$100 \text{ shares} \times [\$48 + (1/16\text{th} \times \$1)] = \$4,806.25$$

Fractions are normally "reduced," so a price of 2/16th of a point would be expressed as 1/8th and 8/16th of a point would be expressed as 1/2. (In the early 1990s the price was rounded off to the nearest 8th of a point instead of the nearest 16th.)

Types of Orders

Investors who wish to buy or sell stock can use several different types of orders and order qualifiers to ensure that their exact wishes are met. The three main types of orders include market, limit, and stop orders. The qualifiers include "all or none," "fill or kill," "good till canceled," and "at the opening" or "at the close."

The most common type of order is the market order. A market order must be executed immediately and completely at the best available price. For example, suppose XYZ, Inc. common stock is currently trading at $60 per share. An investor enters an order to buy 1,000 shares "at the market." The broker receiving this order will immediately go about the task of buying the client 1,000 shares of the stock. The price the investor ends up paying might be $60—or it might be slightly higher or lower than $60, depending upon the momentary balance between supply and demand for the stock at the moment the broker is buying the stock.

Investors who want more control over the price they pay for a stock—or receive from its sale—can instead use a limit order. A limit order specifies either the maximum price an investor is willing to pay for a stock or the minimum price the investor is willing to accept from its sale. For example, again suppose XYZ, Inc. common stock is selling for $60 per share. An investor wants to buy 5,000 shares of the stock but does not want to pay more than $60 per share. In this case, the investor would enter a "limit order" to buy 5,000 XYZ, Inc. at $60.

When the broker receives this order, the broker will buy the client as many shares as possible at a price of $60 or less. If the broker can buy only 1,800 shares at $60 or less, then only 1,800 shares will be purchased. The investor will be informed that only 1,800 shares were for sale at or below the limit price and that the order was partially filled. The broker will then monitor the price of XYZ, Inc. common stock and if, at some later time, its price again drops to a price equal to or less than the limit, the broker will buy more shares until the order has been filled. A limit order is considered to be "good till canceled" unless otherwise specified. This means that the broker will continue to try to fill the order even if it takes months to find enough stock for sale at or below the limit price.

If the investor doesn't want to accept only a partial fill of the order, the investor can enter a limit order on an "all or none" basis. By adding all or none to the order, the investor specifies that if the entire order can't be filled, no stock is to be purchased. Continuing the previous example, a broker receiving this order would not execute the order until the broker was able to buy all 5,000 shares at once—and at a price of $60 or less. Again, the broker might have to hold the order for months before it is possible to execute the order, if ever.

Finally, an investor who did not want to accept a partial fill and wants the stock only if it can be purchased immediately would enter a limit order on a "fill or kill" basis. This order specifies that if the entire order can't be filled immediately, the order should be canceled.

Margin

Because quality stocks are liquid investments, they can serve as collateral for loans. Many investors use the stock they own as collateral for loans that they then use to buy more stock. This is referred to as buying stock on margin—or buying stock with borrowed money. Buying stocks with borrowed money increases both the investor's potential return and the degree of risk.

Investors who borrow money to buy stock pay interest on their loans. The rate they pay is referred to as the margin rate and depends on interest rates in the marketplace, the size of their account, and the broker through which the stock is purchased. Investors who buy stock on margin hope that the return on their stocks exceeds their interest expense so that they have a net profit. For example, an investor who borrows money at 8 percent per year and invests it in a stock that appreciates 30 percent per year would enjoy a pre-tax profit of 22 percent. Of course, an investor who borrowed money at 8 percent and invested in a stock that stayed flat would lose 8 percent per year.

Investors are limited with regard to how much they can borrow against their stock. Currently, that limit is 50 percent. Thus an investor who wanted to buy 1,000 shares of a $20 stock for a total of $20,000 would have to deposit $10,000 in a brokerage account and could borrow the other $10,000 (50 percent).

If the value of stock purchased on margin drops substantially, the value of the collateral behind the loan also declines, making the lender—that is, the brokerage firm—nervous. If this happens, the brokerage firm may insist that the client either deposit additional cash or collateral into the account or sell the stock. When a brokerage firm insists that the client deposit additional collateral, it is called a margin call.

Shorting Stock

While most investors focus their attention on finding stocks that will go up in value, it is just as easy to make money from stocks whose value declines. In order to profit from the decline in a stock's value, investors only need to "short" the stock. Shorting a stock means selling shares that the investor doesn't own, but instead has temporarily borrowed.

The hope of an investor who shorts a stock is to borrow the shares, sell them at a high price, wait for the price to decline, buy the stock back, return the same number of shares that were borrowed to the party that lent them, and pocket the profit. In short, the hope is to first "sell high," then "buy low."

For example, suppose an investor believes that XYZ, Inc.'s common stock, which is currently selling for $60, is substantially overvalued. The investor therefore borrows 1,000 shares from an investor who owns the stock and sells the shares for $60 each. The borrowing of shares is usually arranged by the brokerage firm that the investor uses to execute the short sale. Suppose that, after selling the stock at $60, the market value of the stock falls to $40. At this point the investor repurchases the 1,000 shares, returns them to the party from whom they were borrowed, and retains a profit of $20 per share—less the expense of margin interest and transaction charges.

Shorting a stock always has to be done in a margin account in order to protect the party who lends the securities. In the previous example, the investor is shorting 1,000 shares of a $60 stock. Therefore, the investor would have to deposit $30,000 into a margin account. When the shares are sold for $60 each, the sales proceeds would be $60,000, bringing the balance in the short's account up to $90,000. This money serves as collateral for the short sale by insuring that the party who shorts the stock has ready funds to repurchase the shares so that they can eventually be returned to the lender.

In a short sale, the investor loses if the price of the stock rises. In the previous example, if the stock was subsequently to rise to $75 per share before the investor repurchased the shares, the investor would suffer a $15 per share loss. Because there is no limit on how high the value of a stock can go, shorting a stock is considered to be riskier than buying a stock. (The most an investor can lose by buying a stock for cash is 100 percent of the investment.) If an investor originally shorted a stock at $60, and the company was taken over at $180, the investor could lose much more than 100 percent of the original investment.

Shorting a stock can also entail another risk in that the party from whom the stock is borrowed can insist that the shares be returned at any time. When this happens, the brokerage firm that effected the short sale will endeavor to borrow other shares from a different lender. However, if no other lender can be found, the short will have no choice other than to "cover the short" position by repurchasing the shares in the open market regardless of the then-current market price. When a stock becomes difficult to borrow and the shorts are forced to repurchase the shares, a "short squeeze" occurs. As the shorts try to repurchase the shares they shorted in order to return it to the lenders, their purchase orders can push the stock price higher—the exact opposite of what the shorts want.

ANALYZING STOCKS

This chapter discusses some of the ways in which research analysts and investors analyze stocks in an attempt to determine which stocks might offer superior investment opportunities. There are three schools of thought with regard to analyzing stocks:

- The fundamentalist school, which believes that future earnings can be projected by studying the company's business strategy, competitive position, and financial statements.

- The technical school, which believes that the future movement of stock prices can be projected by studying the past movement of stock prices.

- The academic school, which believes that traditional research is of little, if any, value.

The Fundamentalist School

Investment fundamentalists believe that the future price of a stock is dependent upon two factors: how much the company will earn (that is, its profits) per share, and the multiple (how many times the company's earnings) the market will pay for those earnings. In this section we will look at how analysts/investors project future earnings and/or multiples.

The primary tool that analysts use to project future earnings is a company's income statement(s). The income statement provides an overview of the company's income and expenses for a specified time frame (quarterly, annually). By examining a company's income and expenses over a series of time periods, fundamentalists believe it is possible to learn how a company fared in the past, identify trends that provide insight into how the company will perform in the future, and identify the key factors that may determine the company's future success.

There is no government or Financial Accounting Standards Board's (FASB; pronounced "fas-be") mandated format for income statements, so companies have a certain amount of freedom when it comes to how they format their income statements. While every company's income statement is somewhat different, most have to resemble the example in Figure 3-1.

Figure 3-1
XYZ, Inc. Income Statement (Year 20XX)

Sales (in thousands)	$123,455
Cost of Goods Sold	($62,123)
Operating Expenses	($17,110)
Depreciation & Amortization	($12,445)
Interest	($8,649)
Taxes	($5,251)
Non-Recurring Items	($2,344)
Earnings	$15,533

Before the analysis of a company's income statement can even begin, fundamentalists must "restate" the numbers on the company's income statement. The numbers on the income statement need to be restated because companies have fairly wide latitude with regard to how they report their results. The rules that govern the reporting of results on an income statement have to be flexible because the same rules have to be used by companies as diverse as mining companies and Web designers.

This accounting flexibility can be exploited by company managers to make their companies appear to be either more successful or less successful than they are in reality. Privately owned companies often use the flexibility of the rules to minimize their earnings in order to reduce their taxes. Publicly owned companies often use the rules to manage their earnings in order to boost their share price and multiple, reduce their financing cost, and increase management compensation.

In addition, different companies in the same industry often use very different methodologies for reporting results, and thus their results need to be restated in order to make apple vs. apple comparisons.

INTERPRETING THE INCOME STATEMENT

Sales

The first line in any income statement is the company's sales figure for the reporting period. This number is the dollar value of goods and/or services the company sold—less a reserve for returns and cancellations. In the case of a retail company, measuring sales is fairly straightforward: A sale occurs when a cash register rings and the amount of sales that will be returned can usually be estimated fairly accurately from past returns.

However, reporting sales for manufacturing companies is more complex because different companies have quite a bit of flexibility in deciding when during the sales cycle to actually recognize and report the sale. For example, while one company might choose to recognize its sales when orders are received, another company in the same industry might recognize sales when their orders are shipped, while another might recognize sales when their invoices are mailed, and still another when payment is received. Naturally, when a company chooses to recognize its sales will distort its results relative to its competitors.

When restating a company's income statement, fundamentalists will examine when during the sales cycle a company records that a sale has occurred and whether or not the triggering event has changed. For example, companies that have historically recorded a sale only when they are paid will change their accounting policies and begin to record sales when the order is received in an effort to appear that their sales are either growing faster or declining slower than they are in reality.

In addition to examining the company's accounting policies, fundamentalists will typically ask a variety of questions like the following in order to predict what the company's future sales will be. These questions are answered by talking to customers and competitors, examining marketing research, and a certain amount of gut instinct.

- What has been the historic growth rate of unit sales and how will the growth rate likely change in the future? In other words, what is the size of the market for the company's products and how will the size of the market change in the future?

- What has been the historic level of price increases per unit sold and how will the unit pricing likely change in the future? In other words, how competitive is the company's industry?

- Is the company booking sales while it still has obligations to its customers? For example, a computer company that agrees to provide technical support for two years should not recognize 100 percent of the sale price of a computer sale until its obligation to provide technical support is completed.

- Is the company allowing adequate reserves for returns and cancellations?

- Is the company recognizing sales that are not final, such as equipment shipped to clients on approval?

- Is the company booking as "sales" revenue from sources such as tax refunds, refunds from suppliers, interest income, and so on?

- Is the company increasing its sales by lowering its credit standards without adequately increasing its reserves for credit losses?

- Is the company robbing its future by offering deep discounts before the expiration of the reporting period?

- Is the company robbing its future by booking sales that actually occurred after the reporting period is over?

Because companies can record sales before an order is paid for, or even shipped, "Sales" should not be confused with "Cash Received."

Cost of Goods Sold (COGS)

The second line on an income statement, at least for manufacturing and retail companies, is the "Cost of Goods Sold" or COGS. This entry includes three types of expenses.

1. The cost of either purchasing or manufacturing the goods the company sold during the time period. Included in this category are the costs of raw materials the company used in the manufacturing process, the costs of maintaining the company's manufacturing facilities, and the labor costs associated with producing the goods.
2. Inventory losses that occurred during the period. These losses can result from the company's inventory being damaged while in storage, by spoiling, or by theft.
3. The decline in value of the company's unsold inventory due to obsolescence. Inventory must be carried on the company's books at the lessor of either cost or market value. If the value of inventory drops below its cost of production, the loss should be recognized on the income statement. Goods that are "trendy," such as toys, clothes, and electronics, are particularly susceptible to declines in value. Since inventory rarely becomes obsolete overnight, management teams have some discretion with regard to the timing of when they "write-down" the value of their obsolete inventory. Fundamentalists often look closely at a company's inventory in order to insure that no large write-offs due to obsolescence are imminent.

Another decision that management teams make with regard to their cost of goods sold is deciding which inventory reporting system to adopt. There are four different systems that managers can choose from:

1. Last In, First Out (LIFO). Under this accounting system, the last unit of inventory purchased or produced is assumed to be the first one sold. Thus, when a unit is sold, the COGS recorded is the cost of the last, or more recent, unit produced.

2. First In, First Out (FIFO). Under this accounting system, the first unit of inventory purchased or produced is assumed to be the first one sold. Thus, when a unit is sold, the COGS recorded is the cost of the first, or oldest, unit produced.

3. Average cost. Under this accounting system, the COGS is assumed to be the average cost of producing or purchasing the units the company has in inventory.

4. Pools. Under this accounting system, the inventory is divided into pools based on when the inventory is produced. Management then elects from which pool the inventory came when a unit is sold. (Note that the "pool method" has numerous restrictions on its use and is fairly uncommon.)

During periods when the cost of production is changing rapidly either because of inflation, deflation, or the change in the price of a key raw material, which accounting method is selected for reporting COGS can have a major effect on the company's earnings, return on assets, return on equity, net worth, and taxes. Consider the following example.

Suppose a company buys or builds five units of inventory over time for the following prices: $10, $15, $20, $25, and $30. The company then sells one unit for $25. How much did the company make or lose on the transaction? The answer depends upon the accounting method selected for defining the COGS.

- Under LIFO, the company lost $5, since it sold a unit for $25 that cost it $30.

- Under FIFO, the company made $15, since it sold a unit for $25 that cost it $10.

- Under the average method, the company made $5, because it sold a unit for $25 that cost it $20.

- Under the pooled method, management can select whether to report $15 profit, $10 profit, $5 profit, no profit, or a $5 loss.

In addition to affecting earnings, the choice of which inventory system the company adopts also affects:

- The asset value of the unsold inventory. When a company sells a unit, the value of its inventory declines by a similar amount. In the previous example, under LIFO the COGS is $30, so the value of the remaining inventory declines by $30; however, under FIFO, the value of the remaining industry declines by only $10.

- The return on assets. Inventory is an asset. Since the inventory accounting method selected affects the value of the company's remaining inventory, it also affects the return the company earns on that inventory.

- The company's tax bill and cash flow. Since the inventory accounting method selected affects the value of the company's reported earnings, it also affects the company's tax bill—and cash flow.

For all of these reasons, fundamentalists must look at which reporting method is used for COGS and the affect of that decision on the company's results versus its competitors.

Operating Expenses

The third line on the income statement is the company's "operating expenses." This line item incorporates two types of expenses:

- Overhead or administrative costs, including the cost of maintaining corporate headquarters/administrative buildings, as well as performing administrative functions.

- Sales expenses, including advertising expenses, marketing costs, marketing literature, sales commissions, and so on.

Some companies elect to report these two types of expenses separately, while others combine these numbers into one overall operating expense number. The composition and trend of operating expenses is a topic of tremendous interest to fundamentalists because today some companies are dramatically reducing their operating costs by effectively using the World Wide Web (Web). Companies that use the Web effectively allow their customers to place orders with little or no human intervention—and very little cost. The Web has the potential to do to operating costs what the assembly line did to manufacturing costs.

In addition to looking at the operating expenses themselves, analysts also look at any long-term commitments the company has made in order to determine whether the commitments will help or hurt the company's results and for how long. Some of these commitments include:

- Real estate leases
- Equipment leases
- Power contracts
- Intellectual property rights

Long-term leases at below-market rates will improve future results, while long-term leases at above-market rates can hurt the company's performance for years.

Depreciation, Amortization, and Depletion

The next line on most income statements is depreciation. When a company buys a building or a piece of equipment that has a useful life that is longer than a year, the cost of the equipment cannot simply be included in the COGS or the operating expenses (whichever is appropriate). Instead, the cost of the equipment has to be written off over the period in which the decline occurs.

For example, if a company buys a piece of equipment for $1 million that has a useful life of four years and a salvage value of $400,000, then the $600,000 projected decline in value must be written off over four years. Just as companies can choose among several alternative inventory accounting systems, they can also choose among several alternative depreciation methodologies. The major alternative methodologies are given in Figure 3-2.

Figure 3-2
Alternative Depreciation Methodologies

Straight Line	[Initial Value − Salvage Value] / Initial Life
Declining Balance	[Remaining Value × 2] / Initial Life
Sum of Years	$\dfrac{\text{[Initial Value − Salvage Value]} \times \text{Remaining Life}}{\text{[Initial Useful Life} \times \text{(Initial Useful Life+1)]/2}}$
Production Used	$\dfrac{\text{[Initial Value − Salvage Value]} \times \text{Units Produced}}{\text{Total Number Units Equipment Can Produce}}$

The straight-line method results in the lowest write-offs in the early years and higher write-offs in the future. The other methods increase the size of the write-offs in the early years, but at the cost of lower write-offs in the future. Since write-offs also affect both earnings and taxes, the decision of which depreciation method to use is very important. As an example, consider what the annual write-off is on a $1 million piece of equipment with a five-year useful life and no projected salvage value using the various methodologies above. (See Figure 3-3.)

Figure 3-3
Alternative Amortization Schedules

Year	Straight Line	Declining Balance	Sum of Years
1	$200,000	$400,000	$333,333
2	$200,000	$240,000	$266,666
3	$200,000	$144,000	$200,000
4	$200,000	$108,000	$133,333
5	$200,000	$108,000	$66,666

In addition to depreciating buildings and equipment, companies also have two other types of depreciation.

1. Intangible property and soft assets, such as goodwill, brand names, patents, and so on, are also depreciated. The depreciation of intangible property is referred to as amortization. Soft assets must be written off over the shorter of either the property's legal or market life.

2. The decline in the value of oil fields, mines, and other natural resources as they are consumed can also be written off. The decline in value that results from the consumption of natural resources is referred to as depletion.

Remember that depreciation, amortization, and depletion are all non-cash expenses. While they reduce a company's earnings, they do not actually consume cash.

Interest Expense

The next item is the interest expense. This item includes the interest expense the company incurs during the period and may include any interest income the company earns by investing its cash reserves. Any other income the company receives during the period from refunds, and so on, is also sometimes included in this section. Analysts look to see whether the company is paying a low rate or high rate of interest relative to its competitors, given its credit quality and whether the structure (fixed or floating) and currency mix is helping or hurting the company's results.

Taxes

This number represents the tax liability the company estimates it incurred over the time period. Analysts will examine this number in order to determine if the company has either understated or overstated its actual tax liability. The actual amount the company paid in taxes can be found on another financial statement, the cash flow statement.

Non-Recurring Items

Non-recurring items are transactions that are large enough to be significant to the company's results, but which are one-time events. Some of the types of transactions that fall into this category are the costs associated with shutting down a plant, selling a company division, changing the assumptions in the company's pension plan, settling lawsuits, and so on. Since they are "one-time" events, fundamentalists give them less weight when projecting future results.

Earnings

After subtracting all of the expenses we've identified, the bottom line is earnings. It should be obvious by now that a company's earnings and its cash flow are very different. Analysts look not only at the earnings number but also the quality of the company's earnings. The term "quality of earnings" is a general term that encompasses earnings that have the following characteristics:

- The percentage of the earnings that actually represent cash. The higher the percentage of earnings that represent cash profits, the higher the quality of the earnings. Actual cash is worth more than "paper profits" since cash can be used to buy back shares, pay dividends, fund new R&D, and so on.

- The likelihood that the earnings can be reproduced the following year. Fundamentalists like consistency. Companies with consistent businesses like Coca-Cola and Procter & Gamble trade at higher multiples than cyclical companies like airlines.

- The simplicity of the financial statements and the underlying business. The simpler the financial statements, the lower the possibility of serious error, and the higher the quality of the earnings. There is an old Wall Street axiom "If the company's financials are hard to decipher, it's because the company is trying to hide something."

As earnings quality increases, so does the multiple of earnings that investors will pay for the stock. After analysts have projected what they believe a company's earnings will be, the second step in projecting future value is to project what "multiple" investors will pay for those earnings.

Consider the following situation. XYZ, Inc. is currently earning $1 per share per year and its stock is currently selling for $15 per share. Since:

$$\text{Stock Price} = \text{Multiple} \times \text{Earnings}$$

$$\$15 = 15 \times \$1$$

It is clear that investors are willing to pay 15 times the company's current earnings in order to buy this stock.

If, the following year, the company earned $1.20 and investors were still willing to pay 15 times earnings, the market value of the stock would rise to $18.

$$\$18 = 15 \times \$1.20$$

However, if despite the rise in earnings from $1 to $1.20, the multiple that investors were willing to pay for those earnings declined from 15 to 11, the stock's price would decline to $13.20 despite the higher earnings.

$$\$13.20 = 11 \times \$1.20$$

Investors often get very frustrated when the earnings of the companies in their portfolios rise, but the prices of the stocks decline. Obviously, the ideal situation for an investor is for the company's earnings to rise and for the multiple also to expand. For example, if in the previous example, the earnings rose from $1 to $1.20 and the multiple expanded from 15 to 20, then the price of the stock would rise to:

$$\$24 = 20 \times \$1.20$$

This begs the question, "What factors, besides the quality of earnings, cause the multiple that investors will pay to buy a stock to expand or contract?" While there are many factors that influence investors' decisions regarding what multiple is appropriate besides the quality of earnings, the primary factors include:

The Level of Interest Rates

As interest rates decline, the multiple that investors are willing to pay for the same earnings increases. There are two reasons for this:

1. As interest rates decline, the economy usually expands and company earnings rise at a faster rate (see below).

2. The return offered the main alternative to stocks (that is, bonds) declines when interest rates decline. Therefore, when interest rates are low, stocks become relatively more attractive than bonds. Money flows from bonds into stocks, causing the price of stocks to rise and the multiples at which they trade to expand.

The Projected Growth Rate for the Company's Earnings

The higher the projected growth rate of the company's future earnings, the higher the multiple that investors will pay for the stock. Consider the two companies in Figure 3-4.

Figure 3-4
Projected Earnings

	Year 1	Year 2	Year 3	Year 4
Company XYZ	$1	$1.05	$1.10	$1.15
Company ABC	$1	$1.50	$2	$2.50

If both stocks were selling at $15 per share (that is, 15 times current earnings), every investor would select company ABC because its earnings are expected to rise at a much faster rate. As a result, its price would rise and its multiple would expand. Sometimes stocks with an exceptionally high projected growth rate trade at multiples of 200 times earnings or more.

The Predictability of Earnings

The predictability of earnings also affects a stock's multiple. As a rule, stocks of companies with highly predictable and reliable earnings generally trade at a higher multiple than companies with equivalent but less reliable earnings. This makes sense since the companies with the less reliable earnings are "riskier." Risky investments should sell at a lower price/higher return in order to compensate investors for the higher level of risk.

Ratio Analysis

Once the financial statements are restated, the revised numbers can then be used to calculate and analyze key performance ratios. These ratios can provide valuable insights into a company's past performance and expected future performance. The key ratios that analysts look at include gross margin, operating margin, return on assets, recurring margin, inventory turnover, and cash collection ratio.

GROSS MARGIN

The first key ratio that analysts look at is the gross profit margin. This margin is calculated by dividing the company's gross profit (sales - COGS) by its sales revenue. The higher a company's gross margin, the greater the company's ability to "mark up" the goods or services it produces or sells. In other words, companies with high gross margins have pricing power. Companies with low gross margins have little pricing power and are referred to as "commodity businesses."

A company's ability to maintain a high gross margin is dependent upon a number of factors including:

1. The degree of competition within the industry. The greater the degree of competition within the industry, the more power shifts from producers to customers and the greater the pressure on pricing. The degree of competition within an industry, in turn, depends upon the industry's barriers to entry. These barriers include:

   - An access to capital—Obtaining enough capital to start a Web page design firm is easy; obtaining enough capital to start a aircraft manufacturing firm is extraordinarily difficult.

   - Proprietary technology—Some companies have proprietary technologies that make it very difficult for new competitors to compete against them.

   - Government regulation—Some businesses, such as prescription pharmaceuticals, are subject to a tremendous amount of government regulation, while other companies are subjected to almost none. The high level of government regulation can serve as a barrier to smaller companies.

2. The efficiency of the company's manufacturing and administrative processes. By lowering its manufacturing costs, a company can raise its gross margin without raising its prices.

A declining gross margin is an indication of a future decline in earnings. It is very hard for companies to keep their earnings rising when their gross margins are being squeezed.

OPERATING MARGIN

The second key ratio that analysts look at is the company's operating margin. This margin is defined as the company's operating costs divided by its sales revenue. This margin measures how efficiently the company is administered. Some companies, such as Wal-Mart™, have a reputation for running very efficiently, while other companies are bloated and inefficient. By comparing the operating margins of competitive firms, analysts can determine which firms are the most efficiently administered.

RETURN ON ASSETS

The third key ratio is the company's return on assets. This ratio is cal-culated by dividing the company's earnings by the value of the com-pany's assets used to generate the earnings. This ratio is difficult to calculate because it should be calculated using the actual market value of the company's assets. The company's financial statements reveal only the book value (purchase price - depreciation) of the company's assets, not their market value.

The return on assets is a measure of the company's productivity. If a company is not earning an adequate return on its assets, it should return a portion of its assets to the shareholders so that those assets can be re-employed in a more productive way. Companies that continuously have a low return on assets should be liquidated.

RECURRING MARGIN

The fourth key ratio is the company's recurring margin. This is calcu-lated by dividing the company's recurring margin (earnings before extraordinary items) by its sales revenue. Companies that can maintain their recurring margins while growing rapidly are both very rare and very valuable. Growth stock investors are always seeking companies that fit this profile.

INVENTORY TURNOVER

The fifth key ratio is inventory turnover. It is calculated by dividing sales revenue by the value of the company's inventory. This ratio is yet another measure of efficiency and productivity. If this ratio is equal to four, it means that the company turns over its inventory four times per year. At first glance it may appear that the higher this ratio is, the better. After all, the faster the company turns over its inven-tory, the less capital it has tied up in inventory. However, this con-clusion is superficial.

When a company reduces its inventory level, it also decreases its ability to generate sales. One of the oldest adages in business is that "you can't sell what you don't have." Thus, companies are always trying to optimize their inventory levels so that they minimize their inventory costs without sacrificing too many business opportunities. Determining the optimal inventory level for a company is a highly specialized job for people with advanced degrees in mathematics.

CASH COLLECTION RATIO

The sixth ratio is the cash collection ratio. This is calculated by dividing the cash the company receives from customers by its reported sales. This ratio is a "reality check" on the company's reported sales figures. If the company's sales are genuine and its collection efforts efficient, the ratio will be fairly close to "1." The lower this ratio, the more suspect the company's financial statements become in the eyes of fundamentalists.

Trend Analysis

In addition to using the restated financial statements to calculate and analyze ratios, they can also be used to examine trends in the company's sales, expenses, and profits, as well as to determine the sensitivity of the company's earnings to a variety of key variables. Many analysts regard understanding trends and sensitivities to be the key to predicting future stock prices.

HOW MUCH DATA TO USE

The first issue that has to be addressed when calculating trends is to decide how much data to use. The amount of data that is used to calculate a trend is critical to the result. Consider the data in Figure 3-5.

Figure 3-5
Earnings History

	Year			
	1	2	3	4
Sales	14 million	9 million	12 million	16 million
Earnings	5 million	3 million	6 million	7 million

If the trend in sales and earnings is calculated using four years of data, the growth rate in sales and earnings are, respectively:

Sales growth 3.39%   Earnings growth 8.78%

However, if only three years of data are used, the results are quite different:

Sales growth 21.14%   Earnings growth 32.64%

Obviously, the decision to include or exclude the additional year of data dramatically affects the resulting growth rates—and the stock's valuation. Only the application of common sense can determine whether to use three or four years' worth of data. In the previous example, the decision of whether to use three or four years of data depends upon finding out if some extraordinary event—such as a plant closing—resulted in the large change from year 3 to year 4. If there was an event, then the company changed at that point and only three years' worth of data should be used for analysis. If there was no event, and the change was simply the result of a business downturn, the downturn could repeat itself and four years of data should be used in the analysis.

PERFORMANCE CHARTS

To illustrate and visualize how a company's results are changing, many analysts use performance charts. A performance chart plots a company's results over time on a percentage basis. For example, these charts illustrate how the COGS, operating costs, amount of depreciation, interest expense, and taxes are changing relative to the company's sales. (See Figure 3-6.)

Figure 3-6
Percentage Chart

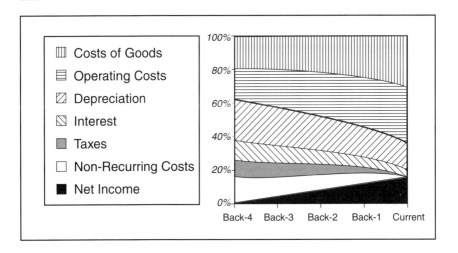

At first glance, this company looks like a stunning success. Its reported earnings have consistently risen over the last five years. A second look, however, reveals that this is, in fact, a company in deep trouble.

- The cost of goods is rising, indicating that it is costing the company a greater percentage of its sales revenue to produce the goods it sells. This may mean that its costs are rising or that the company is not increasing its productivity adequately.

- The operating costs, as a percentage of sales, are also rising. This indicates that the company is becoming less efficient, possibly due to a bloating of the company's headquarters staff.

- The depreciation deduction, as a percentage of sales, is declining. This is boosting the company's earnings but may indicate that the company is not buying any new equipment—perhaps because it is strapped for cash or because it doesn't anticipate generating enough orders in the future to make the investment worthwhile.

- The interest expense as a percentage of sales is also declining. A deeper look reveals, however, that this is because the company has floating rate debt and that interest rates have been declining, not because the company is paying down debt.

- The tax liability as a percentage of sales is also declining. This may mean either that the company is becoming less profitable or that the company has larger deductions. Since the depreciation expense is declining, the company is probably becoming less profitable.

- The non-recurring costs are also declining as a percentage of sales. It is the decline in non-recurring costs that has boosted the company's earnings, not a decline in recurring costs. Since the non-recurring costs have reached zero, there will be no further declines, and thus no more boosts to earnings.

This company's stock should be sold. Its earnings are not only of a low quality, but have also most likely peaked. Selling the stock will not be a problem, since the company's four years of increasing reported earnings will undoubtedly attract many naïve investors who will be anxious to buy when the stock is selling for a very high price.

This example illustrates the futility of simply looking at earnings when making buy and sell decisions. Investors and analysts have to look much deeper.

As a point of contrast, consider Figure 3-7, which illustrates a much healthier company. In this example, the reported earnings are flat. Any quick search of a quantitative database that started with "Show me all the companies whose earnings have risen by more than X percent over the last few years" would exclude this company. However, although the reported earnings are flat, this company has many positive developments that make it an attractive investment candidate. For this company:

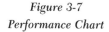

Figure 3-7
Performance Chart

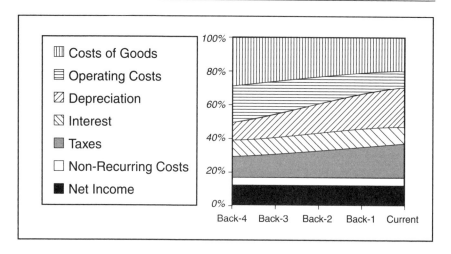

- The cost of goods is declining, indicating that the efficiency of the company's plants is improving.

- The operating expenses are declining, indicating that the efficiency of the company's headquarters and sales operations are improving.

- The depreciation expense is increasing, indicating that the company is purchasing additional equipment—a very bullish sign.

- Non-recurring costs and interest expenses are held constant.

- The company's tax bill is increasing, suggesting increased profitability, especially in light of the increase in depreciation expense.

An analyst might conclude that the company is experiencing many positive developments that will probably result in higher earnings in the future. The time to invest in this company is now, before the earnings rise. After the earnings rise, it may be too late.

SENSITIVITY ANALYSIS

From the restated financial statements, ratios, and trends, fundamentalists try to develop sensitivity profiles for the stocks they follow.

Sensitivity profiles try to answer questions, such as what will be the effect on earnings of a change in:

- The cost of a key raw material
- The cost of labor
- The size of the market
- A key exchange rate

This type of analysis is far more difficult than it would initially appear. The reason is that each change has primary, secondary, and tertiary effects on a company's financial results. For example, consider just some of the questions that have to be answered when the price of a raw material changes:

1. What percentage of the increased cost can be passed on to the company's customers as opposed to being absorbed by the company?

2. If the company passes the price increase along to its customers, how many fewer units will the company sell?

3. How much less labor will the company use if it sells fewer units?

4. What will happen to the production cost per unit as a result of selling fewer units?

Likewise, if a key exchange rate changes, the following questions have to be answered:

1. How will the exchange rate change the company's sales figures?

2. How will the exchange rate change the company's raw material costs?

3. How will the company's competitive position change relative to its foreign competitors?

4. How will the economy be affected by the change in foreign exchange rates?

Once the key sensitivities are performed, fundamentalists can make reasonable estimates of future stock performance.

The Technical School

Another form of analysis is technical. Proponents of technical analysis believe that by studying the "pattern" of how a stock's price has changed in the past, it is possible to predict how the price will change in the future. Proponents of technical analysis fall into one of two schools: those who believe that technical analysis works because it is valid in and of itself, and those who believe technical analysis works because it creates "self-fulfilling prophecies."

Those proponents of technical analysis who believe technical analysis is valid in its own right believe that by studying the pattern of stock prices, it is possible to learn, indirectly, what everyone who does fundamental analysis knows about the stock. They believe that everything fundamentalists know is reflected in the prices at which they were and are willing to buy or to sell the stock. Further, true believers in technical analysis believe that by studying the price patterns of stocks, it is possible to gain valuable insight into the current mass psychology of investors—something that fundamental analysis cannot reveal.

Many investors who do not necessarily believe in the inherent validity of technical analysis still find it to be useful. They believe it is useful because so many *other* people believe in it and that the collective belief of the "true believers" results in a self-fulfilling prophecy. Their reasoning is as follows:

> "If enough people believe that a certain price pattern indicates that a stock will rise, then when a stock's prices exhibit that pattern, the true believers in technical analysis will rush to buy the stock. As a result, the stock's price will rise."

If the stock's price is going to rise as a result of buying pressure from the true believers, then why not go along for the ride?

In order to perform technical analysis, the first step is to create a chart of the stock's historic prices. Naturally, there are a nearly infinite number of ways of plotting the price movements of stocks. One of the most popular ways to chart prices is to use a "bar chart" that is plotted on a "logarithmic scale." (See Figure 3-8.) A bar chart is so named because the trading range of a stock over a given time frame (usually a single trading day) is represented by a simple graphic referred to as a "bar." Each bar can present some or all of the following information:

- The price at which the stock opened during the day (the bar that sticks out to the left—sometimes omitted).
- The low price at which it traded during the day (the bottom of the vertical bar).
- The high price at which it traded during the day (the top of the vertical bar).
- The closing price at which it traded during the day (the bar that sticks out to the right).
- The daily trading range (the length of the vertical line).

Figure 3-8
Sample Bar from a Bar Chart

These bars are plotted on a chart that plots time (on the X-Axis) against price (on the Y-Axis). The scale for the price axis is logarithmic so that the change in price is presented on a percentage basis. Consider the following example:

Suppose Stock A is currently selling for $5 and Stock B is currently selling for $50. Subsequently, the price of both stocks rises by $5. If the scale on which this change was graphed was arithmetic, then both changes would effect to be of equal size—despite the fact that this would distort the real effect of the price change. If the price of Stock A rises from $5 to $10, its price has increased by 100 percent. If the price of Stock B rises from $50 to $55, its price has increased by only 10 percent. On a logarithmic scale, the $5 increase in Stock A will be represented graphically as ten times as large as the $5 increase in Stock B—eliminating the distortion.

Figure 3-9
Volatility Data

	Day 1	Day 2	Day 3	Day 4
Trading Volume	20	30	10	25
High	55	70	90	55
Low	20	40	55	85
Close	30	55	80	75

Because so many technical theories are dependent upon both changes in price and changes in trading volume, the daily trading volume is typically represented along the bottom of the same chart. (See Figure 3-9.)

Putting it all together, a complete bar chart for a very volatile data is illustrated in Figure 3-10.

Figure 3-10
Resulting Bar Chart

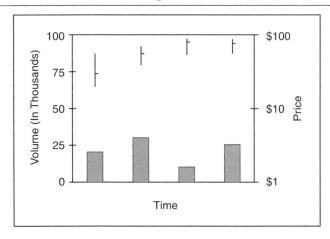

Once a bar chart is created, the resulting patterns need to be analyzed.

Analysis of Bar Charts

Creating charts by hand used to be a tedious and time-consuming process, but personal computers now make the creation of technical charts a process that requires little more than a few mouse clicks. Once the charts are created, investors look for certain patterns that indicate whether the stock's current price trend (bullish or bearish) will either continue or reverse itself. Just a few of the more common patterns are described below.

HEAD & SHOULDERS PATTERN

A head and shoulders pattern (see Figure 3-11) is indicative of a reversal of direction—from bearish to bullish or from bullish to bearish. In a pattern that indicates a reversal from bearish to bullish, a price decline is followed by an equal-sized rise, a larger decline, a larger rise, a smaller decline, and an even larger rise. The volume generally declines as the pattern develops, until the stock's price breaks through the "neckline" where volume rises. The pattern would be flipped vertically if it was the reversal from bullish to bearish.

Figure 3-11
Head & Shoulders Pattern

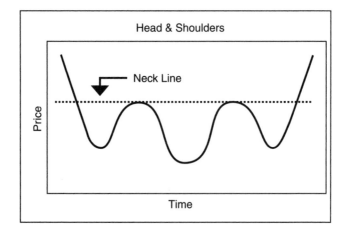

CHANNELS

Stocks often trade over long periods of time within certain price ranges. As the trading range develops, the tops and bottoms of the trading ranges can often be connected by straight lines. The line that connects the tops is referred to as the resistance line. The line that connects the bottoms is referred to as the support line. A trading range is established by the creation of three tops and three bottoms. The longer the stock stays within the trading range and the more times its price reverses when encountering a support or resistance line, the more significant the support and resistance lines become.

Eventually, of course, the price of the stock will either rise above the support line or fall below the resistance line. This is referred to as a "break out" and is typically accompanied by a rise in volume. When the price gets close to the resistance line, proponents of technical analysis sell. If, despite this selling pressure, the stock continues to rise, then, the thinking goes, the fundamentalists must have revised their opinion of the company's future prospects upwards. Once a support or resistance line is broken, a support line tends to become a resistance line and a resistance line tends to become a support line. (See Figure 3-12.)

Figure 3-12
Support and Resistance Lines

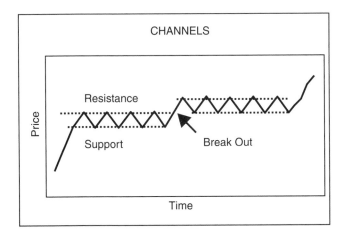

The third common pattern is the flag pattern. The flag pattern often indicates that the current trend is half over. Consider Figure 3-13, in which the flag occurs at the halfway point of the down trend.

Figure 3-13
Channel Pattern

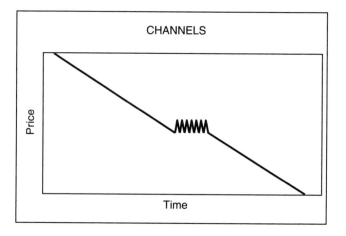

The Academic School

Investors should be aware that despite the fact that a tremendous amount of resources is dedicated to performing both fundamental and technical analysis, many academics and more than a few investors believe that both types of analysis are all but worthless. The reason they believe that research is worthless is because they believe the stock market is at least "weakly efficient."

Investors who believe the market is weakly efficient believe that all the public information that can be known is already reflected in the stock's price. They believe that because stocks today are subjected to so much analysis, both fundamental and technical, by so many analysts/investors, that the chances of finding something new are very small. Since more analysis is neither likely to uncover new or unknown information nor a new perspective on the existing information, the only factor that moves stock prices is those pieces of information that cannot be known in advance, namely, either "private information" or "surprises."

In effect, the very work that analysts/investors perform to find attractive stocks decreases the value of their analysis. Every time analysts/investors examine a stock, their work and conclusions tend to move the value of the stocks towards their "true" or "fair" value. The stocks that are the most likely to be fairly valued are the ones that receive the greatest amount of scrutiny.

Some investors even believe that all "non-public" information is also reflected in the stock price. Those who believe that non-public information is also built into stock prices believe the market is strongly efficient.

Investors who believe the market is efficient believe that whether or not they outperform or underperform the market is purely random. Since academics believe stocks are "fairly priced" and "whether a particular stock outperforms or underperforms is purely random," there is no reason to favor one stock over another. A diversified portfolio of stocks, such as an index fund, will perform as well as any other portfolio on a risk-adjusted basis and is often the cheapest portfolio to acquire and manage on an ongoing basis. The fact that so many investors believe the market is efficient is evidenced by the tremendous growth in the amount of money being committed to equity index funds.

UNDERWRITING STOCKS

The first time a company sells stock to the public, the company goes public. Going public in the U.S. is a complex and sometimes frustrating process that can involve the efforts of many professionals with many specialties. This chapter provides an overview of the process.

Why Companies Go Public

The two primary reasons companies go public is to obtain the capital they need to support their growth and to enable the company's founder(s) to sell the company.

- Supporting growth—Companies often need money to support the roll out of new products, the expansion of their manufacturing facilities, and the creation of distribution networks and sales outlets.

- Owners sell out—Owners of companies pass their companies on to their heirs, sell the company privately, or take the company public. By taking it public, they effectively sell it to the public at large.

Once a company's owners decide to take it public, they must first file a *registration statement* with the Securities and Exchange Commission. Some of the information that must be included in this document is listed in Figure 4-1. An investment banking firm must be selected to help the company go public.

Selecting Investment Banking Firms

Business owners and investment banking firms find each other in a variety of ways.

- Rapidly growing, high-profile companies are deluged with prospecting calls from investment banking firms that seek to do business.
- Companies sometimes call certain investment banks.
- Most commonly, referrals, school ties, the members of the company's board of directors, club members, and neighbors are sources.

Criteria that companies use to select investment banking firms include the firm's reputation, expertise, distribution capacity, pricing structure, and level of commitment they are willing to make to the offering.

- Reputation. As in any business, the reputation of the business is one of the most important issues.
- Expertise. Investment banking firms fall into one of two categories: generalists and specialty firms. Generalist firms, such as Prudential Securities, try to serve firms in many industries. Specialty firms concentrate on specific industries.

  Like law firms, investment banking firms often are built around a few "stars." These rainmakers bring in a large number of clients and have compensation packages that can run into eight figures per year.

- Distribution capacity. Companies sometimes select the investment banking firms they want to use based on their distribution capacity; for example, if a company wants to sell its stock primarily to institutions, individuals, or global companies.

- Pricing structure. As in most industries, competition is fierce, and pricing is becoming a more important consideration.

- Level of commitment. Investment banking firms can support an offering in one of two ways: either on a "firm underwriting" or a "best efforts" basis.

In a firm underwriting, the investment banking firm actually agrees to buy the company's stock from the selling company with its own money. After it has purchased the stock, it then tries to immediately resell the shares to investors at a higher price. The difference between the two prices is called the mark up. It's generally between 1 percent and 5 percent of the share price.

In a firm underwriting, if the investment banking firm cannot resell the shares to investors, the investment banking firm ends up owning them. Since the investment banking firm is putting its own capital at risk, this is a major commitment on the part of the investment bank.

Few investment banking firms are willing to assume a financial risk that might require them to buy an entire company, or may not have enough capital of their own to buy all the shares they underwrite, so the investment banking firm normally shares the risk by forming a "syndicate." A syndicate is a group of investment banking firms that collectively agree to buy a company's stock and then resell it to the public.

Once a company selects its lead investment bank, that bank will then invite other firms to take a piece of the offering. The firm that wins the company's business manages the syndicate, allocates shares among the members, keeps the records, and is normally referred to as the "lead manager." The firms that agree to buy shares are also considered to be underwriters, but are not managers. Some firms may be asked to help sell the stock, but are unwilling or unable to make a firm commitment to buy the shares themselves. These firms are called "members of the selling group."

A stock's mark-up is distributed based on contribution to the sales effort. If, for example, a stock is purchased by the syndicate for $19 and is resold to investors for $20, the mark up is $1. A typical split would be $0.10 for the lead manager, $0.40 for whatever firm underwrites the share, and $0.50 for the firm that sells the share. Thus, if the lead manager sells the share, it will receive the full $1. If another firm sells the share, it will receive either $0.90 or $0.50, depending upon whether it is an underwriter or just a member of the selling group.

Once the investment banking firm is hired, the next step is for the firm to help the company prepare to go public. This involves three steps:

1. Resolving any open legal issues that could scare off potential investors.

2. Restating the company's financial statements. Companies that are privately owned usually try to make themselves seem as poor as the accounting rules will allow. Companies that are publicly owned usually try to make themselves seem as successful as possible to report the highest possible earnings and command the highest possible share price.

3. Resolving any employee issues. Companies often sign up key managers to long-term contracts and sign long-term contracts with any organized labor so that potential investors can count on some stability.

These steps can take anywhere from a few weeks to years, depending upon what issues the company faces. Once the company is ready, the investment banking firm starts to put together a prospectus. The prospectus is a document that provides investors with the information they need to make an informed decision about whether or not they want to invest in the company. The information that companies must provide investors is a matter of law.

While investors should read the entire draft prospectus, some of the most important sections include the sources of stock, use of proceeds, management, and legal issues.

Source(s) of stock. This section of the prospectus discloses whether the stock that is being sold in the offering is being sold by the company, the individuals who own the company, or some combination thereof. For example, suppose Mr. Smith owns 100 percent of ABC, Inc. In order to raise capital, he first increases the number of authorized shares, gifts them to ABC, Inc., and then ABC, Inc. sells the shares. If the company sells the shares, the sales proceeds are added to the company's cash balances, and the company's net worth increases. If Mr. Smith sells any, or all, of the shares he owns personally, the sale proceeds go to Mr. Smith's personal account, and the company's net worth remains unchanged. While investors should not mind if the company's founders sell some of their personal shares in the offering, investors should make sure that the founders are not using the offering to "cash out" by selling all of their shares.

Use of proceeds. This section of the prospectus discloses what the company will do with the sales proceeds. This applies only to shares sold by the company. This section will specify whether the company will use the sales proceeds to make acquisitions, build new plants, expand its marketing efforts, and so on. It is illegal for a company to raise money for one purpose and use the proceeds for another. In order to provide them with maximum flexibility, some companies simply specify that the money will be used for "general corporate purposes."

Management team. This section provides brief resumes of the key company officers. Some of the questions that investors ask include:

- If the company is going to use the money to expand rapidly, does the management team have the expertise necessary to manage rapid growth?

- Does the management team have the depth to survive the death, disability, or departure of some key personnel?

- Does the management team have long-term contracts?

- Is a large portion of the management team's compensation tied to the stock's performance?

Legal questions. This section provides an overview of any significant legal issues that may affect the company's future success. Routine legal problems need not be disclosed.

Once the prospectus is complete (except for pricing the shares), three things happen simultaneously:

1. The investment bank sends a draft copy of the prospectus, along with supporting documentation, to the United States Securities and Exchange Commission (SEC) for approval. The SEC checks the prospectus for completeness, and if it finds it "satisfactory," it issues an approval letter. SEC approval is not an endorsement of the stock as a sound investment. SEC approval means only that the SEC has determined that the prospectus includes sufficient information for investors to make a reasonably informed decision.

2. The investment bank sends the prospectus to the Securities Commissioners of the states in which the issuer expects the stock to be sold so that the states can also approve it. This is called "Blue Skying" the issue.

3. All members of the syndicate and selling group must show copies of the draft prospectus to prospective investors. While investors cannot place firm orders for the stock yet, they are allowed to indicate how many shares they think they would like to buy and the price they would be willing to pay per share. This is called "soliciting indications of interest." Since the prospectus has not yet been approved at this point, the draft prospectus carries a red warning label along the spine saying that the information is preliminary and subject to change. Because of this red warning label, draft copies of the prospectus are called "Red Herrings."

   The feedback that the sales force receives from prospective clients is invaluable in helping the investment banking firm to price the stock. Naturally, the firm wants to sell the stock at the highest reasonable price.

After all the regulatory approvals are obtained, members of the syndicate get together for a final meeting called the "pricing meeting."

Figure 4.1

Information Included in the Registration Statement.

1. The name of the issuer.
2. The name of the state or sovereign power under which the issuer is organized.
3. The location of the issuer's principle office.
4. The names and addresses of the directors and other senior officials.
5. The names and addresses of the underwriters (if any).
6. The names and addresses of persons owning 10% or more of any class of the issuer's stock.
7. The quantities of securities owned by the directors, senior officials, underwriters, and 10% or greater holders.
8. The general character of the issuer's business.
9. A statement of the issuer's capitalization.
10. A statement of securities reserved for options outstanding, with names and addresses of persons allotted 10% or more of these options.
11. The amount of capital stock of each class included in this offer.
12. The issuer's funded debt.
13. The purposes to which the proceeds of this offering will be applied.
14. Remuneration payable to the issuers directly, naming them specifically when annual payments exceed $25,000.
15. The estimated net proceeds to be derived from the offering.
16. The price at which the public offering will be attempted.
17. Commissions, fees, and so on, to be paid to the underwriters.
18. An itemized detail of expenses incurred by the issuer in connection with this offering.
19. The net proceeds derived from any securities sold by the issuer in the preceding two years and pertinent details of those sales.
20. Any consideration paid to a promoter in the preceding two years.
21. The names and addresses of any vendors of property or goodwill to be acquired with the proceeds of this offering.
22. Full particulars of any dealings between the issuer and its officers, directors, and holders of 10% or more of its stock that transpired in the preceding two years.
23. The names and addresses of counsel passing upon the legality of the issue.
24. The dates and details of material contracts created outside the issuer's ordinary course of business within the preceding two years.
25. Certified financial statements of any issuer or business to be acquired with proceeds of this offering.
26. A copy of the underwriting contract or agreement.
27. A copy of the law firm's written opinion attesting to the legality of the issue.
28. A copy of all material contracts referred to in item 24.
29. A copy of the issuer's charter, bylaws, trust agreement, partnership agreement, and so forth, as the case may be.
30. A copy of the underlying agreement or indenture affecting any security offered or to be offered by the issuer.

At this meeting, the syndicate members get their final allotments of stock and the final price is set. The next morning, the offering becomes "effective" and final orders are accepted from investors. The stock also starts to trade in the open market.

From the perspective of the investment bank, the ideal offering is one where the initial shares offered for sale sell out almost immediately and the stock price rises 5 to 10 percent in the open market. Thus if the offering price is $20, the price rises almost immediately to $21 to $22. If the price rises 5 to 10 percent, then both the company that sells the stock and the investors who buy it are happy. Many times this is what happens—but not always.

As soon as the stock is successfully placed, the lead manager announces to the members of the syndicate and selling group that the offering is complete and from then on the stock is worth whatever investors are willing to pay for it in the open market. When the initial offering is complete, the stock is said to have "broken syndicate."

Sometimes the investment bankers overestimate the demand for the stock. Consequently, they price the stock too high and have trouble selling it. The initial investors get worried and immediately start to sell—and the stock goes to a discount in the open market. In this case, it makes it very hard for the syndicate to sell the stock. Often, the syndicate ends up buying back the stock it sold to the initial buyers and then has to try to find new buyers. When the syndicate has the highest bid in the open market, the syndicate is said to be "supporting the stock." This support may continue for a while if the syndicate members think they can find additional investors. Or at some point, the syndicate may simply pull its support and let the price decline.

At other times, the demand for the stock is so strong that demand far outstrips supply. In this case, the stock is called a "hot offering." The stock immediately rises sharply in the secondary market as investors who were not able to get any of the shares on the initial offering compete to buy it in the open market. When this happens, the company is usually unhappy since they obviously could have gotten a better price for the shares they sold.

Anyone who buys stock either during an initial offering or shortly thereafter must receive a copy of the final prospectus. While there are certainly attractive opportunities in the new offerings market, investors should exercise caution. After the initial public offering, any additional public stock offerings are referred to as secondary offerings.

PREFERRED STOCKS

Preferred stock is a specific type of stock that has very different characteristics from the common stock discussed previously. Like common stock, the proceeds a company receives from the sale of shares of preferred stock is recorded by the company on its balance sheet as equity. However, for all practical purposes, investors consider preferred stocks to be just another type of debt security. Specifically, they are debt securities that normally pay a fixed return in the form of quarterly dividends instead of semi-annual interest payments.

However, because preferred stocks are equity, they have three principal differences from bonds.

1. They are "junior" to the company's debt issues. Every security the company issues is ranked in a specific hierarchy from the most senior to the most junior. In the event the company does not generate enough cash flow to service all its debt, then this hierarchy determines who receives the limited cash flow first. Interest payments are made first to the most senior debt holder, then to the next holder, and so on, until the available cash is exhausted. Common stocks are always the most junior security and preferred stocks are always ranked between the most junior debt security and the company's common stock.

2. Unlike debt instruments, the company is not legally obligated to make dividend payments to its preferred holders. Missing an interest payment on a bond issue will cause a "default." If a bond issue is in default, the bondholders can claim breach of contract, force the company into involuntary bankruptcy, and have the board of directors and/or the management team replaced—all in an attempt to protect their interests. Missing a dividend payment, however, is not a breach of contract and will not cause a default.

This begs the question, "If missing a dividend payment will not cause a default, what incentive does the issuer have to make the dividend payments on its preferred?" Usually, under the terms laid out in the offering prospectus, unless and until the company meets its obligations to its preferred holders, the company is prohibited from making dividend payments to its common stockholders or bonus payments to the company's managers. Thus, in addition to the preferred holders, both the company's management and the company's common shareholders usually want to see the preferred holders receive their dividends in full and on time. Usually, only a company that really has a true cash shortage will miss a dividend payment on its preferred.

3. The dividends do not accrue in between dividend payment dates. When bonds trade, they trade with "accrued interest." An investor who buys a bond between interest payment dates must pay the seller not only the agreed-upon price of the bond, but also the interest the bond has earned but not yet paid from the last interest payment date. However, preferred stocks do not trade with accrued dividends. When an investor buys a preferred stock between dividend payment dates, the seller is not entitled to receive a partial or prorated dividend. Whoever owns the stock on its ex-dividend day receives the full dividend regardless of how long they have owned the stock. Since the dividend does not accrue separately, the dividend builds up in the value of the stock between ex-dividend days. This results in a jagged price pattern, where the value of the preferred drops by the amount of the dividend on each ex-dividend date. (See Figure 5-1.)

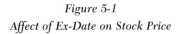

Figure 5-1
Affect of Ex-Date on Stock Price

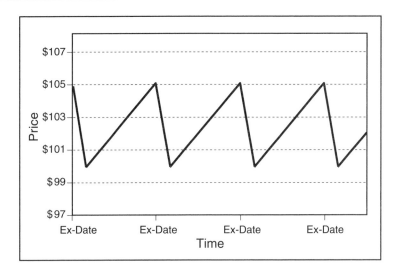

Why Do Companies Issue Preferreds?

Companies issue preferred stocks in order to strengthen their balance sheets. Since the proceeds of preferred stock sales are considered to be equity, the proceeds both strengthen the issuer's balance sheet and improve its debt to equity ratio. Companies often need to strengthen their balance sheets in order to:

- Avoid violating the covenants in their loan agreements.
- Meet legally mandated debt to equity ratios (if they are in regulated industries such as banking or insurance).
- Provide the capital necessary to support expansion plans.

While the issuance of either preferred stock or common stock will strengthen the company's balance sheet, preferred stocks have to offer investors a higher dividend than common stocks because preferred stocks don't offer investors the opportunity to share in the company's growth. Why would companies issue preferred stock if the required dividend payment is higher on the preferred than it would be on the common? The primary reason is that by issuing preferred stock, the company will not dilute the ownership interest of the current common stockowners.

Why Do Investors Buy Preferreds?

Some investors buy preferred stocks:

- As interest rate plays. As with any fixed rate instrument, their prices rise as interest rates fall and fall as interest rates rise. Preferred stocks are sometimes used to speculate on interest rates because of their relatively high sensitivity to interest rates. The interest rate sensitivity of a preferred stock is approximately equal to:

  $$\text{Interest Rate Sensitivity} \cong (1+\text{Yield}) / \text{Yield}$$

  For a preferred stock offering a 7-percent yield, the interest rate sensitivity would be approximately equal to:

  $$\text{Interest Rate Sensitivity} \cong (1+.07) / .07 \cong 15.29\%$$

  Thus, if interest rates rise or fall by 1 percent, the price of the preferred will fall or rise by 15.29 percent. (This assumes that the preferred is perpetual and not subject to being called.)

- To generate a steady income. Many investors, especially retirees, consider "obtaining a high steady income" as their primary investment goal. Preferred stocks are attractive to these investors because they offer a higher yield than debt instruments. The trade-off is that they also offer higher credit risk since they are very "junior" securities.

- To generate tax-advantaged income. Preferred stocks, like common stocks, are subject to the 70-percent dividend exclusion rule. When preferred stocks are owned by a Sub-Chapter C

Corporation, 70 percent of the dividends received are excluded from federal income taxes, provided that the preferred stock is held for more than 45 days.

- To execute a credit play. Preferred stocks are junior-level securities. As such, they generally have lower credit ratings than the more senior securities from the same issuer. The credit ratings of the junior-level securities are also more volatile. If the credit quality of the company improves, the credit rating of the preferred stocks might be upgraded, resulting in some sudden price appreciation. Of course, if the company's credit quality declines, the credit quality of the preferred stock is often the first security to be downgraded.

- To make an option play. Preferred stocks can contain several different types of embedded options. Some options benefit the issuer, while others benefit the investor. They are discussed in the following section.

What Are the Common Embedded Options?

The most commonly employed embedded options in preferred stocks are the call option, the cumulative option, the participating option, the voting rights option, the convertible option, and the exchangeable option.

- The call option. Equity is normally perpetual, meaning that it has no set maturity date. For example, common stock exists until the company either ceases to exist or until the stock is repurchased by the company and retired. Most companies that issue preferred want to have some control over the maturity of their preferred so that they can:

  ➤ Refinance the preferred with a new issue that pays a lower dividend rate if interest rates should decline.

  ➤ Simply retire the preferred if the company has no more need for the funds.

Investors prefer to buy preferreds with a long period of call protection, while issuers prefer short periods of call protection. Issuers compensate investors for short periods of call protection by paying higher dividends. Preferreds whose only embedded option is a call option(s) are referred to as "straight preferreds."

- The cumulative option. If a preferred stock is cumulative, then the unpaid dividends accrue against the preferred in the event the company is unable to meet its preferred dividend payments. This means that before common shareholders can again receive dividends and managers can again receive bonuses, all of the overdue dividends have to be paid to the preferred stockholders. However, if the stock is not cumulative, then any dividend payments that are missed are simply forgotten.

  Suppose an investor buys a cumulative preferred stock from a company that has had problems and that has not paid dividends in five years. If the company then gets back on its feet, the investor will receive all five years' worth of back dividends. Many investors try to find cumulative preferred issues where the dividends are currently in arrears, but may shortly be made current.

- The participating option. If a preferred stock has a participating option, then in the event the company has an especially good year, the preferred shareholders also participate in the company's good fortune—usually by receiving an extra dividend payment. What defines an "especially good year" is described in the prospectus of each issue. Usually it is defined either as the company having "earnings in excess of X dollars" or a "profit margin above a certain percentage."

- The voting rights option. Usually preferred shareholders do not get the right to vote for members of the board of directors. The exception is when the preferred stock has a voting rights option. This option grants the owners of the preferred shares voting rights if, and only if, the issuer is behind on its dividend payments. The preferred holders get these voting rights in order to protect their interests—interests that need protection if the dividends aren't being paid. Sometimes the preferred owners are granted enough votes to effectively seize control of the company—again, only if a dividend payment is missed. The details of any voting right options are found in the offering prospectus.

- The convertible option. Many preferred issues offer investors the right to convert their preferred stocks into a fixed number of shares of the company's common stock. This gives investors the opportunity to participate to some degree in the appreciation of the company's common shares. The trade-off is that convertible preferreds offer a lower dividend yield. The difference in yield is what pays for the option.

- The exchangeable option. A few preferred issues offer the issuer the right to exchange the preferred stock for a more senior debt issue. Consider the following situation. An issuer with a large tax loss carry forward might elect to issue preferred stock instead of debt because:

  ➤ Issuing equity strengthens the balance sheet, while issuing debt weakens it.

  ➤ The company can't make use of the interest expense deduction that is one of the primary benefits of issuing debt securities.

However, once the company's tax loss carry forward is exhausted, the company might want to have debt issued instead of equity. An exchangeable option allows the issuer to replace a preferred stock issue with debt. This can be a win-win option, since the debt the investors receive often has to have either the same or a higher yield and is always a more senior security. An issuer would rather pay 10 percent in interest than 9 percent in dividends if interest payments are deductible and dividend payments are not. However, for most investors, both interest and dividend payments are fully taxable, so the investor would rather receive the 10-percent interest.

CHAPTER 6

TRADING SECURITIES

Securities transactions take place either on an exchange or in the over-the-counter (OTC) market. While the purpose of both the exchanges and the OTC market is to match securities buyers and securities sellers, the way they match up buyers and sellers is very different.

The country's oldest and most prestigious exchange is the New York Stock Exchange (NYSE). The stated purpose of the NYSE is to facilitate the creation of an orderly market.

How a Trade Is Executed

When a customer wants to buy or sell a stock that trades on the NYSE, he or she places an order with a firm that is a member of the exchange. Only firms that are members of the exchange can transact business on the exchange. Being a member of an exchange is referred to as "owning a seat" on the exchange.

The customer's order is transmitted electronically to the firm's floor clerk at the firm's clerk booth. The clerks' booths are located along the perimeter of the exchange floor. The floor clerk hands the order to a floor broker who walks out to the specific location (referred to as the trading post) on the trading floor where that particular stock is traded. Each stock trades at only one location or trading post.

When the floor broker reaches the stock's trading post, the floor broker tries to execute the client's order. The order can be executed either with a floor broker from another firm or with the specialist who is responsible for maintaining an orderly market in the stock. For example, suppose the floor broker for Prudential Securities has an order to purchase 6,000 shares of IBM™. When the floor broker arrives at the IBM trading post, if a floor broker from another firm has 6,000 or more shares for sale, the two floor brokers would negotiate a price and effect the transaction. In actively traded stocks, there are usually several floor brokers at the post looking to execute their client's orders.

If, however, when the floor broker arrives at the trading post, there is no floor broker with shares to sell, the floor broker can transact business with the specialist in the stock. The role of the specialist is to maintain an orderly market and to provide liquidity to the marketplace. Therefore, when no one else is available to buy or sell, the specialist performs that function. Because the specialist stands ready to buy or sell in order to fill customer orders, he or she provides investors with liquidity.

The specialist makes money by making a market with a spread between the bid price and the ask price. For example, a specialist might make a market as 95$\frac{1}{2}$ by 95$\frac{3}{4}$. This means that the specialist will buy the stock at \$95.50 and sell it at \$95.75. Ideally, the specialist would like to buy and sell the same number of shares so as not to end up owning or owing a large number of shares.

Therefore, if investors are buying more shares from the specialist than they are selling to the specialist, the specialist will raise both the bid and asked price for the stock in order to encourage sales and discourage buys. Naturally, if more clients are selling to the specialist than buying from the specialist, the specialist will lower the price in order to discourage sales and encourage buys. The specialists make their money in the "turnover."

Naturally, this process is fairly labor intensive and only suitable for larger orders. Orders for a relatively few shares are executed automatically at the bid price and ask price posted by the specialist via the Super Dot system. Therefore, small orders (1,000 shares or less) can normally be executed instantly.

THE OVER-THE-COUNTER SECURITIES MARKET

Any security transaction that does not take place on a security exchange is said to occur in the over-the-counter (OTC) market. Usually traded in the OTC market are:

- U.S. government securities
- U.S. agency securities
- Corporate bonds
- Municipal bonds
- Stocks of companies with small capitalizations
- Stocks of most banks and savings & loans
- Options on bonds
- Warrants
- American depository receipts

Many investors are initially confused by the OTC market because it has no central location, unlike an exchange with its centralized trading floor. Instead the OTC "market" is a telecommunications market. It consists of firms located throughout the country, any of which can trade with another firm via computer. Since phone lines reach almost everywhere in the country, the OTC market is said to be a market without geographical or physical boundaries.

Many of the brokerage firms in this country are not members of any exchange, and so they cannot transact business on any exchange. Instead they deal exclusively in securities that are traded OTC. In fact, some firms are so specialized that they deal only with one kind of security, such as U.S. government securities or municipal bonds.

Broker/Dealers

In any one OTC transaction, a firm can act as either a broker or a dealer.

When a firm takes an order from a client and then merely executes the order (either in the OTC market or on an exchange), it is said to be acting as the client's *agent,* or as a *broker.* In this type of transaction, the firm never owns the security, but merely performs an order execution service for the client.

When a firm buys securities from its clients (using its own money) or sells securities to its clients (out of its own inventory), it is acting as a principal, or as a *dealer.* In these transactions, the firm itself is on the other side of the client's trade (the contra party). So the firm itself is one of the two principals (the buyer or the seller) in the transaction.

Most firms act in both capacities at different times. They act as brokers when their clients want to buy securities either that the firms do not have in inventory or that are traded on an exchange. They act as dealers when their clients want to sell securities that the firms want to buy or when their clients want to buy securities that the firms inventory.

Firms that act in both capacities are called *broker/dealers*, because they can buy or sell securities either as brokers (agents) or as dealers (principals).

The broker/dealer's compensation depends on its capacity in a transaction. When acting as agent, the brokerage firm charges its clients a *commission* for the services it provides. When acting as *principal*, the firm does not charge commissions, but instead:

- Tries to buy the securities for less than the price at which the firm thinks they can be resold.
- Tries to sell the securities for more than the price paid for them.

Sometimes the firms are successful at making a profit on principal trades, and sometimes they are not.

Example: Dependable Brokerage, Inc., gets three orders from its clients in a given morning.

- The first order is to sell 2,000 shares of an exchange-listed security. The firm sends the order to the floor of the exchange, where it is executed at the best possible price for its client. For its services, the firm charges the client a commission.

- The second order is to buy 500 shares of stock that is traded OTC. The firm itself does not have any of this security in its own inventory, so it has to buy the stock, on the client's behalf, from another firm. The firm contacts a number of firms that have the stock in their inventories to see which firm will sell it for the lowest price. After finding the lowest price, the firm buys the 500 shares and bills the client for the purchase price plus a commission. The firm again acted as its client's agent, but this time in the OTC market.

- The third order is from a client who wants to buy 3,000 shares of a different OTC security. The firm has this security in its own inventory, and so it becomes the seller and fills its client's buy order. Because the firm acted as a principal in this transaction, it cannot charge the client a commission. Instead, the firm "marks up" or raises the price it charges for the securities. If the firm bought these 3,000 shares for less than the price at which it sells them to the client, the firm makes a profit on the transaction. If, however, the firm bought the shares at a higher price than the price at which it sold the shares to the client, the firm incurs a loss on the transaction.

Market Making

When a firm buys and sells securities for its own account, it is said to be *market making*. Before a firm can "make a market" in a security, it has to meet certain qualifications relating to its net capital, as detailed in the

National Association of Security Dealers (NASD) regulations. These regulations are designed to make sure that a firm has enough capital to back up its quotes so that there is no credit risk in the market.

The department that decides which securities to buy and sell and for what prices is called the *trading department.*

Each trader within a firm is assigned certain securities to trade. For example, one trader may be responsible for trading OTC oil stocks, while another may be responsible for trading OTC computer stocks. Every minute of every day that the market is open, these traders decide:

- What prices their firms will pay to buy the securities that they trade.

- The prices at which their firms stand ready to sell the securities that they trade.

The price at which a firm stands ready to buy a security is called its *bid price.* The price at which a firm stands ready to sell a security is called its *offer price.* By offering to both buy and sell a given security, a brokerage firm "makes a market" in the security. As market conditions change during the day, the trader raises or lowers the firm's bid and offer prices. By standing ready to buy or sell securities at their posted prices, these traders play the same role that the specialists and competitive market makers do on the exchange floor.

Example: A trader at Dependable Brokerage, Inc., is responsible for "making the market" in OTC computer stocks. For one of these companies, Wizz Bang Computers, Inc. (WBCI), the trader is currently making the market:

$$29^{3/4} \text{ by } 30$$

In other words, the firm stands ready to buy WBCI stock at $29.75 and to sell it for $30. Note that the price at which the firm stands ready to sell the stock is $0.25 higher than the price at which it will buy it. This $0.25 difference, called the *spread,* is how the firm makes a profit. By buying the stock for $0.25 less than it sells it for, the firm makes a profit of a quarter on every share it buys and then sells.

So if the price stays constant throughout the day and the trader buys 5,000 shares and also sells 5,000 shares, the firm makes a profit of ($0.25 × 5,000) or $1,250.

Unfortunately for the brokerage firms and their traders, trading is not quite this easy. Ideally, traders would like to buy and sell the same number of shares each and every day so that, at day's end, they would not have any inventory to be worried about overnight. If traders are getting "more buyers than sellers" (that is, having more people buy from them than are selling to them), they compensate by raising the bid and asked prices.

Example: The trader was making the market 29¾ by 30. Now, getting "more buyers," she might now make the market:

$$30 × 30¼$$

In other words, the trader is now willing to pay $30 per share and sell for $30.25 a share. By raising the bid price (increasing the price she is willing to pay), the trader hopes to attract more sellers. By raising the offer price (increasing the price at which she is willing to sell), the trader hopes to attract fewer buyers. By attracting more sellers and fewer buyers, the trader hopes to bring the number of buy and sell orders back into balance.

Maintaining balance is important so that the trader does not get caught with a lot of inventory in a bad market.

Example: While making a market in WBCI at 30 by 30¼, the trader receives more sell orders (totaling 10,000 shares) than buy orders (totaling 5,000 shares). By the middle of the trading day, the firm owns 5,000 shares of WBCI. If the market suddenly drops or if a negative news item about WBCI should be announced, the most anyone might be willing to pay for WBCI is, say, $28. In such a case, the market for WBCI falls to 28 by 28¼, and the firm has a loss of $10,000 ($2 per share × 5,000 shares).

The same situation results when the price of the stock moves up sharply after the trader shorts the stock. (Many traders sell stock short to fill buy orders if they do not have any shares in inventory. They then hope to buy the shares at their lower bid price to cover the short position.)

So traders who do not want to speculate with the firm's capital always try to adjust their bid and offer prices so that they are buying and selling approximately the same number of shares at all times. Traders are generally not hurt by a sharply rising or sharply falling market *unless* they build up a substantial long or short position in the security. If they are willing to settle for a small profit on each transaction, little market risk is involved.

But why settle for a small profit? If the firm profits by buying low and selling high, why not widen the spread? For example, instead of bidding 29¾ for WBCI and offering it at 30, why not bid 28 and offer to sell at 34? The firm would then make $6 on every share it bought and then sold.

Widening the spread for greater profit is not feasible for several reasons.

First, the National Association of Securities Dealers (NASD) has the 5-percent guideline prohibiting price differentials of more than 5 percent, except under extraordinary circumstances. Only if a firm incurs an extraordinary expense in trying to fill a client's order can it exceed this 5-percent guideline.

Second, the competition among dealers for each other's business and for clients' business is fierce. Very often a number of firms all make markets in the same securities. Anyone who wants to buy the security—either other firms or clients—of course, buys it from the firm offering it at the lowest price. Likewise, any firm or client wanting to sell a security will sell it to the firm willing to pay the highest price for it. Thus a firm that posts low bids and high offers will just not do any business.

Posting Quotes

How do firms make their prices known to other dealers and to clients? The answer depends on the security itself and on the amount of capital that the issuing company has.

THE PINK SHEETS

If the issuing company is small or the security rarely traded, the security is listed in the *National Quotation Bureau (NQB)* sheets. These daily "sheets" list the securities currently being offered for sale or sought after for purchase and the firms (with their phone numbers) trying to sell them.

- The sheets that contain the stock and warrant listings are called the *pink sheets* because they are printed on pink paper. On any given day, the listings contain about 11,000 different OTC stocks and warrants.

- The sheets that contain the corporate bond listings are called the *yellow sheets* because they are printed on yellow paper.

Because these sheets are printed only once a day, and the value of the securities can change constantly, a prospective buyer or seller of the securities listed on the sheets must call the firms listed on the sheets and get their current bids or offers.

THE NASDAQ SYSTEM

Quotes for more actively traded securities or for securities issued by larger companies can be found on the *National Association of Securities Dealers Automated Quotation System (NASDAQ)*. Founded in 1971, this system is an electronic communication network with hookups for market makers, registered representatives, and regulators. Firms that wish to buy and sell securities can post their bids or offers electronically. Because the system is computerized, firms can change their bids and offers throughout the day as market conditions change.

Because subscribers use this information system for different purposes, not all subscribers need access to the same level of information. For this reason, three different levels of service are available, representing various levels of complexity and, of course, cost.

Level One. This level shows only the highest bid price and lowest offer price for a given security, without disclosing the name of the firm making the bid or offer. It is used by registered representatives to indicate the current "market" to potential buyers and sellers of a security. Often one firm is making the highest bid while another is making the lowest offer. Neither the broker nor the client really cares which firm they buy from or sell to; they care only about price. The highest bid and lowest offer are often called the *inside market.*

Level Two. Service at this level shows what every firm is bidding and offering for every NASDAQ-listed security. Retail traders use it to know not only the best quotes, but also the firms making the quotes. By knowing the firms' names, traders know whom to call to buy or sell the security to fill an order.

Level Three. This service is the same as level two service, except that traders may enter, delete, or update quotations for securities in which they are making a market. Thus, the senior traders who decide their firm's bid and offer prices are the only ones who need level three service. Because every firm that lists a quote on this system must stand ready to buy or sell a round lot of the security at the price it quotes, code letters are used to prevent unauthorized parties from changing a firm's quotes.

Types of Quotations

Securities dealers, particularly those who deal primarily in thinly traded securities, can make or obtain several quotes: firm, subject, and workout.

FIRM QUOTES

Firm bids or offers are prices at which the broker/dealer is committed to buy or sell a specified amount of security. A firm bid or offer is usually good for the moment that the quote is given, but it may also be firm for a longer period. Also, unless otherwise stated, it is good for at least one unit of trading. In other words, the broker/dealer's commitment to buy or sell at the quoted price is limited to 100 shares of stock or 10 bonds at the quoted price. (Bond dealers vary with regard to the size of their firm quotes.) Any quotes on the NASDAQ system are considered firm for one round lot. Orders for more than a round lot are subject to negotiations between the buying firm and the selling firm.

SUBJECT QUOTES

When a broker/dealer gives a quote and says it's *subject,* then the quote is "subject" to confirmation. The broker/dealer needs more information before making the quote firm. Subject quotes can be expressed in several ways including:

- "It's quoted (that is, I'm not quoting it) 10-10½."
- "Last I saw, it was 10-10½."
- "It is 10-10½ subject."

WORKOUT QUOTES

Sometimes there is a very wide spread and the broker follows the quote with the word *workout.* This quote is not firm. It merely provides a range in which the broker/dealer believes a price can be "worked out." These quotes are commonly used for infrequently traded securities.

National Market System (NMS)

National Market System (NMS) stocks, approximately 7,000 at this writing, meet guidelines set by the National Association of Securities Dealers (discussed later in the chapter).

The National Market System consists of stocks for which more information is available than for other OTC stocks. For most stocks traded over the counter, the newspaper listings show the name, dividend, volume, bid/asked, and day-to-day price changes. In addition to this information, listings for NMS stocks include high and low prices for the previous 52 weeks, as well as high and low prices for the day. Trades in NMS stocks are reported within 90 seconds of when they occur.

Third Market Transactions

Over-the-counter trades of stock listed on the New York Stock Exchange (or on any other national stock exchange) are called *third market* transactions. These transactions were very popular prior to 1975 when the NYSE had fixed commission rates. Once the NYSE rates became negotiated (in effect, reduced), the number of third market transactions dropped drastically.

Today, however, third market transactions are again on the upswing. Frequently, a firm that is accumulating shares in a potential takeover target wants first to accumulate a sizable block of its prey's stock in the OTC market before it starts buying large quantities on the exchange floor. The third market offers a way for an acquiring firm to accumulate a large number of shares of a listed security without causing the daily volume figures, as reported by the exchange, to rise sharply.

The third market is now used for trading of exchange-listed securities traded over-the-counter, such as in after-hours trading.

Fourth Market Transactions

Fourth market transactions are over-the-counter trades made directly between large institutional investors, such as insurance companies or pension funds, and bank trust departments. Broker/dealers are not involved in these trades.

Institutional investors interested in buying and selling large blocks of securities do a substantial business in the OTC market for several reasons. For one, they deal a lot in government and municipal bonds, which trade almost entirely over the counter. Second, they are also involved in distributions of new issues, both primary and secondary, which, again, take place in the OTC market. Finally, large block transactions can be executed OTC in such a way as to avoid unduly affecting the price of the security. (Attempting to sell too much stock on an exchange might depress the price.)

The fourth market is composed of transactions without the services of a broker/dealer.

ELECTRONIC COMMERCE NETWORKS

An *Electronic Commerce Network (ECN)* is an automated trading system that allows investors to enter and execute orders in real-time without the intervention of an intermediary, such as a broker. ECNs are technology driven and are rapidly changing the way in which both retail and institutional trading is done. The rapid rise in technology, not only in the workplace, but also in the home with the proliferation of personal computers, has fueled the growth in this new type of marketplace.

ECNs effectively began with the launch of Reuters Group's Instinet, which is still the largest ECN. Instinet began in 1969 as a system for investment managers to execute OTC securities transactions. Instinet allowed mutual funds and other institutional investors to post orders anonymously at prices inside the wide spreads of NASDAQ stocks.

ECNs can act both as a broker or a quasi-stock exchange. On April 21, 1999, Island, an electronic exchange company, filed its submission with the U.S. Securities and Exchange Commission to register as a full-fledged exchange. Once registered, Island will be in a position to rival NYSE and NASDAQ and attract institutional investors that trade in these two markets. Until now, the SEC's interpretation of the definition of exchange reflected relatively rigid regulatory requirements and classifications for "exchange" and "broker/dealers." Advances in technology and the emergence of ECNs have increasingly blurred these distinctions. This has led the SEC to review its interpretation of the term "exchange." The statutory definition of exchange includes "a market place or facilities for bringing together purchasers and sellers of securities or for otherwise performing, with respect to securities, the functions commonly performed by a stock exchange." With ECNs, the natural economic distinctions between stock exchanges and broker/dealers have been broken down. Exchanges and brokers are now doing the same thing.

Advantages of ECNs include cost reduction, faster execution, anonymous trading, and after-hours trading. The best prices are simply determined by the most aggressive order to buy (the highest price) and the most aggressive order to sell (the lowest price). If an order is executed, buy and sell prices are transmitted to broker(s) and/or exchange(s) and posted to the National Market System. If orders cannot be matched, they are routed either to another ECN or to other exchanges for execution.

The major differences between the traditional methods of trading compared to the way in which ECNs operate are in the process, trading times, pricing mechanism, and economics. In the ECNs market, bids and asked quotes are entered and maintained in computer systems either directly by the investor or through his or her broker. When an order to either buy or sell is placed, it is automatically matched with the best available bid/asked quote and automatically executed. If there is no bid/asked quote, the order is transferred to a market making system. In the ECNs market, after-hours trading is available. The market is ready 24 hours a day, 7 days a week. There is direct matching of supply and demand. There are reduced commissions for both the ECN and the broker in the ECN market.

The National Association of Security Dealers (NASD)

The National Association of Securities Dealers (NASD) was organized under the 1939 Maloney Act, an amendment (Section 15A) to the Securities Exchange Act of 1934. Although established by Congress and supervised by the SEC, the NASD operates not as a government agency but as an independent self-regulating organization.

PURPOSES OF THE NASD

The NASD's certificate of incorporation, listing its purposes and objectives, empowers the association to set operating standards to promote just and equitable principles of trade and to require adherence to high standards of commercial honor and integrity.

The NASD's power to regulate lies in its ability to deny membership to any broker/dealers operating in an unethical or improper manner. Because only NASD members have the advantage of price concessions, discounts, and similar allowances, the loss of membership privileges all but prevents a firm from competing in the marketplace. In addition, NASD members are permitted to do business only with other members, although they may deal with foreign banks and dealers.

HOW THE NASD IS ORGANIZED

Board of Governors.   The NASD Board of Governors is comprised of 31 members. Some of the members are elected by the board itself, but most are elected by the membership. Each of the NASD's 13 districts elects one or more governors as representatives on the board for three-year terms. The board as a group administers and manages the affairs of the NASD.

District Committees.   The members in each of the 13 districts elect a committee, which supervises NASD programs in the district. In addition, it serves as a business committee by doing the following:

- Reviewing the reports of NASD examiners
- Investigating complaints against members
- Conducting disciplinary proceedings

- Imposing penalties for violations of federal and state laws and the NASD's Rules of Fair Practice

The chairperson of each district committee also serves as an advisor to the Board of Governors.

Bylaws.   The NASD's bylaws spell out the terms and conditions of everyday operation of the NASD, as well as the classification, qualification, and responsibilities of its members, including the Rules of Fair Practice. The bylaws also deal with such key issues as membership, registration, and qualification standards.

Membership.   Membership in the NASD is open to all properly qualified brokers and dealers whose regular course of business is transacted in any branch of the investment banking or securities businesses in the United States. A *broker* is defined as a legal entity (individual, corporation, or partnership) that effects transactions for the accounts of others. A *dealer* is a legal entity that engages in the buying or selling of securities for its own account. All broker/dealers must be registered with the SEC and the state authorities, as required by law, to be eligible for membership in the NASD. By definition, banks are not broker/dealers and therefore not eligible for NASD membership.

Some broker/dealers may not become members of the NASD, according to the bylaws. Because the main purpose of the NASD is to promote high standards of commercial conduct, broker/dealers convicted of violations of law are barred from membership in the NASD. Specifically, membership is denied to the following:

- Broker/dealers that have been suspended or expelled from a registered securities association or exchange for acts inconsistent with just and equitable principles of trade.
- Broker/dealers whose registration with the Securities and Exchange Commission has been revoked or denied.
- An individual who has been named as a "cause" of a suspension, expulsion, or revocation, or one whose registration as a registered

representative has been revoked by the NASD or a national securities exchange.

- An individual who has been convicted within the preceding 10 years of any crime arising out of the securities business and involving embezzlement, fraudulent conversion, misappropriation of funds, or the abuse or misuse of a fiduciary relationship.

- A broker/dealer whose partner, officer, or employee is not qualified for NASD membership.

- A broker/dealer with officers, partners, or employees who are required to be registered representatives but who are not.

NASD Rules of Fair Practice

The Rules of Fair Practice are a part of the NASD bylaws designed to promote and enforce the highest ethical conduct in the securities business. The most basic of the rules is Section 1, Article III, which states the fundamental philosophy of the NASD: "a member in the conduct of his business, shall observe high standards of commercial honor and just and equitable principles of trade."

The broad-based Rules of Fair Practice include specific rules on many areas of the securities business. Some of the areas addressed by the rules follow.

NASD MEMBER FIRM ADVERTISING

The Rules of Fair Practice consider it a violation for a member to publish, circulate, or distribute any advertisement, sales literature, or market letter that a member knows to contain untrue, false, or misleading statements. Similarly, no material fact or qualification can be omitted from advertising material if such an omission causes the material to be misleading. In short, all advertising, sales, and market literature must be based on the principles of fair dealing and good faith.

EXECUTION OF RETAIL TRADES

So that all customers may benefit from a free and open market, NASD members must use "reasonable diligence"—that is, consider all pertinent factors—to make sure that the customer gets the best possible price under prevailing market conditions. The rules also state that a member's obligation to do the best for customers is not fulfilled by channeling business through another broker/dealer, unless using a third party reduces costs to the customer.

RECEIPT AND DELIVERY OF SECURITIES

No member may accept a customer's purchase order for any security without first making sure that the customer agrees to receive those securities against payment. On the sell side, no member may sell securities for a customer without being reasonably sure that the customer possesses the securities and will deliver them within three business days. To satisfy the requirement of "reasonable assurance," the broker/dealer or registered representative should note on the order ticket the present location of the securities to be sold.

FORWARDING OF REPORTS AND PROXY MATERIAL

When securities are held for a customer by a brokerage firm, they are usually held in *street name* (that is, in the name of the broker/dealer). In these cases, the issuer of the security sends all literature, including reports and proxies, to the brokerage firm, not to the customer. If NASD member firms do not promptly forward such material to customers, their conduct can be regarded as inconsistent with high standards of commercial honor.

RECOMMENDATIONS TO CUSTOMERS

According to the Rules of Fair Practice, all recommendations to a customer to purchase, sell, or exchange securities must be based on reasonable grounds and be suitable for the customer's account: The controlling factor is the best interest of the customer. To determine suitability, the member is expected to learn about the specific financial condition and needs of each customer.

NASD Uniform Practice Code

The Uniform Practice Code (UPC) is a part of the NASD bylaws whose purpose is the uniformity of the customs, practices, and trading techniques used among all NASD members. The code includes rules for trade terms, the delivery of securities, payment, rights, stamp taxes, computation of interest, and due bills.

The administration of the UPC is the responsibility of the National Uniform Practice Committee and the District Uniform Practice Committees. Any changes in the rules by district committees must be approved by the board. Any contact between NASD members (except transactions in exempt securities or on national exchanges) is subject to the Uniform Practice Code.

If a situation arises that is not specifically covered by the written code, it is referred to the appropriate District Uniform Practice Committee for action. Controversies about an interdistrict trade are referred to the National Uniform Practice Committee.

Some of the important sections of the UPC follow.

DELIVERY OF SECURITIES

For each security transaction, there are two key dates: the trade date and the delivery date.

Trade Date.   The transaction takes place on the trade date. The NASD code requires that all ordinary transactions be confirmed in writing on or before the first full business day following the trade date.

Delivery Date.   The delivery date is the date on which payment is due. There are several types of delivery:

- *Cash:* Settlement occurs on the same day as the trade itself. Cash settlement is used when the client has to settle a transaction before a certain date, such as year-end for tax purposes.

- *Next day:* The contract is settled the first business day after the trade date.

- *Regular way:* The seller agrees to deliver the securities to the office of the buyer on the third full business day following the transaction date.

- *Seller's option:* For securities other than U.S. government securities, this type of delivery allows the seller to have the securities at the buyer's office on or before the business day that the seller's option expires.

  Example: If securities are sold "seller's 30," the seller can deliver up to 30 days from the trade date, as long as one day's notice is given and three business days have elapsed from the trade date.

  This type of delivery is often requested by sellers who have difficulty getting possession of their securities.

- *Buyer's option:* This type of delivery gives the buyer the option to receive securities on a specific date.

Three-day (regular way) delivery applies to most trades in over-the-counter securities and securities listed on an exchange. All corporate, municipal, and most federal agency securities trade the regular way. United States government securities are usually settled on a next-day basis.

DON'T KNOW (DK) PROCEDURES

After a trade, each broker/dealer sends the other a notice to confirm the details. If both parties recognize and acknowledge the trade, it is *confirmed,* or *compared.* Sometimes, however, the contrabroker (the broker/dealer with whom the trade was made) sends back a signed DK, a *don't know* notice, telling the confirming broker that the contrabroker does not "know"—or recognize—the trade. If the contrabroker does not respond to the confirming broker by the close of two business days from the trade date, the following procedures can be used:

- Not later than the 15th calendar day after the trade date, the confirming member sends a DK notice to the contrabroker.

- The contrabroker then has four business days after the notice is received either to confirm or to DK the transaction.

- Failure to receive a response from the contrabroker by the close of four business days constitutes a DK, and the confirming member has no further liability.

- All DK notices sent by either party must be signed by authorized persons.

A DK is sometimes referred to as a *questioned trade (QT)*.

DIVIDENDS

When a corporation declares a dividend, there are four significant dates as follows:

1. The *declaration date* is the date on which the corporation declares a dividend to common or preferred shareholders.
2. The *record date* is the date on which the corporation's recorded shareholders are listed for the purposes of paying the declared dividend.
3. The *ex-dividend date* is the date on or after which the buyer of stock is *not* entitled to receive a declared dividend.
4. The *payment date* is the day on which the dividend is actually paid to shareholders.

Securities normally go *ex-dividend* (that is, without dividend) on the second business day preceding the record date. *Anyone purchasing the securities on or after the ex-dividend date is not entitled to receive the dividend.*

Example: Gyrus Corporation declares a dividend to be paid to holders of record on February 10, a Monday; this is the record date. Anyone buying stock has to buy it at least two days before the record date in order to take delivery and be recorded as the owner. To be the holder of record, you have to purchase Gyrus on or by February 5 (five calendar days or three business days before delivery.) Gyrus starts trading ex-dividend on February 6.

Due Bills

Occasionally, a security is sold before the ex-dividend date but is delivered too late for the buying broker to record ownership and get the dividend. In this case, the selling broker receives the dividend but is actually not entitled to keep it. At the time of the sale, the buyer can demand a promise from the seller to pay the dividend. This claim on dividends is called a *due bill.*

Good Delivery

To assure clear ownership, the NASD Uniform Practice Code requires that all transactions must be for *good delivery*—that is, the security must be in proper form so that the record of ownership may be readily transferred. The qualifications for good delivery are as follows:

1. Stock certificates must be accompanied by an assignment. For example, if a stock certificate is registered in the name of John A. Smith, the owner must endorse the certificate exactly that way. The assignment (endorsement) can be made in the appropriate space on the back of the certificate. Or if a registered stockholder does not have the certificate available, a stock power can be used. If a certificate is issued in the name of joint tenants or tenants in common, the delivery is good only if the certificate is signed by all

co-tenants. Sometimes a *power of substitution* is used, in which the owner assigns power of attorney to the broker to facilitate transfer.

2. The certificate must be in good condition.

3. When a contract is for more than 100 shares, the delivered certificates must be in denominations from which units of 100 shares can be made. For example, a trade for 300 shares can be satisfied by three certificates for 100 shares or six certificates for 50 shares. But four certificates for 75 shares are not good delivery because the pieces cannot be bunched into lots of 100 shares. For odd lots, the exact number of shares must be delivered.

4. A certificate in the name of a deceased person is not good delivery, even if it is properly assigned. Such certificates must be transferred to the executor of the estate or to street name.

5. A bond or preferred stock that is called for redemption is not good delivery unless the entire issue has been called.

6. Temporary certificates are not good delivery if permanent certificates are available.

7. Delivery of bonds should be in denominations of $1,000 or in multiples adding up to $1,000.

OPERATIONS

U ntil the late 1960s, securities transactions were processed on a "cash and carry" basis. For every transaction, the selling firm, on the trade's settlement date, delivered the securities by messenger to the purchasing firm. This delivery usually occurred before 11:30 A.M. The messenger delivering the securities was given a receipt for the securities and then moved on to the next delivery.

The firm receiving the securities then checked them to make sure that the delivered securities were the same ones that were purchased and that all of the other paperwork was complete. Once it determined that everything was in order, the receiving firm "cut a check" to the selling firm and arranged for the securities to be re-registered in the new owner's name.

Around 2:30 P.M. the same day, the delivering firm's messenger came back to the purchasing firm, presented the receipt, picked up the check, and returned it to the selling firm in time for the firm to:

- Verify that the check was for the correct sum.
- Deposit the check in the firm's bank.

This system left very little time for trades to be verified for accuracy and for errors to be corrected. It also required separate paperwork, messenger pickups, check cutting, and security re-registrations to be done for every single securities transaction. No matter how hard the brokerage firms' employees worked, there was a limit to how many transactions they could correctly process in a day. This became abundantly clear in the early 1970s when the New York Stock Exchange had to shorten its trading hours in an attempt to reduce the number of transactions occurring in a day—just so that the firms could keep up with the paperwork.

During this time, many firms went out of business not because they ran out of money, but simply because they couldn't keep up with the mountains of paperwork created by the cash and carry system of settlement. Clearly a new system was needed.

The system that evolved from this mayhem is still used today. The cornerstone of the system is a *securities depository* that acts as a central depot for most firms' securities. A depository holds in its vaults most of the actual security certificates owned by the firms that use the depository's services, as well as the securities owned by those firms' clients. In addition, most firms maintain a cash balance at their depository.

To process a trade, the selling firm electronically instructs the clearinghouse to transfer the securities from its account at the depository to the purchasing firm's account there. The purchasing firm notifies the clearinghouse to pay the selling firm from the cash reserve in its account. When the clearinghouse has instructions from both firms, it verifies that they are correct and then transfers the securities and the money. With this system, no messengers need to be sent and no checks between firms need to be cut.

To simplify matters even further, the clearinghouse (discussed later in the chapter) "pairs off" trades.

Example: For their respective clients, Firm A sells 100 shares of XYZ, Inc., to Firm B, and Firm B sells 100 shares of XYZ to Firm C. The net effect is that Firm A has 100 shares less and Firm C has 100 shares more. The total for Firm B does not change because it has both bought and sold 100 shares of XYZ. Because Firm B has both bought and sold 100 Shares of XYZ, these trades can be paired off. The clearinghouse simply instructs Firm A to deliver 100 shares to Firm C to settle all three transactions, thus reducing the number of transfers from three to one. Any price differentials are subtracted from, and/or added to, the firms' cash accounts, and each firm has the securities re-registered in the new owners' names.

Brokerage firms can process today's incredible volume of transactions only because of this depository/clearinghouse arrangement. In June of 1995, the securities industry changed regular way settlement from five business days to three business days after trade date. As of this writing, there is a move in the industry to change regular way settlement for corporate and municipal securities again; this time to be the next business day. Advances in technology with the growing interconnectivity of computer systems is the driving force this time.

Operations Departments

The departments within a firm that collect, store, process, and maintain all the paperwork associated with a securities transaction are collectively referred to as the *back office* or as *operations*. These departments support the sales department, which interacts with the firms' clients, and the trading department, which executes the buying and selling of securities. The operations departments and their functions follow.

NEW ACCOUNTS (NAME AND ADDRESS) DEPARTMENT

When a registered representative (account executive or financial advisor) in the firm's sales department establishes relationship with a new client, at least three forms must be completed:

1. The *new account agreement* contains information on where the client's statements are to be sent, the client's investment objec-

tives, usually some information about the client's employer, and/or some credit references.

2. In the *W-9 form,* clients disclose their social security numbers or tax identification numbers for the firm's and the government's tax records.

3. The *client agreement* authorizes the firm to act as the client's representative in the marketplace and establishes the terms and conditions of the client–firm relationship.

To expedite business, the new account form can be filled out over the phone by the salesperson asking the new client questions and recording the answers on the form itself. The other two forms must be mailed to the client who must sign them and return them promptly.

In addition:

- To open a margin account, the client has to sign a *margin account agreement.*

- To authorize the broker to make the decisions on what to buy and sell, and/or when to buy or sell, without first having to check with the client, the client has to sign a *discretionary account agreement.*

- To trade options, futures, or commodities, additional forms have to be completed.

If the client is a corporation, partnership, charity, or any entity other than an individual, still more forms need to be completed.

All these forms are then sent to the new accounts department, which checks to be sure the forms are completed properly, stores the paperwork, and opens an electronic file for the client on the firm's computer system.

The new account department also makes sure that the information is kept up to date. It changes the client's file information whenever the client moves, gets a new phone number, changes employer, and so on.

ORDER DEPARTMENT

The order department acts as a "go-between" for the firm's salespeople and its traders. All orders solicited by the firm's sales force are sent to the order department. If the firm is a small one, the orders may simply be carried to the order department as they are received. In a large firm, with offices all over the country, the brokers forward their orders via an electronic mail system called a *wire*. (For these reasons, large firms with multiple offices are often called *wire houses.*)

If a branch office sends an order to the order room via the electronic mail system, the order quickly prints out in the order room on a *teletype.* The order department quickly checks the orders for any obvious errors (missing account numbers, missing office numbers, and the like). Then, since speed is of the essence, it quickly forwards the order (either electronically or via phone) to the right person in the trading department so it can be executed.

It is essential that the order be sent to the right person or exchange, because securities are traded on different exchanges or by different traders in the over-the-counter market. If the security is traded on the exchange, the order is sent to the floor clerk, who passes it on to the firm's floor trader. If the security is traded OTC, the order is forwarded to the individual within the trading department who trades that security.

In the meantime, the order department keeps a copy of the order in its file. When the client's order is executed (which may take seconds or months depending on the type of security and the type of order), the floor clerk or trader then reports the execution price back to the order department. The order department then:

- Records the execution price on its copy of the order.
- Notifies the broker (via the same wire system) of the execution and of the execution price, so that the broker can, in turn, notify the client.
- Advises the purchase and sales department when the order is executed.

PURCHASE AND SALES DEPARTMENT

The purchase and sales (P&S) department performs several tasks when it is notified that a trade has been executed:

1. Records the trade
2. Prepares the customer's confirmation
3. Figures the total billing to the client
4. Compares the trade with the contrabroker

Recording.   The P&S department records the trade on the firm's master records. These records are used by the firm as the basis for later notifying the clearinghouse of which securities have been bought and sold by the firm—so accuracy is a must.

Figuration.   The P&S department computes (or figures) how much money the client owes the firm for a purchase or how much the firm owes the client for a sale. In deriving this total, the department includes not only the sale or purchase price of the security, but also:

1. Any commission the client owes the firm if the firm acted as the client's agent is *added* to the client's bill or *subtracted* from the client's sale proceeds.
2. Any accrued interest (if the security traded is a bond) is *added* to the client's bill or to the client's sale proceeds.
3. Any "ticket charges" (processing fees charged by some firms) are *added* to the client's bill or *subtracted* from the sale proceeds.
4. Any applicable state and/or federal securities transfer taxes are *added* to the client's bill and/or *subtracted* from the sale proceeds.

A statement called a *confirm* discloses each of these itemized charges, as well as the final total that the client owes the firm or the firm owes the client. *The confirm is prepared and mailed to the client the same day as the trade.*

Comparison. The P&S department also compares the details of the trade, from its firm's point of view, with the P&S department of the firm with which the trade was executed (the so-called *contrabroker*), to be sure that both firms' understanding of the trade is identical. Because of the sheer speed at which orders are executed and the number of trades performed each day, some misunderstandings are inevitable.

Example: Firm A thinks it sold Firm B 200 shares of a given stock, whereas Firm B thinks it bought only 100 shares of the stock from Firm A.

It's important that these disagreements be discovered, resolved, and corrected prior to settlement day. Otherwise the trade does not settle when it is supposed to settle.

Confirming the details of each and every trade with every other firm would be an overwhelming task for any P&S department. So catching the majority of these disagreements prior to the settlement date is the responsibility of the appropriate clearing organization. Each day every firm submits to the clearing organizations (via various electronic means) its data on the trades it executed.

The five main clearing organizations are the following:

1. The Securities Industry Automation Corporation (SIAC) clears trades generated on the New York Stock Exchange.

2. The American Stock Exchange Clearing Corporation (ASECC) clears trades generated on the American Stock Exchange. (Note: Many of the computer operations of both the SIAC and ASECC are performed by the Stock Clearing Corporation [SCC], a wholly owned subsidiary of the NYSE.)

3. The National Clearing Corporation clears most OTC trades of NASDAQ securities.

4. The Option Clearing Corporation (OCC) clears most listed option transactions.

5. The National Securities Clearing Corporation (NSCC) is now the largest securities clearing corporation in the United States.

The trade is submitted to the clearing corporation, which pairs off the trades as reported. If there is no disagreement, there is no problem. However, after most of the trades are paired off, usually some trades are left over with no identical countertrade.

Example: Firm A reports a sale of 200 shares of XYZ at 43½, and Firm B reports a purchase of 200 shares of XYZ at 43⅜. There is no countertrade for either trade, which means that, most likely, one firm or the other made a price error.

In this case, both firms are notified that their trades do not match up, and it is left to them to decide how the error is going to be resolved. Perhaps one firm can prove to the other that it is right by comparing the price at which the transaction occurred to the price at which the stock was trading in the market at the time the order was executed. Or maybe one firm finds that it made a paperwork error and corrects the report it sent to the clearing corporation. If neither firm can prove it is correct, then the two traders of the firms involved negotiate a settlement. Either each trader or firm assumes half the difference, or the firms take turns assuming errors.

While anyone can (and does) make an occasional mistake, if a trader or a firm gets a reputation for making too many "errors," the risk is of being ostracized by the rest of the traders and firms on the street. A trader that no one will trade with is of limited usefulness to anyone.

It's important to note that the firm, not the client, suffers the loss resulting from an error.

Example: A firm reports a purchase to a client at 43⅜ when it actually bought the stock for 43½. The client pays only 43⅜. The extra eighth of a point comes out of the firm's pocket (or the trader's annual bonus).

Trades that are not submitted to a clearinghouse are called *ex-clearinghouse trades (XCH)* and must be compared manually. This means one firm, usually the seller, must contact the other firm and verify the security traded, the quantity traded, the price, and the settlement terms. This is typically done by means of a written confirmation that the selling firm delivers to the buying firm and that the buying firm signs to signify its agreement on the details.

CASHIERING DEPARTMENT

One of the departments that receives a copy of the firm's confirmation notices is the cashiering department, which is sometimes referred to as the *cage*. This department has a number of duties:

1. Receiving securities sent to the firm by other firms or by the firm's clients.
2. Delivering securities to other firms or to the other firm's clients.
3. Transferring the name on the security from the old owner to the new owner.
4. Borrowing and loaning shares of stock for short sales.
5. Arranging to borrow money from banks to support the firm's margin activities.
6. Reorganizing, that is, converting one security into another.

Receive or Deliver. The receive and/or deliver section of the cashiering department receives or accepts delivery of certificates from customers, other firms, or depositories. When receiving or delivering the securities, the firm must make sure that they are in *negotiable form.* To be negotiable:

1. The securities must be signed on the back of the actual certificate by the owner. If a certificate has more than one owner (such as a husband and wife), both must sign the certificate just the way their names appear on the front of the certificate. Without the appropriate signatures, the securities cannot be delivered to the new owner.
2. If the stock certificate is held by the broker, the client(s) must sign a separate form (called a *stock power*), which the firm must attach to the actual certificate.
3. If the security is a bearer certificate (that is, there is no name on it), the person delivering the security must provide proof, such as a purchase confirmation, that he or she acquired the certificate legally.

Transfer.   Every time a security changes hands, it has to undergo *transfer.* That is, the existing certificate, which carries the name of the former owner, must be canceled and a new certificate, which reflects the name of the new owner, must be issued. This is the job of the *transfer agent,* usually a bank or other organization outside the brokerage firm.

Another outside agency, often a trust company or bank, acts as *registrar.* Its duty is to keep track of the number of shares or bonds an issuer has in circulation. It verifies that no more shares are issued than are destroyed, so that the total number of outstanding shares remains constant. (Often, the transfer and register duties are handled by the same bank or agency.)

When a brokerage firm receives securities that have been sold, it passes them on to the transfer agent, so that they can be re-registered in the name of the new owner.

If the firm has the old certificates at a depository, the depository sends them to the transfer agent to be re-registered.

Vaulting.   When a brokerage firm receives securities, it must place them in a vault or depository. Actively traded securities are usually placed in the depository. Thinly traded securities are typically held in the firm's own vault, or "box."

Whether held at the depository or in the vault, the securities must be divided into two groups: (1) securities that are owned outright by the firm's clients and (2) securities that the firm itself owns or that the firm's clients have borrowed against (that is, margined). By law, securities that are owned outright by the firm's clients must be segregated from the other securities, regardless of whether the certificate is registered in the clients' name or in the broker's name. For that reason, these securities are said to be *in seg* (short for "segregation").

The Depository Trust Corporation (DTC) is the world's largest securities depository, providing post-trade clearance and settlement systems to both the domestic and international financial services communities. DTC is a central securities repository where stock and bond certificates are exchanged, performing securities custody services for its participating banks and broker/dealers. Most of the certificate exchanges now take place electronically and few paper certificates actually change hands. The DTC is owned by most of the brokerage houses on Wall Street, called "participants," and, at one time, had been owned by the New York Stock Exchange. It is a clearinghouse for the settlement of trades in corporate and municipal securities.

Lending and Borrowing Stock. The securities that the firm itself owns, as well as the margined securities owned by clients, can be lent out by the firm to short sellers. The short sellers can be either clients of the same brokerage firm or other firms. The stock loan clerk arranges to lend surplus securities and to borrow, from other firms and sources, the securities that the firm's clients want to sell short.

Bank Loan. The bank loan section of the cashiering department arranges to borrow money from the firm's banks. The employees of this section arrange to borrow money from commercial banks, either to finance the purchase of securities for the firm's own account and/or to provide funds for margin loans to customers.

MARGIN DEPARTMENT

The margin department supervises all the money in all of the firm's accounts, regardless of whether they are margin accounts. (In this respect the name "margin department" is something of a misnomer.) The margin department is responsible for ensuring that the firm's accounts meet all the financial requirements required by the various regulatory bodies.

In addition to supervising cash and margin accounts, the margin staff has the following responsibilities:

- It instructs the cage to issue checks or to deliver securities.
- It files for extensions.
- It closes out positions when necessary.

DIVIDEND DEPARTMENT

The dividend department is responsible for accepting, allocating, paying, and/or claiming dividends and interest distributions on securities held by the firm. The clerks in this department must be sure that the firm and its clients receive all the interest and dividends to which they are entitled. This task is complicated by the dividend-paying process.

Cash Dividends. For cash dividends, the dividend process depends on four dates.

1. The *declaration date* is the date on which the company's board of directors announces that the company will pay a dividend. On this date, the company also declares the size of the dividend payment and the record date.

2. The *record date* is the date when the company asks its registrar to provide a list of its current shareholders so that it knows who is entitled to the dividend checks. To receive the dividend, the stockholder has to be on the company's books as a shareholder as of this date.

3. On the *payment date*, the company actually cuts the dividend checks. This date is usually about two weeks after the record date, so as to give the company time to generate all the dividend checks.

4. The *ex-dividend date* comes two business days before the record date, when the investors who purchase the stock for regular way (three-day) settlement are no longer entitled to receive the dividend.

Because an investor who buys the stock on the ex-dividend day does not show up on the company's books as a shareholder until the day after the record date, the dividend is mailed to the stock's previous owner. As a result, the market value of the stock generally drops by the value of the dividend when it opens for trading on the ex-dividend date.

Example: Consider the following calendar:

May

S	M	T	W	T	F	S
	1	2	3	4	5	6
7	8	9	10	11	12	13
14	15	16	17	18	19	20
21	22	23	24	25	26	27
28	29	30	31			

The board of directors puts out a press release on May 2 saying that it will pay a $0.50 dividend to the owners of record as of May 17, with checks to be mailed as of May 26. Then:

- May 2 is the declaration date.
- May 17 is the record date.
- May 26 is the payment date.

The ex-dividend date is May 15. If an investor buys the stock on May 15 for regular way settlement, the trade does not settle until May 18. The investor is not recorded as the owner of the stock on the company's books (maintained by the registrar) until May 18. Thus, the *seller* is still entitled to receive the dividend.

Of course, other settlement options have other ex-dividend dates, but the vast majority of stock trades are regular way trades. For example, for cash settlement the ex-date is the day after the record date, since a cash trade on the record date would entitle the new owner to receive the dividend.

Sometimes, however, the dividend check is mailed to the wrong person. Either the firm does not get the information about the new owner to the registrar in time, the registrar does not process the information in time, or there is simply a human error somewhere along the line. If the dividend check is inadvertently mailed to the wrong party, that party must return it so it can be correctly routed.

Stock Dividends. For large stock dividends (20 percent or larger) and all stock splits, the sequence of these dates is different. The ex-dividend date now called the *ex-distribution date,* is positioned after the payment date instead of after the declaration date. Thus, the sequence for a stock distribution is as follows:

1. Declaration date.

2. Record date.

3. Payment date.

4. Ex-distribution date.

The ex-distribution date is usually the business day following payment by the corporation.

Example: Use the following calendar:

January

S	M	T	W	T	F	S
	1	2	3	4	5	6
7	8	9	10	11	12	13
14	15	16	17	18	19	20
21	22	23	24	25	26	27
28	29	30	31			

If the company declares a 25-percent stock dividend on January 2, for payment on January 24, then the stock starts to trade ex-distribution on January 25. Anyone who buys the stock so as to receive delivery before January 25 is entitled to receive the stock dividend.

Thus, any trades entered into after the record date and settled before the payment date must have *due bills* attached. These due bills entitle the buyer to claim the additional shares when they are distributed. Shares without due bills attached cannot be delivered to settle a trade during this period. The dividend department is responsible for checking every security in every account to make sure that all clients receive the dividends to which they are entitled (*and* to make sure clients do not keep any dividend to which they are not entitled).

The dividend department also allocates dividend payments paid to the firm by the company to their rightful owners. Many clients do not have their securities registered in their own name but instead have them registered in the name of their brokerage firm. By so registering the securities, they do not have to worry about signing the securities or a stock power when they want to sell. Instead all they have to do is call their broker and say "sell," and an officer of the firm endorses the certificate.

Of course, if 100 clients, each of whom owns 100 shares of a given stock, should then decide to register their stock in their brokers' names, then the company's books show that the firm "owns" 10,000 shares, even though those shares are actually being held for the benefit of the firm's clients. (The clients' claims are called *beneficial ownership*.) When it's time to pay a dividend, the company makes one check payable to the firm, since the company has no way of knowing the actual beneficial owners. The firm, when it receives the check, must then distribute the proceeds on a proportional basis to all of the actual owners. This task falls to the employees of the dividend department. The dividend department also allocates interest payments that it receives on bonds held in the name of the firm, or *street name.*

PROXY DEPARTMENT

The proxy department is closely related to the dividend department. The proxy department distributes corporate publications (including financial reports), notices of meetings, and voting information to the beneficial owners who have their securities in street name.

Proxies. The most important of these distributions is an "advisory and voting solicitation," which is mailed at least once a year. It gives the shareholder the right to elect the members of the board of directors and decide on other important matters brought before an annual, or special, meeting of the company. Owners, whose shares are in street name, cannot cast their votes directly. The company recognizes only the brokerage firm as its shareholder, because that's the name on the stock certificates according to the firm's registrar.

To allow the real owners of these shares to vote on these matters, the proxy department sends a request form, called a *proxy*, to each of the beneficial owners. As the real owners return their proxies, the firm tallies the owners' votes and reflects the owners' wishes when it votes its shares at the annual meeting.

Example: Two owners leave their stock in street name. The first owner has 200 shares and the second owner has 100 shares. The firm receives the right to cast 300 votes at the annual meeting. The firm sends proxies to the owners, collects their responses, and votes as they would have voted if they had actually attended the annual meeting and voted by themselves. If Investor A votes yes and Investor B votes no on a certain proposal, then the firm casts 200 yes votes and 100 no votes at the annual meeting.

Sometimes the beneficial owners do not bother to advise the proxy department about their preferences. This can be a waste. Exchange regulations prevent a firm from voting on crucial issues unless it receives instructions from its clients. (However, firms can vote unreturned proxies on routine matters.)

Solicitations of Stockholders. The proxy department also acts as an agent for anyone or any group that wishes to communicate with the beneficial owners whose shares are in the firm's custody, providing the group has registered its proxy statement or solicitation with the SEC, per Section 14 of the Securities Exchange Act of 1934, and agrees to reimburse the brokerage firm for postage and other out-of-pocket expenses connected with a mailing.

A stockholder solicitation may be a simple plea for a vote to effect a reform or to change the company's present management. Or it may be a request for the beneficial owners to tender their shares in response to a purchase proposition. The latter often leads to another function of the proxy department, although in larger firms it is assigned to a separate unit known as the reorganization department.

REORGANIZATION DEPARTMENT

The reorganization department (reorg) is responsible for handling:

1. Redemption calls.
2. Conversions.
3. Exchanges.
4. Rights offerings (subscriptions).
5. Tender offers.

Redemption Calls. A *redemption call* is the exercise by the issuer of a call privilege on a stock or bond. An *absolute,* or *full,* call requires all holders to submit their bonds or shares for redemption. In a *partial call,* only the holders of specific certificate numbers must respond. These certificate numbers are chosen at random by the company, often by electronic means. If the called securities are held in safekeeping and segregated by owner through individual identification methods, reorg simply submits the appropriate certificates to the company and credits the customers with the cash received. But if the securities are segregated in bulk form, the firm must either (1) record the specific certificate numbers for each customer account or (2) adopt an impartial lottery system.

Conversions. The reorganization department processes requests to convert convertible bonds and convertible preferred stock into the underlying common stock, which sometimes results from a full or partial call in a convertible issue. The issuing company forces the holders to exchange their securities for the common stock or accept the call price, which is typically lower than the market value of the comparable common shares. In a typical bond call, the bondholder is advised that, unless some personal action is initiated before the close of business on a given day, (1) the conversion privilege is revoked, (2) accrued interest on the bond ceases, and (3) the holder must accept the redemption price. In the meantime, the reorganization department must contact the beneficial bond owners and solicit instructions from them.

Exchanges. When one class of security is exchanged for another of the same issuer, it is called *reorganization.* Sometimes, if a corporation is in dire financial straits, bondholders may accept an equity security exchange for their debt instruments to avoid prolonged and expensive bankruptcy proceedings. Or such an exchange may be directed as a result of a decision in bankruptcy court. Either way, the reorg department submits the old certificates on behalf of the owners and accepts the new ones in satisfaction. If the exchange is voluntary, reorg needs a voluntary exchange request—that is, written instructions from the beneficial owner. In an involuntary exchange, no instructions are needed.

When one company's securities are exchanged for those of another, it is known as a *merger.* In a merger, reorg submits its customers' shares for shares in the surviving company or for shares of a newly organized third company. Records of the holdings of the firm and its customers are adjusted at the completion of the exchange. If the merger is an outright acquisition for cash, the customers' accounts are credited with the funds received after the reorganization department submits the old shares and obtains payment.

Preemptive Rights (Subscriptions Privilege). In a preemptive rights offering, the reorganization department uses these rights and supplementary funds from a customer's account to subscribe to the new stock from the company. If additional rights are needed to satisfy the customer's written instructions, they are purchased either from the issuing company's agent or in the open market. Conversely, if certain customers decide not to subscribe or if they own rights in excess of the amount needed to subscribe for the number of shares they want to buy, the reorganization department disposes of the extra rights before they expire. It may either sell them to the company's agent bank or standby underwriter, or accept someone else's bid in the open market. Either way, the appropriate customer accounts are credited with the net proceeds of that sale.

Purchases by means of subscription *warrants* are handled similarly. Reorg needs written instructions from the beneficial owner before taking action. These purchases also entail a ratio formula set by the company.

Tender Offers.   A *tender offer* is a formal solicitation by means of a proxy statement to shareholders to induce them to sell their shares. A tender offer can be a successful method for acquiring large amounts of stock without upsetting the supply/demand equilibrium in the marketplace. It is often used by corporations or large institutions to effect a merger with, or to gain control of, another company at reasonable cost. If not enough shares are submitted for sale, the offering company is denied its desired objective. Under these circumstances, the offerer usually reserves the right to refuse the purchase of any shares tendered—a valuable privilege not available in open-market transactions. Similarly, if a tender offer produces more than enough shares to satisfy the offer, the offerer can accept all the shares, any portion of them, or only the amount specified in the proxy statement. If only some of the shares are to be purchased, they can be bought either on a first-come/first-served basis or on a prorated basis.

STOCK RECORD DEPARTMENT

The position lists used by the dividend, proxy, and reorganization departments are a part of the records that are prepared and maintained by the stock record department. This part of operations serves as a control and reference source for monitoring securities under the brokerage firm's jurisdiction. Although its title is "stock record," it keeps records of all securities—stocks and bonds alike. An individual record is maintained for each issue. For financial and regulatory reasons, these records must be unquestionably current and accurate. The stock record ledger shows the following:

- Name of the security
- Owner of the security
- Location of the certificate

In terms of location, the stock record has to identify whether that security is in one of the following:

- Safekeeping
- Segregation
- A loan arrangement at a bank or to another broker/dealer
- Re-registration proceedings at the transfer agent
- Transit to the customer's agent bank or broker versus payment
- Fail-to-receive status from a contrabroker/dealer or customer

During the course of trading each day, the status of the securities under the firm's care changes constantly. Certificates arrive from and go out to customers and other brokers. Others go to the transfer agent, and still others come back. Book-entry changes of ownership occur, even though the certificates do not change hands.

Throughout all this change, the stock record has to remain balanced at all times. A *break* in the record indicates that a mistake has been made. Given the amount of activity surrounding this document, errors must be corrected immediately—or they might never be corrected at all.

To ensure that record books are kept to a minimum size and corrected as soon as possible, the stock record department issues a daily report and a weekly report. The *daily stock record* reports the movement of all securities involved in any kind of movement: sale, purchase, transfer into or out of the vault, received from a customer, and so on. The *weekly stock record* is a balance sheet of all securities under the supervision of the firm, whether or not they were involved in a transaction the preceding week. Both of these reports must balance—like a balance sheet. Stock may not be removed from a part of the record without being accounted for in some way or another.

ACCOUNTING DEPARTMENT

The accounting department in a brokerage firm performs all the tasks that it would in any other type of company. Basically, its responsibilities are as follows:

- Keeping the firm's journals and ledgers
- Preparing periodic trial balances
- Issuing the firm's balance sheet and income statement
- Generating reports for management as necessary

In addition to its quarterly and annual reports to stockholders, the accounting department also issues special reports for regulatory bodies such as the SEC or NASD. Sometimes the regulatory authority calls for a report as the result of a special audit. Other reports are generated periodically, such as the *Financial and Operational Combined Uniform Single (Focus) Report*. This statement gives regulators vital statistics regarding the financial health of the brokerage firm that might not be available from the company's other reports.

Customer's Statement. The accounting department is also involved in the very last step in customer operations activity—the preparation of the statements of account. Under federal law, if there has been any transaction activity, security position, or money balance in an account within the preceding calendar quarter, the customer must receive a statement of account. Many firms comply by sending their customers (particularly margin account customers) monthly statements instead of the mandatory quarterly report.

Whether monthly or quarterly, the statement summarizes all that has occurred in the customer's account during the period. All purchase expenses are debited to the account, and sales proceeds are credited. However, each purchase and/or sales transaction is posted on the contract settlement date, whereas all other activities are posted on the day they occur.

Example: A check received from a customer is credited to the account on the day it is received, and money delivered out of the account is debited on the actual day of reimbursement. But a regular way sale of a corporate security on June 26 is not posted until July 1, three business days later.

This difference is often a point of confusion for customers, especially when they receive their monthly statements of account without certain month-end trades posted on it.

Despite the best efforts and intentions of the accounting department, mistakes occur. Perhaps an issue is not carried forward to the following month's position listing, or duplicate entries are processed accidentally and both items posted in the account. A typical customer statement, therefore, carries a self-protective legend, *"E&OE,"* which means, *errors and omissions excepted.* This statement allows the brokerage firm an opportunity to correct the mistake without legal liability.

The statement may also carry a legend advising customers of financial protection afforded them under SEC Rule 15c3-3. Free credit balances must be maintained in a "special reserve bank account for the exclusive benefit of customers," a rule that denies the brokerage firm the right to use those funds in the speculative conduct of its own business. The accounting department, employing a formula approved by a stock exchange or the NASD, supervises the firm's compliance with this rule and ensures that customer money is used only for customer purposes.

In Closing...

When they think of the securities industry, many people call to mind the busy floor of the stock exchange, the electronic trading screens, and the Wall Street area. Not many can picture the sometimes feverish back office work that is necessary to keep the records and books straight, to comply with regulations, to protect the interests of customer and firm alike, and, through it all, to make a profit.

THE MONEY MARKET

Money market instruments are those investments that are suitable for investors with an investment horizon of a year or less. The money market instruments are divided into two categories: traditional and nontraditional. The traditional instruments include:

- Treasury bills (T-bills)
- Certificates of deposit (CDs)
- Bankers acceptances (BAs)
- Commercial paper (CP)
- Repurchase agreements (repos)

The nontraditional instruments include:

- Floating rate notes (FRNs)
- Adjustable rate preferred stocks (ARPs)
- Money market preferreds (MMPs)

Treasury bills are covered in Chapter 10.

Insured Certificates of Deposit

An insured certificate of deposit represents a loan from an investor to a bank or a savings & loan (S&L). The loan is usually for a fixed time period ranging from 30 days to seven years. The first $100,000 that an investor deposits in most banks and S&Ls, including CDs, is insured by the Federal Deposit Insurance Company (FDIC). Because FDIC insurance is limited to $100,000, most investors elect not to put more than $100,000 in any one bank at any one time. Banks issue fixed rate, floating rate, and zero coupon CDs. Many securities dealers make a secondary market in certificates of deposit.

Negotiable Certificates of Deposit

Negotiable certificates of deposit are large $5 million-plus certificates of deposit that are issued by America's largest and "safest" banks. These certificates of deposit are sold exclusively to large institutional investors such as money market funds. Again, only the first $100,000 is insured.

Bankers Acceptances

Bankers acceptances are pieces of short-term bank loans that are sold to investors. Consider the following example. A U.S. company that imports furniture from Asia applies for a line of credit at a U.S. bank. The bank checks on the credit quality of the importer and grants the company the line of credit. The company borrows $980,000 from its bank to finance a transaction and agrees to pay the bank back $1,000,000 in 120 days. The importer signs a document that looks like a check that evidences its promise to pay the bank $1,000,000 in 120 days. This receivable is an asset of the bank.

Like any other asset the bank owns, the bank can elect to either hold the asset or sell it. Although the bank may be comfortable with the credit quality of the importer, other investors will not be—and will not be interested in doing the extensive credit analysis required to determine the credit quality of the issuer. Thus, in order to make the asset sellable, the bank first has to eliminate the credit risk. The bank can eliminate the credit risk of this asset by guaranteeing its credit quality. The bank does this by stamping the back of this instrument with the word "Accepted" and by having an officer of the bank sign the instrument. Hence the name "Bankers acceptance." Since the bank accepts the credit risk, the instrument trades on the credit quality and rating of the bank, not the investor.

Bankers acceptances are usually sold in multiples of $1 million. Bankers acceptances smaller than $1 million are referred to as odd-lots.

Commercial Paper

Commercial paper (CP) represents an unsecured short-term loan from an investor to a corporation. CP is sold to investors at a discount to its face value and is redeemed at face value by the issuer upon maturity. Most of the CP that is issued has a very short-term maturity of between 30 and 90 days. The maximum maturity for CP is 270 days. The 270-day maximum maturity stems from the fact that any public debt offering with a maturity longer than 270 days has to be registered with the Securities and Exchange Commission (SEC)—a time-consuming and expensive procedure that most corporations try to avoid.

CP comes in two varieties: direct paper and dealer paper. Direct paper is issued by those companies that have such a large and continuous need for short-term financing that it pays them to have an in-house sales operation to raise money from investors by issuing CP. These issues directly market their paper to investors both by using in-house salespeople and by posting offerings on their Web page. Some examples of direct issues include General Electric Credit Corp (GECC) and General Motors Acceptance Corporation (GMAC).

These companies generally post the rates they are willing to pay to borrow money for many different maturates. Many direct issuers also allow lenders to specify the term of the loan they would like to make. For example, a wealthy investor may want to invest $5 million for exactly 44 days. The investor could inquire—via the Web—what rates various direct issuers would pay to borrow the $5 million for 44 days.

The second type of CP is dealer paper. This paper is issued by dealers instead of being sold directly by the issuing company. The companies that hire dealers to issue their CP tend to be small or have only seasonal borrowing needs.

Because CP usually represents an unsecured loan from an investor to the issuer, the issuer's credit rating is particularly important to the lender. The rating agencies rate the credit strength of CP issuers on a scale from 1 to 4, with issuers rated 1 being the most credit worthy. A growing trend is for companies to sell commercial paper that is backed not only by the full faith and credit of the issuer, but also by specific assets. These assets include receivables, securities, and even real estate.

CP is purchased by a wide range of investors, including individuals, institutions, and money market funds.

Repurchase Agreements

Repurchase agreements are very short-term secured loans that securities dealers use to finance their fixed income inventory. Consider the following example. A securities dealer buys $100 million of Treasury bonds from a client. The dealer has to pay for the securities the next business day, regardless of whether the dealer resells the bonds or not.

The dealer can obtain the money it needs to pay the client for these bonds by either borrowing $100 million from a bank or by borrowing money from investors. Usually the cheaper source of financing available to a securities dealer is to borrow the money from investors. In order to borrow money at the lowest rate possible, dealers usually collateralize the loans by allowing the investors from whom they borrow to hold the collateral they are financing. In the unlikely event that the dealer does not repay the loan, the client can sell the collateral in the open market and use the sales proceeds to recoup the investment.

Repo transactions are usually $1 million-plus in size. The term of the loan is usually overnight. Longer-term transactions—two to 30 days—are referred to as "term repos." Repos appeal to institutional investors and money market funds.

Sometimes the transaction is reversed: A client borrows money from a securities dealer and allows the dealer to hold high-quality securities as collateral. Often this form of short-term secured transaction represent a client's cheapest source of short-term funds. In effect, the client "pawns" his or her securities to raise cash. When the client borrows money from the dealer, the transaction is referred to as "reverse repo."

Floating Rate Notes

Floating rate notes (FRNs) are corporate notes that pay an interest rate that "floats" in response to changing market interest rates. For example, a formula for the coupon might be:

"The three-month T-bill rate plus 110 basis points (1.10%)"

The interest rate that the note pays might change every six months. The date the rate changes is called the "reset date." If on the reset date the three-month T-bill rate was 5 percent, the coupon for the next interest rate period would be 6.10 percent.

Since the interest rate the note pays rises and falls as market interest rates rise and fall, the market value of the note stays reasonably constant. The coupon rate is usually defined by a formula tied to a widely publicized "index rate." The most commonly used index rates are the LIBOR rate, Prime rate, and T-bill rate.

- The LIBOR rate is the "London Inter-Bank Offering Rate." It is the rate at which banks in London lend each other money.

- The Prime rate is the rate at which U.S. banks lend money to their largest and highest credit-quality clients.

- The T-bill rate is the rate at which the U.S. Government can borrow money.

While most short-term interest rates move in "tandem," the T-bill rate often moves the opposite way of other short-term interest rates. This "divergence" happens because political and economic shocks result in a "flight to quality." During times of war, political uncertainty, and economic turmoil, investors become more concerned about the credit quality of their investments, so they rush to move their money from other short-term instruments into T-bills. Thus, the price of T-bills rise (yield falls) and the price of other instruments fall (yield rises).

Since these rates move in the opposite direction, the coupons on FRNs tied to these rates also move in opposite directions. Many investors elect to diversify their portfolios by buying FRNs tied to different indicies. While it is possible to buy just one FRN for about $1,000, most FRNs are purchased in $1 million or larger amounts.

Adjustable Rate Preferreds

Adjustable rate preferreds (ARPs) are similar to FRNs in that the dividend rate they pay floats in response to changing market interest rates. The rate that ARPs pay is usually tied to the highest of the three following rates. The highest of these rates is called the "basis rate."

1. 90-day Treasury bill

2. 10-year Treasury note

3. 20-year Treasury bond

The attraction of ARPs as money market instruments is that when a corporation buys another company's preferred and holds it for at least 45 days, then 70 percent of the dividends the company receives is excluded from federal income tax. Thus, if a company receives $10,000 in dividends, only $3,000 would be subject to tax.

The major issuers of ARPs are banks, utilities, and insurance companies that want to match their assets against their liabilities.

Money Market Preferreds

Another type of preferred stock that is specifically designed to be a money market instrument is the money market preferred (MMP). These stocks are auctioned every 49 days on a yield basis. As with adjustable rate preferreds, they offer corporate investors the same tax advantage.

INTRODUCTION TO FIXED INCOME

The "fixed income" or "bond" market is composed of securities that represent pieces of loans made by investors to borrowers. The borrowers that issue the bonds can be governments, agencies, states, political subdivisions of states, or corporations. The lenders who buy the bonds are individuals, banks, insurance companies, and pension plans. The majority of these loans are at a fixed rate—referred to as the coupon rate—and for a fixed term.

The borrowers pay interest periodically (usually either semi-annually or annually) to the bondholders until the loan comes due and the principal is repaid by the borrower. Bonds are typically sold in $1,000 denominations. A bond is typically identified by quoting the interest rate it pays, the entity that issued it, and its maturity date. For example, a bond might be described as the:

9% IBM of January 15th 2012
or
6.25% Treasury of March 1st 2020

The bonds that evidence the loans trade freely in the open market and may change hands many times between the time the bond is first issued and when it matures. Each time a bond changes hands, it may do so at a different price.

Buying Bonds

Bond prices are quoted in points, where each point is equal to $10. Thus, if a bond is priced at "92," that means 92 points or 92 × $10 = $920. A price of 113 likewise means a price of $1,130. Partial points are quoted in 1/8th, 1/10th, or 1/32nd of a point depending upon the market conventions for that particular type of bond.

While many factors contribute to the value the market places on a particular bond, its market value rises and falls primarily in response to two factors:

1. The relationship between current interest rates and the bond's coupon. For example, a bond that pays investors 10% per year will be very desirable if new bonds being issued are only paying 6% because interest rates have declined. Investors would be willing to pay a premium (i.e., a price above the bond's face or par value) to buy this bond because it pays an above-market rate of interest. Its price would rise until it offered an overall return—i.e., a yield to maturity (YTM) that was competitive with new bonds being issued.

   However, if interest rates rise and new bonds being issued are paying 14%, then the relative attractiveness and value of a bond that pays only 10% will decline. Investors would not be willing to pay anything close to full value for a bond that pays only 10% interest when bonds paying 14% are available. The value of a 10% bond will have to decline until its overall return becomes competitive with new bonds. Almost on a minute-by-minute basis, bond prices change as market interest rates change.

2. The probability that the borrower will be able to meet its interest and principal payments in full and on time. Bonds backed by financially strong issuers are more desirable than bonds backed by issuers whose credit quality is suspect. As the issuer's credit quality changes, so will the value of the issuer's bonds.

Quoting Bond Yield

The first thing most investors want to know when considering buying a bond is "What does the bond yield" or "What return can I expect if I invest in this bond?" This is an easier question to ask than it is to answer, because a bond has a minimum of two yields: the current yield and the yield to maturity. To illustrate the difference between these yield measures, let us examine an 8% $1,000 bond with a remaining time to maturity of 10 years.

The current yield is the return the bond offers on a "cash on cash" basis. It is calculated by dividing the annual interest the bond pays by the bond's current price. If, for example, the bond was currently selling for either 91 or 114, the current yield will be respectively:

$$\$80 / \$910 = .0879 = 8.79\%$$
$$\$80 / \$1,140 = .0702 = 7.02\%$$

The weakness of a bond's current yield is that it does not account for the fact that when the bond matures it will return $1,000 to the investor, regardless of the price the investor paid to buy the bond. If an investor purchased the bond for $910 and held it until maturity, the investor would not only earn $80 per year in interest, but would also experience a $90 gain over the 10-year holding period ($1,000 received at maturity minus $910 cost). Likewise, an investor who purchased the bond for $1,140 would experience a $140 loss over the 10-year holding period.

The yield measure that not only accounts for the interest the investor receives, but also incorporates the effect of the gain or loss the investor experiences over the investment horizon as the bond approaches maturity is referred to as the yield to maturity. Naturally, a bond purchased at a discount to its face value will have a yield to maturity that is higher than its current yield. A bond at a premium to its face value will have a yield to maturity that is lower than the coupon yield. For the above example the YTM would be:

9.41% if the bond was purchased for $910
6.11% if the bond was purchased for $1,140

Investors normally make decisions about which bonds to buy and sell based on their respective YTMs.

The yield to maturity the bond offers when it is purchased only measures the return the investor earns on the original investment. Naturally, each interest payment the investor receives along the life of the bond has to be reinvested—and may be reinvested at either a higher or a lower rate, depending upon which way interest rates move. Naturally, the rate(s) at which the interest payments are reinvested will affect the investor's overall return over the life of the bond. Investors need to be aware that the YTM is not the same thing as a projected return.

Accrued Interest

Bonds pay interest "in arrears." This means they pay interest only *after* it is earned. Consider a bond that pays interest in March and September. The interest paid in March compensates the investor for lending the issuer money from the previous September until March. The September interest payment compensates the investor for lending money to the company from the previous March until September.

Even though bonds pay interest only in arrears, the investors who own bonds earn interest for each day they own the bond. When investors trade bonds, the seller of the bond is entitled to receive any interest earned, but not yet received. Looking at the previous example, suppose the owner of the bond sold it in June. The seller would be entitled to receive the interest earned from March, when the last payment was made, until the day the bond is sold in June. The interest an investor has earned to date—but has not yet been paid—is referred to as "accrued interest."

There are two possible ways to handle accrued interest. The first would be for the issuers to track everyone who owns their bonds and for how long they own them. If six different investors happened to own a bond during the six months between the two interest payment dates, the issuer could cut six different interest payment checks with prorated amounts paid to each investor based on the percentage of the six months for which each owned the bond.

The second way is for the buyer of a bond to pay the seller of the bond any interest the seller has earned, but has not yet received. In other words, any accrued interest is simply added to the purchase price. The buyer is then reimbursed for the accrued interest on the next interest payment date because the buyer receives the entire interest payment even though the buyer only owned the bond for part of the period. Using the previous example, if a seller sold the bond in June, the buyer would pay the seller the interest accrued from March until June. The buyer will then receive the full six-month interest payment in September.

Embedded Options

In addition to a maturity date, many bonds also include provisions that allow either the investor or the issuer to shorten the bond's life. These provisions are called "embedded options."

PUT OPTIONS

When the investor has the option of shortening the bond's life, the option is referred to as a "put" option, since this option allows the issuer to put the bond back to the issuer. When the investor puts a bond back to the issuer, the issuer pays the investor the bond's par value or $1,000, regardless of what the bond is worth in the open market.

Investors elect to put their bonds back to the issuer for one of two reasons:

1. The credit quality of the issuer declines and the investor becomes worried that the issuer will not be able to make the required interest and principal payments in full and on time.

2. When interest rates rise the market value of bonds decline. By putting bonds back to the issuer, the investors not only receive the

full face value of the bond, but are also able to reinvest the money at a higher interest rate.

The specifics of when the put option, if any, can be used varies with each bond issue. Some bonds give the bondholder the right to put the bond at anytime while others only allow the bondholders to put the bonds after a certain period of time has passed or during a certain time period.

For example, suppose XYZ, Inc. issued a 15-year 9% bond that included a put option. The provisions of this option provide that the:

- Bonds can't be put until at least three years after the bond is first issued. The time frame from when the bond is issued until it can be put is referred to as the period of put protection.

- Bonds can be put only during the fourth year after the bond is issued. The period during which the option can be used (exercised) is referred to as the option window.

Naturally, since put options can provide investors with a way to get out of a bad investment without taking a loss, they can be quite valuable to investors. Investors "pay" for the embedded options not by writing a separate check, but by accepting a lower rate of interest on the bond. For example, suppose an investor with a 15-year investment horizon has the choice of buying either of these bonds at par:

- A 15-year bond with a 9% coupon that can be put in year four.

- A 15-year bond with a 10% coupon that has no put option.

Naturally, if interest rates decline, the 10% bond with no embedded option will be the better performer over the next 15 years, since it pays 10% interest instead of 9% interest and the put option would be of no value. However, should interest rates rise to 12%, the 9% putable bond might result in a higher return over the 15-year investment horizon, since the investor could:

- Earn 9% for the first three years.
- Put the bond back to the issuer and receive par value.
- Reinvest at 12% for the next 12 years.

Most major securities firms have highly trained fixed income analysts. These analysts use very sophisticated computer models to quantify how much yield investors should be willing to sacrifice to buy a bond with a put option instead of an otherwise identical bond without a put option.

CALL OPTIONS

When the issuer has the right to shorten the life of a bond, the embedded option is referred to as an embedded "call" option. Issuers elect to shorten the life of bonds when interest rates decline. Issuers call in their bonds for one of three reasons:

1. They no longer need the money.
2. They elect to obtain the money they need from some other source, such as a bank loan, the sales proceeds of a stock offering, or the proceeds of an asset sale.
3. Interest rates decline and the company can refinance its debt at a lower rate by calling in its existing bonds and issuing new ones that pay a lower interest rate.

Of the three reasons listed, the third is by far the most common. By calling in its bonds, an issuer forces its bondholders to accept the return of the money they lent to the issuer. Because the investor's money is returned prematurely, the investors are effectively forced to reinvest their money at a lower rate.

Obviously, the right to shorten the maturity of a bond issue can be very valuable to issuers and very detrimental to investors. In order to entice investors into buying bonds that have embedded call options, issuers have to pay a higher interest rate. Thus, investors might be faced with the choice of investing either in:

- A 15-year bond that pays 11% interest, but is callable in three years.
- A 15-year bond that pays 10% interest, but is not callable.

Naturally, if interest rates rise, the issuer will not call the bond, and the callable bond will be the better performer for the investor since it pays 11% instead of 10%. However, if interest rates decline and the first bond is called, then the noncallable bond will be the better investment since the investor would not be forced to reinvest at a lower rate.

Often, when a bond is callable, the provisions of the call option require the issuer to pay a slight premium to an investor over par if the issuer calls the bond. This premium is referred to as the call premium and it usually declines over time. For example, XYZ, Inc. might issue a 20-year bond with five years of call protection and the following call price schedule:

Figure 9-1
Call Schedule

Year	Call Price	Call Premium
1-5	NA	NA
6	$1,030	$30
7	$1,020	$20
8	$1,010	$10
9-20	$1,000	$0

Conditional Call

Some bonds have embedded call options that can be exercised only if some specified condition is first met. For example, a bond may be callable only if:

- Interest rates decline by more than 2%.
- The issuer's credit quality drops below some specified level.

Naturally, if the option is conditional, its value tends to be lower. How much lower it is than a nonconditional option depends upon what the probability is that the condition will be met.

Call Frequency

The second characteristic of a call option is the call frequency. After the period of call protection expires, the call frequency determines how often the bond can be called. Some bonds can be called only on:

- A single day—Usually the day the period of call protection expires. This type of option is a "use it or lose it option."

- An infrequent schedule—For example, on the day the period of call protection expires and each five-year anniversary thereafter. Each call date is a separate option and the total value of the embedded option is the sum of the values of the individual call options.

- An annual schedule—Typically on the day the period of call protection expires and each one-year anniversary thereafter.

- A continuous basis after the period of call protection expires.

The more frequently the bond can be called, the higher the value of the embedded call option and the higher the bond's yield.

Partial Calls

The third characteristic of an embedded call option is whether the option allows for partial calls. If a partial call is permitted, the issuer has the option of calling in only a portion of the bond issue instead of having to call in the entire issue at once. This feature would make the option more valuable for the issuer because the issuer would not have to wait until it had the funds necessary to call in the entire issue before it could start retiring it.

Naturally, if partial calls are permitted, investors need to be concerned about the order in which the bonds will be called during a partial call. In some cases, the order in which the bond will be called is simply random, while in other cases, the bonds are called in a specific order.

Hidden Calls

The fourth characteristic is whether the bond includes any hidden calls. A hidden call is a call that is very unlikely to be used. The circumstances under which it can be used are typically buried in the fine print of the offering memorandum. For example, a bond may contain a hidden option that allows it to be called if the value of some collateral drops below a predefined value. Since even hidden options have value, the yield of a bond with hidden options should be higher in order to reflect the value of these hidden and rarely used options.

In Closing . . .

The previous discussion is applicable to most bonds. In the next chapters, the characteristics of specific types of bonds are presented.

U.S. TREASURY BONDS

The market for U.S. Treasury securities is a five-plus-trillion-dollar market. The U.S. Treasury securities is the largest, most important, and most liquid fixed-income marketplace in the world. Treasury securities appeal to a wide spectrum of U.S. investors, including individuals, banks, insurance companies, and pension plans. Further, because so much of the world's commerce is denominated in U.S. dollars and the U.S. dollar functions as the de facto reserve currency of so many nations, U.S. Treasury securities also have broad appeal to non-U.S. citizens. Because of the wide appeal of the U.S. dollar and the position of the U.S. as the leader of the free world, U.S. Treasury securities are not only the benchmark fixed-income security in the United States, but are the benchmark fixed-income security for the world.

Advantages of U.S. Treasury Securities

The reason U.S. Treasury securities are so popular with investors is that they offer many advantages.

- Credit Quality—Many investors regard U.S. Treasury securities as one of the safest investment vehicles available in the world. This is because they are backed by the full faith and credit of the United

States Government and, as such, the U.S. Government is required to do whatever it takes to meet its obligations in full and on time. If the government has to raise taxes, it will raise taxes; if it has to cut spending, it will cut spending.

The U.S. Government is considered an excellent credit risk because of the size and diverse nature of the U.S. economy, and the stability of the U.S. political system, and because the U.S. Government can print as many dollars as it needs to insure that it makes all its interest and principal payments in full and on time.

- High Liquidity—The U.S. Treasury market is the most liquid fixed-income market in the world. Buyers and sellers of Treasury bonds are almost always able to transact business in quantity and at a fair price because the market is so active and has so many buyers, sellers, and dealers. The daily trading volume in U.S. Treasury securities exceeds an average of 200 billion dollars per business day.

- Small Spread—Dealers make their money by buying the bond at one price and selling it at a slightly higher price. The difference in the price at which a dealer will buy (the bid price) and the price at which a dealer will sell (the offer price) U.S. Treasury securities is very small. The low spread not only minimizes transaction costs, but it also increases the profitability of trades and makes it possible to profitably implement a greater variety of strategies.

- Transparent Pricing—Because of the tremendous amount of liquidity and immediate price dissemination in this market, investors can always determine what the fair value of any Treasury bond is at any moment. Markets where the prices are known and widely disseminated are said to have "transparent pricing."

- Book Registration—U.S. Treasury bonds are traded and stored electronically. There are no actual paper bond certificates to store, keep track of, or lose. Because dealers do not have to process a lot of paper, the dealers' costs are low—allowing them to keep transaction costs low. Eventually, all securities will trade electronically.

- Limited Taxation—The interest on U.S. Treasury securities is subject only to federal income tax and is exempt from state and local income tax. This limited taxation is of greatest benefit to those investors in high tax states.

- Excellent Call Protection—Unlike most other types of bonds, corporate bonds, and mortgage-backed securities, almost all U.S. Treasury bonds are noncallable. As such, they protect investors from call risk and allow investors to lock in returns for longer periods of time.

- High Leverage—Because of their high credit quality and liquidity, U.S. Treasury securities make excellent loan collateral. Investors can normally borrow up to 90 percent of their value.

While U.S. Treasury securities offer many advantages, they also have two key disadvantages that investors who consider investing in U.S. Treasuries should be aware of: low YTM and political risk.

1. Treasury bonds offer a relatively low YTM when compared to other investments. Because of their many advantages, investors are willing to accept a lower yield from Treasury securities than from other bonds. For investors who simply want to "buy and hold," other fixed-income securities usually offer a higher return.

2. Treasury bonds are exposed to political risk. These bonds do not have traditional credit risk because the government can print as many dollars as it needs to avoid defaulting on its debt. However, the government constantly needs to issue new debt in order to pay off its maturing debt and the Senate must authorize the issuing of the new debt. It is possible that, because of a political dispute, the Senate could refuse to reauthorize the issuance of debt and that this would cause a technical default.

Types of U.S. Treasuries

U.S. Treasury securities come in four varieties: Treasury bills, Treasury notes/bonds, Treasury strips, and Treasury Inflation Protection Securities.

TREASURY BILLS

The first type of U.S. Treasury security is the Treasury bill. Treasury bills are simply short-term U.S. Government discount notes. The government sells these notes at a discount to their face value, and when they mature, the government pays investors the notes' full-face value. The difference between the discounted price at which the notes are sold and their face value at which they are redeemed represents the investors' return. The government issues T-bills with three different maturates that are commonly referred to as the three-month, six-month, and one-year T-bills. Note that their actual maturity is 13, 26, and 52 weeks. (See Figure 10-1.)

Figure 10-1
T-Bill Maturity Schedule

Name	Actual Maturity
Three-Month	13 Weeks / 91 Days
Six-Month	26 Weeks / 182 Days
One-Year	52 Weeks / 364 Days

The dollar amount of the discount from par is calculated as follows:

$$\text{Discount} = \text{Face Value} \times \text{Discount Rate} \times (\text{Days Until Maturity} / 360)$$
$$\text{Face Value} - \text{Discount} = \text{Market Price}$$

For example, a $1 million T-bill that matures in 142 days and is priced at a 6.12 percent discount would be priced at:

$$\text{Discount} = \$1,000,000 \times .0612 \times (142 / 360)$$
$$\text{Discount} = \$24,140$$
$$\text{Price} = \$1,000,000 - \$24,140 = \$975,860$$

Figure 10-2
Daily T-Bill Chart reprinted from The Wall Street Journal

Maturity	Days to Mat.	Bid	Asked	Chg.	Ask Yld.
Mar 23 '00	7	5.09	5.01	....	5.08
Mar 30 '00	14	5.30	5.22	− 0.02	5.30
Apr 06 '00	21	5.04	4.96	− 0.01	5.04
Apr 13 '00	28	5.04	4.96	− 0.11	5.05
Apr 20 '00	35	5.41	5.37	− 0.06	5.47
Apr 27 '00	42	5.70	5.66	....	5.78
May 04 '00	49	5.59	5.55	+ 0.02	5.67
May 11 '00	56	5.58	5.54	− 0.01	5.67
May 18 '00	63	5.54	5.52	− 0.06	5.65
May 25 '00	70	5.61	5.59	− 0.03	5.73
Jun 01 '00	77	5.65	5.63	− 0.01	5.78
Jun 08 '00	84	5.68	5.66	− 0.01	5.82
Jun 15 '00	91	5.69	5.68	− 0.02	5.84
Jun 22 '00	98	5.68	5.66	− 0.02	5.83
Jun 29 '00	105	5.68	5.66	+ 0.01	5.83
Jul 06 '00	112	5.69	5.67	− 0.01	5.85
Jul 13 '00	119	5.63	5.61	....	5.80
Jul 20 '00	126	5.70	5.68	+ 0.01	5.88
Jul 27 '00	133	5.68	5.66	+ 0.01	5.86
Aug 03 '00	140	5.72	5.70	− 0.01	5.91
Aug 10 '00	147	5.73	5.71	− 0.02	5.93
Aug 17 '00	154	5.79	5.77	....	6.00
Aug 24 '00	161	5.82	5.80	+ 0.01	6.04
Aug 31 '00	168	5.82	5.80	....	6.04
Sep 07 '00	175	5.83	5.81	− 0.01	6.06
Sep 14 '00	182	5.85	5.84	− 0.01	6.10
Oct 12 '00	210	5.87	5.85	− 0.01	6.12
Nov 09 '00	238	5.90	5.88	....	6.16
Dec 07 '00	266	5.89	5.87	− 0.01	6.16
Jan 04 '01	294	5.90	5.88	+ 0.02	6.19
Feb 01 '01	322	5.89	5.87	− 0.01	6.20
Mar 01 '01	350	5.85	5.84	+ 0.01	6.19

Because the investor is buying the note at a discount, the effective return is higher than the stated discount. For example, if an investor wanted to determine what his or her true return is from the above T-bill, which offers a 6.12 percent discount, the investor could calculate it by using the following formula:

$$Yield = (Discount / Price) \times (360 / Days\ Until\ Maturity)$$
$$Yield = (\$24{,}140 / \$975{,}860) \times (360 / 142)$$
$$Yield = 6.27\%$$

Thus, buying a T-bill at a discount of 6.12 percent is the equivalent of earning a 6.27 percent return on the money invested. T-bills are widely regarded as the safest and most liquid investment available in the world. The prices, maturates, and yields are readily available in most major newspapers and financial Web sites.

TREASURY NOTES AND BONDS

A Treasury with an initial maturity longer than one year is referred to as either a Treasury note (T-note) or Treasury bond (T-bond). The only difference between the two is that T-notes have initial maturates of between one and 10 years, while T-bonds pay interest on a semi-annual basis. Both Treasury notes and bonds pay interest on a semi-annual basis instead of being sold at a discount.

Notes and bonds with specific maturity dates are auctioned off on a predetermined schedule. The schedule changes frequently as the government's need for financing changes. Starting in the late 1990s the U.S. Government started running a budget surplus. Therefore, both the total volume of Treasury securities sold and the number of times per year the securities are sold have declined. (See Figure 10-3.)

The most recently auctioned issue of each maturity of Treasury note and bond is referred to as the "on the run" issue. The on the run issues are distinctive in that they are more liquid than the other Treasury issues and, therefore, offer lower yields than the other Treasuries. For example, the most recently auctioned five-year note is referred to as the "on the run five-year." It will remain the on the run issue until the government auctions off the next five-year note, which will then become the new on the run five-year issue. As with T-bills, the prices, yields, and maturates of T-bonds are widely available.

Figure 10-3
Revised Treasury Auction

Issue	Old Schedule	New Schedule
Two-Year	Monthly	Monthly
Three-Year	Quarterly	Canceled
Five-Year	Monthly	Quarterly
Ten-Year	Quarterly	Quarterly
Thirty-Year	Three Times Per Year	Semi-annually

Figure 10-4 Treasury Listing reprinted from The Wall Street Journal

TREASURY BILLS, BONDS AND NOTES

PRICES IN 32ND OF A POINT, BILL YIELDS IN BASIS POINTS. THURSDAY, MARCH 16, 2000

TREASURY BILLS

Date	Bid	Ask	Chg	Yield
Mar 23 00	5.05	5.03	+0.01	5.12
Mar 30 00	5.21	5.19	+0.01	5.29
Apr 06 00	5.06	5.04	+0.01	5.14
Apr 13 00	4.92	4.91	...	5.01
Apr 20 00	5.26	5.24	+0.01	5.35
Apr 27 00	5.66	5.64	+0.01	5.77
May 04 00	5.58	5.56	+0.01	5.70
May 11 00	5.59	5.57	+0.01	5.71
May 18 00	5.58	5.56	+0.01	5.71
May 25 00	5.64	5.62	+0.01	5.78
Jun 01 00	5.67	5.65	+0.01	5.81
Jun 08 00	5.67	5.65	...	5.82
Jun 15 00	5.70	5.68	+0.02	5.86
Jun 21 00	5.72	5.70	+0.03	5.89
Jun 29 00	5.69	5.67	−0.01	5.86
Jul 06 00	5.70	5.68	−0.01	5.88
Jul 13 00	5.65	5.63	−0.01	5.83
Jul 20 00	5.71	5.69	...	5.90
Jul 27 00	5.69	5.67	...	5.89
Aug 03 00	5.73	5.71	−0.01	5.94
Aug 10 00	5.74	5.72	−0.01	5.95
Aug 17 00	5.80	5.78	...	6.02
Aug 24 00	5.82	5.80	...	6.05
Aug 31 00	5.83	5.81	−0.01	6.05
Sep 07 00	5.84	5.82	...	6.07
Sep 14 00	5.84	5.82	−0.01	6.09
Oct 12 00	5.86	5.84	...	6.12
Nov 09 00	5.89	5.87	...	6.16
Dec 07 00	5.89	5.87	...	6.18
Jan 04 01	5.89	5.87	...	6.20
Feb 01 01	5.88	5.86	...	6.20
Mar 01 01	5.83	5.81	−0.01	6.15

BONDS AND NOTES

Month	Rate	Bid	Ask	Chg	Yld
Mar 00 p	5½	99.31	100.01	...	3.84
Mar 00 p	6⅞	100.01	100.03	...	3.13
Apr 00 p	5½	99.30	100.00	...	5.16
Apr 00 p	5⅝	99.30	100.00	...	5.51
Apr 00 p	6¾	100.02	100.04	...	5.49
May 00 p	6⅜	100.02	100.04	...	5.34
May 00 p	8⅞	100.15	100.17	−0.01	5.14
May 00 p	5½	99.29	99.31	...	5.57
May 00 p	6¼	100.02	100.04	...	5.50
Jun 00 p	5⅜	99.26	99.28	...	5.70
Jun 00 p	5⅞	99.31	100.01	...	5.69
Jul 00 p	5⅜	99.24	99.26	+0.01	5.86
Jul 00 p	6⅛	100.00	100.02	...	5.86
Aug 00 p	6	99.30	100.00	...	5.97
Aug 00 p	8¾	101.02	101.04	...	5.87
Aug 00 p	5⅛	99.17	99.19	...	6.04
Aug 00 p	6¼	100.00	100.02	−0.01	6.05
Sep 00 p	4½	99.02	99.04	...	6.17
Sep 00 p	6⅛	99.31	100.01	...	6.06
Oct 00 p	4	98.20	98.22	...	6.21
Oct 00 p	5¾	99.22	99.24	+0.01	6.16
Nov 00 p	5¾	99.21	99.23	...	6.18
Nov 00 p	8½	101.13	101.15	...	6.13
Nov 00 p	4⅝	98.28	98.30	+0.01	6.19
Nov 00 p	5⅝	99.17	99.19	...	6.19
Dec 00 p	4⅝	98.22	98.24	+0.01	6.28
Dec 00 p	5½	99.11	99.13	+0.01	6.28
Jan 01 p	4½	98.13	98.15	...	6.32
Jan 01 p	5¼	99.02	99.04	+0.01	6.30
Feb 01 p	5⅜	99.04	99.06	+0.01	6.30
Feb 01 p	7¾	101.06	101.08	...	6.28
Feb 01	11¾	104.24	104.26	...	6.19
Feb 01 p	5	98.24	98.25	+0.01	6.34
Feb 01 p	5⅝	99.10	99.12	...	6.31
Mar 01 p	4⅞	98.15	98.16	...	6.39
Mar 01 p	6⅜	99.31	100.01	...	6.34
Apr 01 p	5	98.16	98.18	+0.01	6.35
Apr 01 p	6¼	99.26	99.28	...	6.34
May 01 p	5⅝	99.03	99.05	...	6.37
May 01 p	8	101.23	101.25	...	6.35
May 01	13⅛	107.12	107.14	−0.01	6.31
May 01 p	5¼	98.20	98.21	...	6.41
May 01 p	6½	100.01	100.03	...	6.39
Jun 01 p	5¾	99.04	99.06	+0.01	6.41
Jun 01 p	6⅝	100.06	100.08	...	6.41
Jul 01 p	5½	98.24	98.26	+0.01	6.42
Jul 01 p	6⅝	100.07	100.09	+0.01	6.40
Aug 01 p	7⅞	101.27	101.29	...	6.42
Aug 01	13⅜	109.05	109.07	...	6.39
Aug 01 p	5½	98.21	98.23	...	6.43
Aug 01 p	6½	100.01	100.03	...	6.42
Sep 01 p	5⅝	98.24	98.26	+0.01	6.45
Sep 01 p	6⅜	99.26	99.28	...	6.45
Oct 01 p	5⅞	99.02	99.04	+0.01	6.45
Oct 01 p	6¼	99.20	99.22	+0.01	6.44
Nov 01 p	7½	101.17	101.19	+0.01	6.45
Nov 01	15¾	114.10	114.12	...	6.43
Nov 01 p	5⅞	99.00	99.02	+0.01	6.45
Dec 01 p	6⅛	99.12	99.14	+0.01	6.45
Jan 02 p	6¼	99.18	99.20	+0.01	6.45
Jan 02 p	6⅜	99.25	99.27	+0.01	6.45
Feb 02	14¼	113.23	113.25	...	6.44
Feb 02 p	6¼	99.18	99.20	+0.01	6.46
Feb 02 p	6½	100.01	100.03	+0.01	6.45
Mar 02 p	6⅝	100.08	100.10	+0.01	6.46
Apr 02 p	6⅝	100.08	100.10	+0.01	6.46
May 02 p	7½	101.31	102.01	+0.01	6.47
May 02 p	6½	99.31	100.01	...	6.47
Jun 02 p	6¼	99.15	99.17	+0.01	6.46
Jul 02 f	3⅝	99.15	99.17	...	3.84
Jul 02 p	6	98.30	99.00	+0.02	6.46
Aug 02 p	6⅜	99.23	99.25	+0.01	6.47
Aug 02 p	6¼	99.13	99.15	+0.01	6.48
Sep 02 p	5⅞	98.17	98.19	+0.01	6.48
Oct 02 p	5¾	98.07	98.09	+0.02	6.47
Nov 02	11⅝	112.04	112.06	+0.02	6.53
Nov 02 p	5¾	98.04	98.06	+0.03	6.49
Dec 02 p	5⅝	97.24	97.26	+0.01	6.49
Jan 03 p	5½	97.12	97.14	+0.02	6.49
Feb 03 p	6¼	99.09	99.11	...	6.49
Feb 03	10¾	110.27	110.29	...	6.56
Feb 03 p	5½	97.10	97.12	+0.01	6.49
Mar 03 p	5½	97.08	97.10	+0.01	6.49
Apr 03 p	5¾	97.28	97.30	+0.01	6.49
May 03	10¾	111.21	111.23	+0.02	6.57
May 03 p	5½	97.03	97.05	+0.01	6.49
Jun 03 p	5⅜	96.23	96.25	+0.02	6.48
Aug 03 p	5¼	96.08	96.10	+0.02	6.47
Aug 03 p	5¾	97.23	97.25	+0.02	6.48
Aug 03	11⅛	113.19	113.21	+0.02	6.58
Nov 03 p	4¼	92.30	93.00	+0.03	6.43
Nov 03	11⅞	116.30	117.00	+0.02	6.56
Feb 04 p	4¾	94.07	94.09	+0.03	6.43
Feb 04 p	5⅞	97.31	98.01	+0.02	6.45
May 04	12⅜	120.20	120.22	+0.02	6.59
May 04 p	5¼	95.19	95.21	+0.03	6.46
May 04 p	7¼	102.20	102.22	+0.02	6.49
Aug 04 p	6	98.06	98.08	+0.03	6.46
Aug 04 p	7¼	102.26	102.28	+0.03	6.49
Aug 04	13¾	126.31	127.01	+0.03	6.58
Nov 04 p	5⅞	97.21	97.23	+0.04	6.45
Nov 04 p	7⅞	105.12	105.14	+0.03	6.50
Nov 04 k	11⅝	119.30	120.00	+0.03	6.56
Feb 05 p	7½	104.02	104.04	+0.04	6.50
May 00-05	8¼	100.12	100.14	...	5.23
May 05 p	6½	100.00	100.02	+0.03	6.48
May 05 k	12	123.13	123.15	+0.04	6.55
Aug 05 p	6½	99.30	100.00	+0.04	6.50
Aug 05 k	10¾	118.23	1.18.25	+0.04	6.56
Nov 05 p	5⅞	96.31	97.01	+0.03	6.51
Feb 06 p	5⅝	95.23	95.25	+0.05	6.49
Feb 06 k	9⅜	113.17	113.19	+0.04	6.56
May 06 p	6⅞	101.24	101.26	+0.05	6.51
Jul 06 p	7	102.14	102.16	+0.05	6.51
Oct 06 p	6½	99.29	99.31	+0.05	6.50
Feb 07 p	6¼	98.23	98.25	+0.06	6.47
Feb 02-07	7⅝	101.18	101.22	+0.02	6.66
May 07 p	6⅝	100.24	100.26	+0.06	6.48
Aug 07 p	6⅛	97.29	97.31	+0.05	6.47
Nov 02-07	7⅞	102.25	102.27	+0.03	6.68
Jan 08 f	3⅝	96.08	96.10	+0.01	4.18
Feb 08 p	5½	94.05	94.07	+0.06	6.44
May 08 p	5⅝	94.24	94.26	+0.05	6.45
Aug 03-08	8⅜	104.30	105.00	+0.03	6.70
Nov 08 p	4¾	88.30	89.00	+0.06	6.43
Nov 03-08	8¾	106.12	106.14	+0.04	6.73
Jan 09 f	3⅞	97.21	97.23	−0.02	4.18
May 09 p	5½	93.21	93.23	+0.07	6.42
May 04-09	9⅛	108.14	108.16	+0.04	6.74
Aug 09 p	6	97.05	97.07	+0.06	6.39
Nov 04-09	10⅜	114.11	114.13	+0.05	6.72
Jan 10 f	4¼	100.20	100.22	...	4.16
Feb 10 p	6½	101.26	101.28	+0.08	6.24
Feb 05-10	11¾	120.28	120.30	+0.05	6.67
May 05-10	10	114.03	114.05	+0.05	6.70
Nov 05-10	12¾	128.06	128.08	+0.09	6.67
May 06-11	13⅞	135.29	135.31	+0.10	6.65
Nov 06-11	14	138.31	139.01	+0.12	6.64
Nov 07-12	10⅜	122.02	122.04	+0.12	6.64
Aug 08-13	12	134.01	134.04	+0.10	6.64
May 09-14	13¼	144.24	144.26	+0.12	6.64
Aug 09-14k	12½	140.15	140.17	+0.09	6.63
Nov 09-14k	11¾	136.10	136.12	+0.04	6.59
Feb 15 k	11¼	145.16	145.18	+0.10	6.45
Aug 15 k	10⅝	140.15	140.17	+0.10	6.44
Nov 15 k	9⅞	133.19	133.21	+0.11	6.43
Feb 16 k	9¼	127.27	127.29	+0.11	6.42
May 16 k	7¼	108.18	108.20	+0.10	6.39
Nov 16 k	7½	111.08	111.10	+0.10	6.39
May 17 k	8¾	124.06	124.08	+0.11	6.40
Aug 17 k	8⅞	125.24	125.26	+0.12	6.39
May 18 k	9⅛	129.02	129.04	+0.11	6.39
Nov 18 k	9	128.07	128.08	+0.11	6.38
Feb 19 k	8⅞	127.05	127.07	+0.11	6.38
Aug 19 k	8⅛	119.13	119.15	+0.11	6.36
Feb 20 k	8½	123.28	123.30	+0.11	6.36
May 20 k	8¾	126.27	126.29	+0.12	6.36
Aug 20 k	8¾	127.01	127.03	+0.11	6.36
Feb 21 k	7⅞	117.17	117.19	+0.11	6.34
May 21 k	8⅛	120.18	120.20	+0.11	6.34
Aug 21 k	8⅛	120.22	120.24	+0.11	6.34
Nov 21 k	8	119.16	119.18	+0.12	6.33
Aug 22 k	7¼	111.01	111.03	+0.11	6.32
Nov 22 k	7⅝	115.16	115.18	+0.11	6.32
Feb 23 k	7⅛	109.23	109.25	+0.10	6.31
Aug 23 k	6¼	99.12	99.14	+0.10	6.30
Nov 24 k	7½	115.01	115.03	+0.11	6.28
Feb 25 k	7⅝	116.24	116.26	+0.12	6.28
Aug 25 k	6⅞	107.18	107.20	+0.11	6.27
Feb 26 k	6	96.24	96.26	+0.10	6.25
Aug 26 k	6¾	106.13	106.15	+0.12	6.25
Nov 26 k	6½	103.08	103.10	+0.11	6.24
Feb 27 k	6⅝	104.29	104.31	+0.12	6.24
Aug 27 k	6⅜	101.24	101.26	+0.11	6.23
Nov 27 k	6⅛	98.21	98.23	+0.11	6.22
Apr 28 f	3⅝	91.28	91.30	−0.01	4.11
Aug 28 k	5½	90.17	90.19	+0.11	6.21
Nov 28 k	5¼	87.10	87.12	+0.10	6.20
Feb 29 k	5¼	87.13	87.15	+0.09	6.18
Apr 29 f	3⅞	95.31	96.01	−0.01	4.11
Aug 29 k	6⅛	99.15	99.17	+0.09	6.16
Feb 30 k	6¼	102.25	102.27	+0.09	6.04

Source: Street Software/Bear Stearns via The Associated Press

TREASURY STRIPS

A Treasury strip, commonly referred to either as a "strip," "Treasury zero," or "Zero coupon bond (ZCB)," is very similar to a T-bill in that it is sold at a discount and when it matures, it pays the investor its face value. In effect, a strip is nothing more than a long-term discount note. The name "strip" comes from the way in which the securities are created—by stripping the individual cash flows away from interest-bearing T-notes and bonds. Consider the following example:

T-notes and bonds are just collections of individual cash flows. For example, 20 two-year 10 percent T-notes would generate the cash flows shown in Figure 10-5.

Figure 10-5
Treasury Cash Flows

–$20,000	+$1,000	+$1,000	+$1,000	+$21,000
Today	Six Months	12 Months	18 Months	24 Months

Each of these cash flows can be sold separately as a strip—provided they are offered at the appropriate discount rate.

Figure 10-6
Repackaged Cash Flows

Time	Cash Flow	Sold As
6 Months	$1,000	6-Month ZCB
12 Months	$1,000	12-Month ZCB
18 Months	$1,000	18-month ZCB
24 Months	$21,000	21 24-Month ZCBs

The $1,000 payment in six months could be discounted at the appropriate six-month rate and sold as a separate investment. Likewise, the $1,000 payment in 12 months could be discounted at the 12-month rate and sold separately, and so on.

When compared with Treasury notes and bonds, Treasury ZCBs have the following distinctive characteristics:

- ZCBs have no reinvestment risk. Since ZCBs generate no cash flows prior to the day they mature, there are no cash flows to reinvest and, therefore, no risk that the cash flows will have to be reinvested at a lower rate. Of course, they also eliminate the possibility of reinvesting interest payments at a higher rate. So, investors who want to be absolutely sure of having a certain number of dollars on a certain day in the future find Treasury zeros to be very attractive.

- ZCBs generate tax liabilities without generating any cash with which to pay the taxes. Each year investors have to pay taxes on the accretion towards par, even though the bond does not generate any cash flow with which to pay the taxes. For this reason, many investors prefer to buy strips inside tax-deferred accounts such as IRAs and retirement plans.

- ZCBs have very high interest rate sensitivities. As interest rates change, the price of a ZCB will change more than any other bond with a similar maturity. Thus, they are attractive vehicles for speculating on the direction of interest rates.

The prices, maturates, and yield of Treasury strips are widely available.

TREASURY INFLATION PROTECTION SECURITIES

The most recent innovation in the Treasury securities market is the creation of Treasury inflation protection securities (TIPS). These Treasury securities do not pay a fixed rate of interest. Instead, the rate they pay is a fixed percentage over the inflation rate. If the TIPS paid the rate of inflation plus 3 percent, then if inflation was at 4 percent, the TIPS would pay 7 percent. The rate is adjusted semi-annually as inflation changes. Because the interest rate that TIPS pay fluctuates with inflation, the market value of TIPS should remain reasonably constant as time passes—making them a very low-risk form of Treasury security.

Treasury Yield Curve

Investors frequently plot the various Treasury notes and bonds (exclusive of TIPS) on a yield versus maturity graph. (See Figure 10-7.) Once the data points are plotted, a statistical methodology called regression analysis is used to determine the shape of the line that "best fits" the data. This line is referred to as the Treasury yield curve. Many investors consider the Treasury yield curve to be a graphical representation of the trade-off between risk and reward in the Treasury market.

Figure 10-7
Creating the Treasury Yield Curve

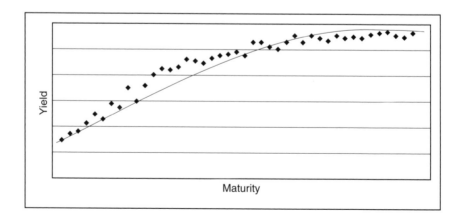

Investment Strategies

Investors who purchase U.S. Treasuries often do not have to just hold them and collect interest. They can also try to outperform the return available from simply buying and holding Treasuries by implementing a number of strategies and tactics.

STRATEGY ONE—TRADE ON INTEREST RATE OUTLOOK

For investors who want to speculate on interest rates, Treasury bonds are the investment vehicle of choice. Their high liquidity, transparent pricing, low transaction costs, and in the case of Treasury zeros, high volatilities, make them the ideal fixed-income-trading vehicle for speculators. Investors should buy (sell) Treasury zeros at whatever point along the yield curve they believe offers the best (worst) trade-off between risk and reward.

For example, suppose an investor expects inflation to decline sharply. If inflation declines sharply, then long-term interest rates, which are driven by inflation, will also decline. If long-term interest rates decline, investors should buy long-term ZCBs, since they will have a higher volatility than any other Treasury bond. Thus, as interest rates decline, they will experience more capital appreciation (on a percentage basis) than any other security.

As another example, if an investor expects the five-year interest rate to rise, the investor could short the five-year zero coupon bond. As rates rose, the price would fall and the investor could cover the short position and profit.

STRATEGY TWO—PROFITING ON FINANCING

Another way investors can hope to profit is by borrowing money at a low rate and using the money to buy Treasuries that offer a higher yield. In effect, the investor hopes to make money by earning the spread between the rate the investor pays on the borrowed money and the rate the investor earns on the Treasury. In order for this strategy to be profitable, the yield curve has to be very steep. When the yield curve is very steep, investors can borrow money for the short term at low rates and use the money to buy high-yielding long-term Treasuries. For example, if investors are able to borrow at 6 percent and invest at 10 percent, they can make a 4 percent financing spread.

Naturally, the higher the spread between short- and long-term rates, the greater the profit from a financing strategy. In order to reduce their borrowing costs, most investors who pursue this strategy collateralize their loans with Treasuries. After all, investors can borrow at a lower rate when they put up collateral to guarantee the loan—especially high-quality collateral like Treasuries. The market where securities are used to collateralize short-term loans is referred to as the repurchase agreement (or repo) market.

Figure 10-8
Yield Curve

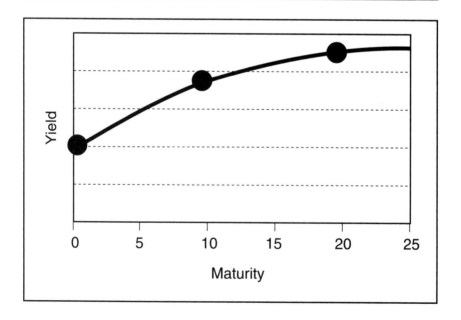

STRATEGY THREE—YIELD CURVE SPECULATION

Another commonly used strategy is to speculate on how the shape of the yield curve will change. (See Figure 10-8.) By taking both long and short positions that have the same volatility at different points along the yield curve, investors can speculate on changes in the shape of the curve—without being exposed to general interest rate risk.

For example, if an investor expected the yield curve to steepen, the investor would take a long position in short-term Treasuries and a short position in long-term Treasuries. This position would generate a profit if the yield curve steepened, and a loss if it flattened. A parallel shift of the yield curve up or down would have no affect on the value of the overall position. An investor who expected the yield curve to flatten would take a short position on short-term treasuries and a long position in long-term.

STRATEGY FOUR—BULLET, LADDER, AND BARBELL

One very popular trade is to shift money among bullet, ladder, and barbell positions. Consider the following example, in which an investor is interested in building a bond portfolio that has an average life of 10 years out of cash, a 10-year bond, and a 20-year bond. (See Figure 10-9.)

Naturally, there are a variety of ways to build this portfolio. For example, the investor could use any of the following three portfolios—among many others.

Portfolio A is a "bullet portfolio," since all the bonds mature at the same time.

Figure 10-9
Alternative 10-Year Average Life Portfolios

	Cash	10-Year	20-Year
A	0%	100%	0%
B	33%	33%	33%
C	50%	0%	50%

Portfolio B is a "ladder portfolio," since the bonds mature all along the yield curve, and the distribution among short-term, intermediate-term, and long-term is even.

Portfolio C is a "barbell portfolio," because the cash flows are concentrated at the ends of the yield curve.

Because the average maturity of each portfolio is 10 years, how should an investor decide among them? The answer lies in what the investor's outlook is for interest rate volatility. If the investor expects interest rates to remain unchanged, the investor would prefer the bullet portfolio, since it offers the highest yield. Because of the curvature of the yield curve, the barbell portfolio would offer the lowest yield. The ladder portfolio's return is, of course, between the bullet and barbell.

If the bullet portfolio offers the highest return, why would anyone buy the barbell? The answer lies in how the portfolios will perform if interest rates change. While the barbell offers the lowest yield today, it will offer the largest gain if interest rates decline and the smallest loss if interest rates rise. Thus, if interest rates change, the barbell portfolio will offer the highest total return. If interest rates remain stable, the bullet portfolio will offer the highest return. If an investor does not want to try to forecast how volatile interest rates will be, he or she can simply buy the ladder portfolio, which will always be an intermediate performer.

CORPORATE BONDS

Investors who seek a higher return than the return offered by Treasuries and Agencies, and who are also willing to take more risk to obtain it, should consider investing in bonds issued by corporations. While corporate bonds pay a higher interest rate than government bonds, they do expose investors to additional risks, including event, credit, and tax risk. Therefore, investors who consider buying corporate bonds should either make sure to do their homework or rely on the opinions of corporate bond experts.

Why Companies Issue Bonds

There are several reasons companies elect to issue bonds instead of raising the capital they need from some other source. Some of these reasons include:

- Bond buyers are often willing to lend companies money for a longer period than banks. Most banks are not willing to make loans that are longer than about five to seven years. Since banks generally borrow money from depositors for short periods of time, they don't want to relend it for long periods of time. However, companies frequently want to borrow money for terms as long as

20 years and, therefore, have no alternative other than to issue bonds.

- Companies often do not want to dilute the percentage ownership of the existing common stock by issuing additional shares. Instead, they issue debt.

- Sometimes the rate at which companies can borrow in the bond market is the lowest cost source of financing available to the company.

When a company elects to issue corporate bonds, it can either sell the bonds to the public at large via public offering or sell them to a limited number of banks, insurance companies, pension planners, and other "institutional investors" via so-called "private placement."

In a public offering, a company generally hires an investment bank to help it prepare a loan document that spells out the terms of the loan it is seeking from investors. This loan document, called the bond indenture, can be quite complex and lengthy (500-plus pages of legalese are common). Like any loan documents, these agreements spell out the terms of the loan and the promises that the borrower makes to the lenders. These promises, referred to as covenants, fall into two main categories: affirmative and negative. Affirmative covenants are the promises the company makes regarding things it will do. Typical affirmative covenants include promises concerning:

- What it will do with the proceeds. For example, will it use the money to make acquisitions, or build a new plant, or for working capital? The company is obligated to use the proceeds from the sale of bonds for whatever purpose it says it will use them in its indenture. A company cannot say it is borrowing to build a new plant and then turn around and use the money instead to make acquisitions.

- What steps it will take to protect investors. For example, the company may agree in its indenture to maintain a certain debt to equity ratio, to not pay dividends if the company's cash reserves drop below a certain level, and so on. The interests of bondholders and stockholders are often opposed. Shareholders often want to pull money out of their companies, while bondholders want money to stay in the company to secure their debt.

Typical negative covenants include promises concerning:

- Issuing additional bonds that are more senior to the debt. Most lenders want guarantees that if they lend the company money by buying its bonds, the company will not then turn around and issue new bonds or obtain bank financing that is senior.

- Promising not to change its corporate structure or state of incorporation. State laws vary widely with regard to the level of protection afforded lenders, and so lenders often want protection against companies changing their state of incorporation.

- Disposing of any significant assets. Lenders want companies to agree not to sell assets, because they are afraid that the sale proceeds could be squandered instead of acting as security for their loans.

Naturally, most investors lack the time and expertise required to read and understand all of the provisions in the indenture, much less monitor whether the company adheres to its various covenants. Most investors elect to rely on the opinions of bond experts when determining which bonds have attractive deal terms and which do not.

To monitor whether the company adheres to its covenants on an ongoing basis, each public deal is assigned a "corporate trustee." This trustee is normally a commercial bank. Bondholders can have legal recourse against the corporate trustee if it fails to notice a violation of a loan covenant and, consequently, the bondholders suffer a loss.

Corporate Bonds and Credit Ratings

One of the most important factors that investors must consider when evaluating corporate bonds is the current and projected future credit quality of the bond. (See Figure 11-1.) The higher a bond's credit qual-

Figure 11-1
Ratings of Bonds

Investment Bracket	Fitch	Moody's		Standard & Poor's
Top quality	AAA	Aaa		AAA
	AA	Aa		AA
	A	A		A
Medium quality	BBB	Baa.	1–2–3°	BBB
to speculative	BB	Ba		BB
	B	B		B
Poor quality	CCC	Caa		CCC
	CC	Ca		CC
	C	C		C
Value is	DDD			DDD
questionable	DD			DD
	D			D

°The number 1 added to these ratings indicates the *high* end of the category, number 2, the *mid-range* ranking, number 3, the *low* end.

ity, the greater the probability that it will make its interest and principal payments in full and on time. Most major securities firms, as well as a number of independent companies (such as Standard & Poor's and Moody's), analyze companies' financial results, business prospects, management quality, and so on, in an attempt to determine how likely it is that the issuer will be able to meet its commitments. They assign credit ratings to each bond offering based on their analysis.

Bonds that have a rating of BBB or higher are considered to be "investment grade." The probability of default with bonds that have a credit rating this high or higher is so low, that banks are permitted to buy them to secure depositors. Bonds that have a lower credit rating are referred to as "high-yield bonds" by their fans, and as "junk bonds" by their detractors.

The vast majority of bond offerings are high yield bonds. While any single high-yield bond issue has a higher probability of default, historically, a well-diversified portfolio of high-yield bonds has offered a higher total return than a portfolio of Treasuries, agencies, and/or investment-grade corporate bonds.

Investors who buy corporate bonds must periodically reevaluate the credit quality of the corporate bonds they own, as well as the bonds they are considering buying. Investors always try to buy bonds whose credit quality they think will improve and to sell bonds whose credit quality they think will decline. In other words, corporate bond investors make "credit bets."

When a bond's credit quality is upgraded, its price rises. When it is downgraded, its price declines. However, in order to be successful, investors need to be right far more often than they are wrong. This is because an upgrade will generate a smaller gain in a price than the loss in price that results from a credit downgrade. Thus, credit risk has a type of "negative convexity," meaning the loss from an unfavorable change is greater than the gain from a favorable change. Consider the following example involving a bond with a current rating of BBB+.

According to Figure 11-2, if the bond is upgraded, its yield will decline by 30 basis points. This decline in yield will result in a rise in the bond's market value. If the bond is downgraded, its yield will rise by 45 basis points and the bond's market value will decline. Thus, the loss due to a downgrade is 150 percent of the gain due to an upgrade. Thus, an investor would have to have three "credit upgrades" for every two "credit downgrades" simply to break even.

Figure 11-2
Effect of Rating Change on Yield

Bond Rating	Total Yield
A–	8.10%
BBB+	8.40%
BBB	8.85%

Types of Corporate Bonds

Corporate bonds are divided into categories based on the type of collateral, if any, that secures the company's debt. The major categories include:

- Mortgage bonds—*Mortgage bonds* are secured not only by the full faith and credit of the issuer, but also by a lien against some real property, such as an office building, manufacturing plant, warehouse, or acreage. In the event the issuer fails to make an interest or principal payment in full or on time, the bondholders—acting through the corporate trustee—can legally force the company into bankruptcy, seize the property, and sell it in the open market. Hopefully, the proceeds from the sale of the property will allow the investors to recoup their original investment plus any unpaid interest.

  Sometimes companies issue several bond deals secured by the same piece(s) of real estate. In this event, the bonds are ranked in a specific order regarding the order in which the bondholders are to receive any sales proceeds. The first bonds to be paid off are referred to as first mortgage bonds, the second bonds to be paid off are referred to as second mortgage bonds, etc.

- Collateral bonds—*Collateral bonds* are backed by some form of high-quality, reasonably liquid, collateral, such as securities or receivables. Again, in the event the issuer defaults, the collateral can be seized and sold by the bondholders.

- Equipment trust certificates—*Equipment trust certificates* are secured by liens against specific equipment or inventory, such as aircraft, rail cars, automobiles, and so on. Again, in the event the issuer defaults, the equipment can be seized and sold by the bondholders.

- Debentures—*Debentures* are bonds that are not backed by any specific collateral, but instead are backed only by the company's full faith and credit. The majority of all bonds issued are debentures. Companies frequently have several different debenture issues outstanding at the same time. As with mortgage bonds, the various debenture issues are ranked according to the order in which they will be paid off in the event the company goes bankrupt. The first bond to be paid off is referred to as the senior debenture. The next most senior is the first subordinated debenture, then the second subordinated debenture, and so on.

- Income bonds—*Income bonds* are a special category of bonds. Unlike every other type of bond, the issuers of income bonds promise to pay interest only if they can afford to pay it. If they cannot afford to make an interest payment when it comes due, they simply do not pay it. Unlike every other category of bond, where missing an interest payment creates a "default" that can allow the bondholders to force the issuer into bankruptcy, income bonds provide their owners with no such power. Naturally, the only reason any investor would buy an income bond is if it offered a substantially higher yield. In addition, the indentures of income bonds usually prohibit the company from paying bonuses to managers or dividends to shareholders unless it is current on its interest payments on its income bonds.

Note that while the bond indentures for each bond offering clearly state where the particular issue ranks with regard to seniority relative to the issuer's other outstanding bond issues, the bankruptcy court is not bound to honor those commitments. Bankruptcy court judges in the U.S. have sweeping powers and have ignored the stated seniority order of bond offerings when they have imposed settlements.

Expressing the Yield of Corporates

Over the last 10 years, the way the yield of corporate bonds is expressed has changed. This change has been empowered by the rapid advances of technology. Ten years ago, bond returns were quoted only on a yield basis, such as 10.14 or 6.67 percent. Today, while dealers still quote corporate bond yields this way, they also quote yields by comparing the corporate bond yields with the yield of the equivalent Treasury bond. The difference in the yields is referred to as the "bond spread." For example, when asked to make a market in a particular corporate bond that matures in five years, a dealer might respond with "I make the market at 55 by 65." This response means that the dealer is willing to:

- Buy the bond at whatever price equals a yield that is 65 basis points (.65 percent) higher than the current yield to maturity of the five-year Treasury.

- Sell the bond at whatever price equals a yield that is 55 basis points (.55 percent) higher than the current yield to maturity of the five-year Treasury.

Thus, if the five-year Treasury was currently offering a yield to maturity of 6 percent, the dealer is saying that he or she is willing to buy the bond at whatever price equals a yield to maturity of 6.65 percent and is willing to sell it at whatever price equals a yield of 6.55 percent. If this corporate bond had a 7-percent coupon, the prices at which the dealer would buy and sell would be $1,014.63 and $1,018.93, respectively.

Note that there is no legal standard for what exactly defines the "equivalent" Treasury and, therefore, there are several ways to do so. Some of these include quoting the spread to the Treasury whose maturity is the closest to the maturity of the corporate, or to the "on the run" Treasury whose maturity is the closest to the maturity of the corporate.

Each way of quoting the spread will result in a different value for the spread. While any of the above methods can work, it is important to use a consistent method and to apply it to all bonds when trying to determine which corporate bond offers the best relative value.

Components of Spread

In addition to having more credit risk, there are other reasons corporate bonds yield more than Treasuries. Some of these other reasons include:

1. Liquidity risk—Even the most liquid corporate bonds are less liquid than the least liquid Treasury bonds. Because these bonds have less liquidity and, therefore, may be harder to sell, investors demand a higher yield as compensation. Thus, some part of the spread in yields between Treasuries and corporates is compensation for the difference in liquidity.

2. Tax difference—The interest received from U.S. Treasury bonds is subject only to federal income tax. The interest received from corporate bonds is subject to federal, state, and city income tax. Because most U.S. taxpayers pay higher taxes on corporate bonds than they do on Treasury bonds, corporate bonds have to offer some additional compensation to account for this difference.

3. Calendar difference—The calendar convention that is used to calculate interest for Treasury bonds and corporate bonds is different. Treasury bonds are quoted on an actual/actual calendar, while corporate bonds are quoted on a 30/360 calendar. Thus, an 8-percent Treasury bond can generate a different amount of interest than an 8-percent corporate bond over the same partial payment period. The spread in yields needs to reflect this difference. (See Figure 11-3.)

4. Call risk—While almost all Treasury bonds are noncallable, almost all corporate bonds are either openly callable or can be called under certain circumstances (so-called hidden calls). Because a call always works against the investor, corporate bonds have to offer a higher return in order to compensate investors for selling these embedded call options. Valuing the embedded options is one of the major challenges facing corporate bond investors, and is discussed in greater detail in the following section.

Figure 11-3
Composition of Yield Curve

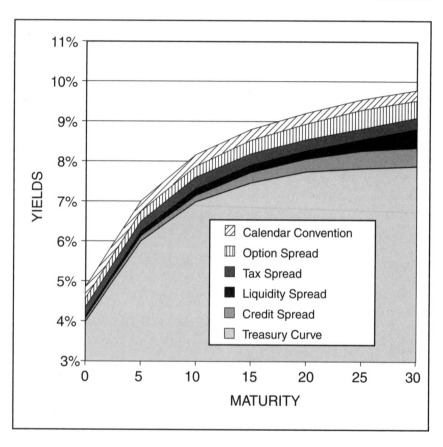

Option Adjusted Spread

A further refinement of the way in which corporate bonds are valued and quoted is their option adjusted spread (OAS). This is the spread between the yield of the corporate bond and the equivalent treasury after the value of the option is subtracted from the spread. When an investor buys a corporate bond that is "callable"—that is, contains an embedded call option—the investor really has two positions:

1. The investor will receive whatever cash flows are generated by the bond.

2. The investor grants the issuer the right to shorten the bond's life.

While the investor pays the seller to receive the bond's future cash flows, the issuer pays the investor for the right to shorten the bond's life. Thus, the overall yield spread reflects the value of both of these positions. OAS analysis attempts to separate the two so investors can make a more informed decision regarding the relative value of different corporates.

This OAS concept is best illustrated with an example.

Assume the 10-year Treasury bond currently offers a yield of 9 percent, and an investor is trying to decide which of the two otherwise identical corporate bonds is a better value—Bond A or Bond B.

- Bond A: 10-year AA rated corporate bond that offers a yield of 10.20 percent and is callable at par in three years.

- Bond B: 10-year AA rated corporate bond that offers a yield of 9.80 percent and is callable at 103 in five years.

In this example, Bond A offers a 120 basis point spread (10.20 – 9 percent) to the equivalent Treasury, while Bond B offers only an 80 basis point spread (9.80 – 9 percent). At first glance, it might seem that Bond A offers a better relative value than Bond B.

However, this analysis does not take into account the differences in the embedded options. Bond A offers just three years of call protection, while Bond B offers five years of call protection. Further, if Bond A is called, the investor receives just $1,000, while if Bond B is called, the investor receives $1,030.

Thus, the embedded option in Bond A is much more valuable to the issuer than the embedded option in Bond B. The right to take the bond away from the investor at $1,000 in just three years is more valuable than the right to take the bond away from the investor for $1,030 in five years. Therefore, an investor who buys Bond A should receive a higher yield as compensation for selling an option with a higher value. The fair value of both embedded options can be valued using option pricing models. The fair value of both options (expressed in terms of yield) can then be subtracted from the absolute spread in order to determine the option adjusted spread.

Figure 11-4
Nominal vs. Option Adjusted Spread

	Bond A	Bond B
Absolute Spread	120 basis points	80 basis points
Value of the Option	70 basis points	20 basis points
Option Adjusted Spread	50 basis points	60 basis points

For example, if the fair value of the first option was determined to be 70 basis points of yield per year and the fair value of the second option was determined to be 20 basis points of yield per year, then the option adjusted spreads of the two bonds would be 50 basis points and 60 basis points, respectively. (See Figure 11-4.) The option adjusted spread is just the total spread minus that portion of the spread that represents a fair return to the investor for selling the issuer the embedded option.

The OAS, then, represents the spread that the investor receives for accepting credit, liquidity, and tax risk. In this example, Bond B offers 10 basis points higher OAS than Bond A and, as such, offers the investor a better relative value. OAS is the current standard by which the relative value of corporate bonds is evaluated.

As with any option valuation model, the least certain input is the volatility input. The higher the volatility assumption used in the calculation, the greater the value of the embedded option. The greater the value of the embedded option, the lower the OAS. If the volatility measure is high enough, the value of the option can exceed the absolute spread. When this happens, the OAS can actually become negative.

CHAPTER 12

MUNICIPAL BONDS

Municipal bonds are bonds issued by states and political subdivisions of states, including counties, cities, water authorities, publicly owned power authorities, protectorates, colonies, and U.S. territories. Because there are so many issuers of municipal bonds, there are also many municipal bond issues (more than 1.5 million) outstanding at any time. Most of the issues are quite small, privately placed, and are only of local interest. Because there are so many different issues outstanding, the municipal bond market is the least efficient of the major fixed income markets. Investors who invest carefully can exploit this inefficiency for their own benefit.

Tax Treatment of Municipals

(While the following discussion applies to the majority of municipal bond issues, the tax treatment of municipal bonds can be quite complex. Investors should have tax experts verify the tax status of every individual bond issue prior to making any investments.)

For individuals, the primary benefit of municipal bonds relative to other investments is that the interest received is exempt from federal income tax. This exemption applies only to the interest received, not any capital gains. If the bonds are sold (or mature) at a higher value than the purchase price, the increase in value is taxed as a capital gain. However, if the bonds are sold (or mature) at a lower value than the purchase price, the tax treatment depends upon whether the bonds were purchased at a premium, at par, or at a discount.

- If the bonds were purchased either at par or a discount, any loss can be claimed as a capital loss.

- If the bonds were purchased at a premium, then the premium must be amortized over the remaining life of the bond. The investor can take a capital loss only if the bonds are sold at a price below the amortized value. Sales above the amortized value will be taxed as a gain.

Consider the following example. A municipal bond with an above-market coupon and 10 years of remaining life is purchased for a price of $1,200. Each year, the accreted value of the bond declines by $20. Thus, five years later, the bond has a tax basis of $1,100. If the bond was sold at $1,080 in five years, the investor would be able to claim only a $20 capital loss. The theory behind this tax treatment is that since the federal government can't tax the above-market coupon payments that caused the bond to be priced at a premium, the investor can't deduct the loss of the premium.

Interest payments are also normally exempt from state income tax, provided the investor buys a bond issued by an issuer within the individual's state of residence. Almost all states require that income taxes be paid on interest received from bonds issued by "out of state" bonds. The tax treatment of capital gains and losses on municipals at the state level is very similar to the federal tax treatment in most states.

For corporate investors, the tax treatment is somewhat different.

- Interest payments are exempt from federal income tax.

- Interest payments are exempt from state income tax if the bonds are from the same state in which the tax return is filed. Many companies file tax returns in several states. In each state, the interest received from the bonds of that state is exempt from federal income tax.

As a result of the favorable tax treatment, investors are willing to accept a lower coupon from municipal bonds than they are from other types of debt. For example, an investor in the 30-percent tax bracket would receive as much after-tax income from a 7-percent municipal bond (issued in the investor's home state) as from a 10-percent corporate bond.

General Obligation Versus Revenue Bonds

There are two forms of municipal bonds: general obligation bonds and revenue bonds. They differ with regard to the backing that secures the bonds.

1. General obligation (GO) bonds are backed by the full faith, credit, and taxing power of the issuer. For example, if a city issues GO bonds, theoretically at least, the city obligates itself to raise its property taxes, to raise its user fees, to cut its services, or to take whatever other actions are necessary in order to meet its interest and principal payments in full and on time. Of course, taxpayer revolts, such as the one that occurred in California, can negate even the most binding obligations created by politicians.

2. Revenue bonds are not backed by an issuer's full faith and credit. Instead, revenue bonds are backed by the cash flow of a specific project. Normally, the cash flow comes from a project the bonds were used to finance. For example:

   • The interest and principal due on bonds that are issued by cities to build our water systems and sewage lines comes from the fees that homeowners and businesses pay to receive water and hook up to the sewage system.

- The interest and principal due on bonds that are issued by cities to build airports are serviced by the revenue generated by renting out concessions within the airport, charging parking fees to the passengers, charging landing fees to the airlines, and renting ticket counter and baggage space.

- The interest and principal due on bonds that are issued by states to build bridges and turnpike bonds are serviced by the tolls collected to use them.

Often, the maturity of revenue bonds is staggered to match the expected cash flows generated by the project. For example, a state might build a new toll bridge for $100,000,000. If the state expects it to take three years to build the bridge, and expects the tolls collected to generate a surplus of at least $4,000,000 per year, then the maturity schedule of the revenue bonds might resemble the one in Figure 12-1.

The bonds that mature early are referred to as "serial bonds," because they mature in a series. The bonds that mature at the end of the financing are referred to as "term bonds," since they are outstanding for the entire term of the offering. Naturally, the yield of each bond reflects its respective maturity, with longer-term bonds generally offering a higher coupon.

If the revenue from the project is not sufficient to service the debt, the bonds will go into default. Unfortunately, bondholders cannot repossess a bridge or sewer system if a revenue bond defaults.

Figure 12-1
Maturity Schedule of Bonds

Year	Coup	Amt	Year	Coup	Amt	Year	Coup	Amt
1	NA	0	6	4.15%	4 Million	11	4.30%	4 Million
2	NA	0	7	4.20%	4 Million	12	4.30%	4 Million
3	NA	0	8	4.25%	4 Million	13	4.40%	4 Million
4	4%	4 Million	9	4.25%	4 Million	14	4.40%	4 Million
5	4.10%	4 Million	10	4.25%	4 Million	15	4.50%	66 Million

Underwriting Municipal Bonds

There are two ways that municipal bonds are underwritten: competitive and negotiated.

1. In a competitive underwriting, the issuer announces a proposed bond offering in the trade press, such as *The Bond Buyer.* The advertisement states the amount the issuer wishes to borrow, the purpose for the borrowing, and the term for which the municipality wants to borrow the money. Municipal bond firms then submit sealed bids to buy the bonds from the issuer. The firm (or firms if several firms elected to bid together as a syndicate) that is willing to pay the most for the bonds wins the bidding and buys the bonds. In effect, the firms compete for the right to sell the bonds. The winning firm(s) then tries to sell the bonds to investors at a slightly higher price. Frequently, however, the winning firm ends up taking a loss on the initial underwriting and counts on subsequent trading of the issue to turn an eventual profit. General obligation bonds have historically been underwritten on a competitive basis.

2. In a negotiated underwriting, the issuer negotiates terms of the offering with underwriting firms directly, instead of using sealed bids. The issuer is under no obligation to accept the lowest bid. Awarding deals on a negotiated basis came under severe criticism in the early 1990s, since it was often the underwriting firm that made the largest political contributions that was awarded the business. Recently, the municipal bond industry agreed to a near-total ban on political contributions in order to clean up the industry's image.

MORTGAGE-BACKED SECURITIES

One of the largest and fastest-growing fixed income markets is the mortgage-backed securities market. Mortgage-backed securities are backed by mortgage loans that are, in turn, backed by liens against real property. For example, when a homebuyer buys a $200,000 house, the buyer typically makes a down payment of 20-25% and borrows the balance of the purchase price from a bank or mortgage company. The lender secures its loan by allowing the bank to retain the title to the property. In the event that the buyer defaults on the mortgage loan, the bank will seize the property (i.e., foreclose) and sell it in order to recover the funds it lent.

Historically, banks raised money from depositors to make their mortgage loans and they held the loans as assets in their portfolios. Banks paid their depositors 3%, made mortgage loans at 6%, and had consistent profit margins. (See Figure 13-1.)

Figure 13-1
Profitable Mortgage Lending

Figure 13-2
Unprofitable Mortgage Lending

The world of banking was turned upside down in the 1980s, when interest rates skyrocketed, and consequently banks found themselves in the unenviable position of earning 6% on their assets and paying 12% to their depositors. (See Figure 13-2.) Because the capital banks raised from depositors was borrowed for the short term from checking accounts, saving accounts, certificates of deposit, and so on, and the money it lent was for terms as long as 30 years, the banks' interest expense rose much faster than its interest income. This asset liability mismatch caused many banks to fail.

Since the 1980s, banks have been wary of allowing the average life of their assets (loans) to exceed the average life of their liabilities (funding). One of the ways they have reduced the life of their assets is to sell their long-term mortgage loans to investors, instead of holding them in their portfolios. However, individual mortgage loans are not especially liquid and, therefore, can be difficult to sell.

Problems Associated With Selling Individual Mortgages

Individual mortgages have several characteristics that hinder their liquidity and their appeal as potential investments.

- High cost of assessing the credit risk of mortgage loans. When lenders consider making mortgage loans, they usually have a number of reports prepared so that they have the information necessary to assess the credit quality of potential loans. These reports usually include:

1. A report by a professional appraiser on the property's actual market value and an assessment of whether the appraiser expects property values in the area are expected to rise or fall.

2. A report by one or more credit agencies on the loan applicant's credit history.

3. A report by the loan applicant's employer(s) on the likelihood of the applicant's continued employment.

4. An environmental report that details any hazards such as radon gas, old oil storage tanks, and so on.

The cost of having these reports prepared can be more than $1,000 per loan application. In addition, every time the loan is sold to a new investor, the perspective buyer will have to have the same reports prepared and will have to incur the same $1,000 plus in costs. This makes the transaction charges associated with transferring individual mortgages prohibitively high and results in very little liquidity for mortgages.

- Large size. The median size of a new mortgage in the U.S. is more than $100,000. Most investors cannot afford to put $100,000 into a single investment. This makes individual mortgages prohibitively expensive to most individual investors.

- Accounting issues. Most mortgage loans in the U.S. are both fixed rate and fully amortizing. The fact that they are fixed rate means that the interest rate the homeowner pays remains fixed over the life of the mortgage. The fact they are fully amortizing means that each month the homeowner not only pays the interest on the borrowed money, but also repays a part of the principal. When the last of the equally sized mortgage payments is made, the final unpaid balance of the principal is repaid. If the mortgage loan is partially amortizing, then less than 100% of the principal is repaid over the life of the mortgage. The unpaid balance that remains when the loan comes due is referred to as a balloon payment.

This balance needs to be repaid or refinanced when the loan comes due.

Fixed rate mortgage loans are normally structured so that the overall payment stays the same from month to month. Since each month the outstanding principal declines, the amount of interest that must be paid also declines. In order to keep the overall monthly payments flat, the amount of principal that is repaid each month increases. The portion of principal and interest in each of the 360 $1,467.53 monthly payments of an 8% 30-year fixed year mortgage is illustrated in Figure 13-3.

- Each month, a mortgage lender receives one check from the borrower that includes both interest and principal. The investor must separate the interest and principal each month for both accounting and tax purposes. Therefore, compared to a normal bond, mortgages require far more detailed and onerous record-keeping.

Figure 13-3
Percentage of Interest and Principal in Each Monthly Payment

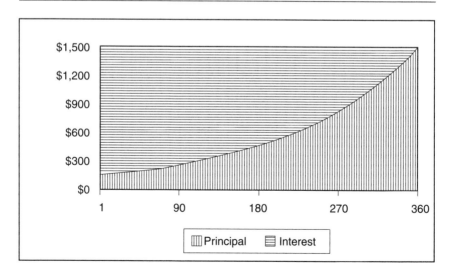

Role of the Mortgage Agencies

Of all of the problems associated with increasing the liquidity of individual mortgages, the most important one is the problem of assessing the credit quality of the mortgage. To overcome this problem, the U.S. Government has facilitated the creation of a number of agencies, quasi-agencies, and public corporations with lines of credit from the government. These agencies and quasi-agencies guarantee the credit quality of mortgages in order to make them easier for mortgage originators to package them and sell them to investors. By making it easier for mortgage originators to sell their mortgages, the government lowers the risk of making mortgage loans, which in turn lowers mortgage rates—thereby making it easier for citizens to buy homes.

The three government-sponsored guarantors of mortgages are the Government National Mortgage Association (GNMA or "Ginnie Mae"), the Federal National Mortgage Association (FNMA or "Fannie Mae"), and the Federal Home Loan Mortgage Corporation (FHLMC or "Freddie Mac"). These three entities are collectively referred to as "the agencies," although they are not technically agencies of the U.S. Government.

They all either buy mortgage loans from originators in order to package and sell them to investors or provide credit guarantees for mortgage loans so that the loan originators can sell the mortgages to investors themselves. The mortgages that the agencies insure must meet certain criteria concerning the size of the required down payment (expressed as a percentage of the property value), the loan to property value ratio, and the maximum loan size. Mortgages that meet the agency criteria are referred to as "qualifying mortgages."

Creation of a Pool of Mortgages

The creation of a pool of mortgages starts with a mortgage originator who extends mortgage loans to homebuyers. Assuming the mortgage loans meet the agency's criteria, the agency then either buys the mortgages or extends a credit guarantee to the mortgages. The pool of mortgages is then purchased by a securities firm that subsequently resells "undivided interests" in the pool to investors. (See Figure 13-4.) An undivided interest means that an investor who buys a 4% interest in the pool owns 4% of 100% of the mortgages in the pool, not 100% of 4% of the mortgages in the pool—an important distinction.

In the following example, suppose that an originator creates ten $100,000 9.% 30-year fixed rate "qualifying" mortgages. The mortgages are then sold to an agency. The agency extends its credit guarantee to the mortgages for which it receives a fee—usually around 0.50% per

Figure 13-4
Creation of a Pool of Mortgages

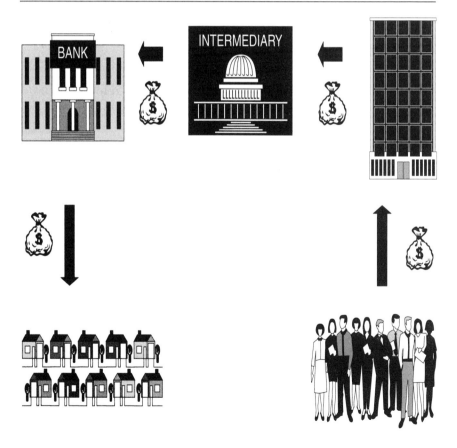

year of the outstanding principal balance. The mortgages are then sold to a securities firm that, in turn, sells interests in the pool—called "participation certificates"—to investors. Suppose that this pool was sold to five investors who purchased the percentage of the pool listed in Figure 13-5. Thus, the capital that is lent to the homebuyers ultimately comes from the five investors and is passed through the two intermediaries: the originator and the agency.

After the loans are extended, the homeowners make their monthly mortgage payments to the lender. The lender collects and records the payments, sends any late notices, executes foreclosure proceedings, and maintains any escrow accounts. Providing these collective services is referred to as "servicing the mortgages" and for providing these services, the lender (or other agent if the servicing is handled by a third party) is paid a fee usually .50% of the outstanding principal.

The lender then passes the mortgage payments, minus its servicing fees, on to the agency. The agency takes out its fee for providing its credit guarantee, and then distributes the payments to the investors on a prorated basis, based on the investor's initial investment. Therefore, Investor A receives 50% of the interest and principal the agency can pay out while Investor E receives 2.50% of the interest and principal the agency can pay out.

The homeowners pay off a portion of their loans each month as part of their mortgage payments. Therefore, each month, the investors

Figure 13-5
Percentage Ownership

Investor	Percentage	Investment
A	50%	$500,000
B	25%	$250,000
C	15%	$150,000
D	7.50%	$75,000
E	2.50%	$25,000

receive back a portion of their principal. If any of the homeowners whose mortgages are in the pool pay off their loans early, the principal that is paid off is again distributed on a prorate basis to the investors.

This structure allows investors to invest in mortgages without having to devote any time or incur any of the expenses associated with originating and servicing mortgage loans. It also allows them to eliminate the credit risk from their mortgage investments.

The cost of eliminating these problems is the approximately 1% paid to the lender and agency. Thus, in the previous example, while the homeowners were paying 9% interest on their mortgages, the investors received only 8%. Many investors believe that the 1% paid to the intermediaries for the services they provide is money well-spent.

Analyzing Pools

Because agency pools are insured, there is little need for investors to perform any credit analysis on potential investments. Instead, most of the analysis involving mortgage pools revolves around trying to predict the speed at which the pools will "prepay." The vast majority of 30-year mortgages do not remain outstanding for 30 years. People move, die, refinance, get divorced, and so on, and when these events occur their homes are often sold and their mortgages are paid off ahead of schedule. Pools in which the mortgages are paid off quickly, relative to the average pool, are referred to as "fast pools" and those that return principal slowly are referred to as "slow pools."

The most important objective for investors who buy agency mortgage pools is to find pools with the appropriate prepayment speed given their outlook for interest rates. Investors seek out pools that will prepay quickly when interest rates are expected to rise and pools that will prepay slowly when interest rates are expected to decline. Investors want to invest in slow pools when they expect interest rates to decline. Slow pools are preferred, since the principal that is received would only have to be reinvested at a lower rate. Likewise, investors want fast pools when they expect interest rates to rise, so that they can reinvest it at a higher rate.

Several factors influence the speed at which pools of mortgages prepay principal:

- Level of interest rates. As interest rates decline, homeowners with fixed rate mortgages often refinance their existing mortgages. Refinancing means the homeowners take out new mortgages and use the money to pay off their older, higher-rate, mortgages. Generally, interest rates have to drop by 1.50%-2% before homeowners save enough money to offset the expense and hassle of refinancing.

- Size of the mortgages. All other factors being equal, larger mortgages generally prepay faster than smaller mortgages. There are two reasons for this. First, larger mortgages are taken out by a wealthier and more mobile segment of the population. Executives frequently change jobs and move from city to city to take new assignments.

- Whether the mortgage is assumable. An "assumable" mortgage can be transferred from one borrower to another, provided the new borrower meets the lender's underwriting criteria. An assumable mortgage is valuable when interest rates rise, because homeowners who want to sell their homes can offer prospective buyers the option of assuming the existing low-rate mortgages, instead of having to take out new higher-rate ones. Mortgages that are not assumable have a "due on sale clause." This clause requires that the mortgages be paid off whenever the property is sold. During periods when interest rates are high, the prepayment speed of pools of assumable mortgages will be lower than pools of nonassumable mortgages.

- Regional economic strength. The prepayment rate of mortgages from a given region of the country is dependent upon the level of the economic activity in that region. If the level of economic activity is either very high or very low, the prepayment speed of the mortgages from the region will increase. If the regional economy is very strong, a high percentage of homeowners will be able to trade up to larger homes, while if the economy is very slow, there will be a high number of defaults and foreclosures. Defaults increase the prepayment speed of the pool, because the mortgages are insured and the insurance pays them off.

Quoting Prepayment Speed

In order to compare the prepayment speed of various mortgage pools and in order to measure the change in prepayment speed over time, there needs to be a way to quantify the rate at which mortgages prepay. The standard way to measure the prepayment speed of a pool of mortgages is to compare the speed with a theoretical mortgage pool. This theoretical pool initially prepays at 0%, has its prepayment speed increase by .2% per year for the first 30 months until it reaches 6% per year, and then continues to prepay at this rate for the remaining life of the mortgages. This benchmark mortgage pool is referred to as a 100% PSA pool. (See Figure 13-6.) It is named for the Public Securities Association study that defined it.

Figure 13-6
100% PSA pool

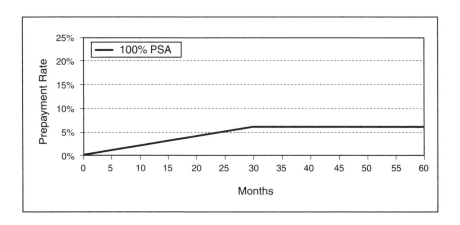

The speed of other pools is expressed relative to this benchmark pool. For example, a pool that was 90 months old that was prepaying at a 12% rate would have a prepayment speed of 200% PSA. A pool that was 12 months old and was prepaying at a rate of 7.20% would be prepaying at a 300% PSA rate. (See Figure 13-7.)

Whole Loan Pools

In addition to the agency pools described, there is another type of mortgage pool called a "whole loan pool." The credit quality of these pools is not guaranteed by an agency. Instead, the buyers of these pools either assume the credit risk associated with the underlying mortgages or arrange for a private credit guarantee from an insurance company or bank.

Collateralized Mortgage Obligations

In addition to mortgage pools, there is another type of mortgage-backed security, referred to either as a "REMIC" (Real Estate Mortgage Invest-

Figure 13-7
Various PSA Speeds

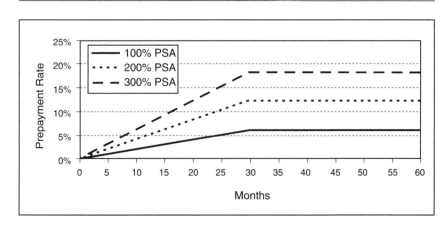

ment Conduit) or a "CMO" (Collateralized Mortgage Obligation). CMOs are bonds that are collateralized by a pool of mortgages. CMOs come in many varieties, including "sequentials," "planned amortization certificates," "floaters," and "strips."

A CMO always starts with a pool of mortgages. The pool of mortgages is purchased and held by a Special Purpose Corporation (SPC) that is, in turn, owned by a financial services firm. The only purpose for this corporation is to hold the pool of mortgages as collateral and to issue the CMOs. For illustrative purposes, let's assume that the collateral is a $1 million pool of 8% fully insured mortgages that is expected to have a prepayment speed of 200% PSA. A $1 million pool of 8% mortgages with an expected PSA speed of 200% will generate the cash flows shown in Figure 13-8.

The cash flows that the SPC receives from the pool of mortgages can be modified into other series of cash flows that are more appealing to investors. The process of converting one series into another series of cash flows is referred to as "financial engineering."

Figure 13-8
Interest and Principal from Pool

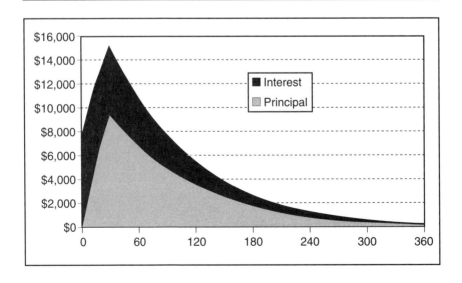

Sequentials

One type of financial engineering that can be performed on the cash flows from the pool of mortgages is to make them more closely resemble traditional bonds. Some investors are uncomfortable with the complicated pattern of cash flows that mortgage pools generate and prefer a more traditional structure in which interest is paid periodically and the entire principal is returned at the same time.

Suppose the SPC issues $1 million face value of 7.80% bonds that are secured by the collateral in the SPC. The interest from the mortgage pool can be used by the SPC to pay the interest on the bonds. As the homeowners pay down their mortgages, the returned principal from the normal pay down of mortgages as well as any prepayments can be used to call the bonds. If no call order is specified, the bonds will simply be called on a random basis. Normally, the SPC will call one of the bonds as soon as it accumulates $1,000 of principal from the homeowners paying the mortgages.

In this structure, the investors are willing to accept a return that is .20% lower than the yield on the mortgages in exchange for the simpler structure. This leaves a gross margin of .20% for the SPC to compensate it for structuring and administering the deal.

The big problem with this structure is that, since the call is random, any bond in the issue can either be the first one called or the last one called. Thus, investors have little control over the maturity of their investments. In order to provide investors with more control over the maturity of their investments, the deal can be restructured so that instead of issuing one class of bonds, several classes of bonds can be issued.

The difference between the various classes—typically referred to as tranches (from the French word for "slice")—is that they have different priorities regarding the order in which they are called. For example, the deal can be redesigned so that the securities firm issues five evenly sized tranches of bonds labeled Tranche-A through Tranche-E. (See Figure 13-9.)

Under this structure, as the homeowners pay down and prepay their mortgages, the principal collected by the SPC is first used to call

Figure 13-9
Tranches

Tranche	Size
A	$200,000
B	$200,000
C	$200,000
D	$200,000
E	$200,000

the bonds in Tranche-A. After $200,000 of principal has been received by the SPC, and all of the bonds in Tranche-A have been called, the principal will then be used to call the bonds in Tranche-B. After all of the bonds in Tranche-B have been called, the SPC will start to call the bonds in Tranche-C, and so on. The last 200,000 of principal received is used to call the bonds in Tranche-E.

By dividing the bonds into different tranches based on the sequence in which they are called—hence the name "sequentials"—the issuer provides investors with greater control over the expected maturity of their investment. Within each tranche, however, the bonds are still called on a random basis, so the maturity can only be estimated if interest rates and prepayment speed remain constant.

Given an expected prepayment speed, the average life of each tranche can be estimated as Figure 13-10 illustrates.

Figure 13-10
Average Life of Tranches

Tranche	Size	Maturity
A	$200,000	22 Months
B	$200,000	45 Months
C	$200,000	74 Months
D	$200,000	117 Months
E	$200,000	202 Months

Figure 13-11
Spread Curve

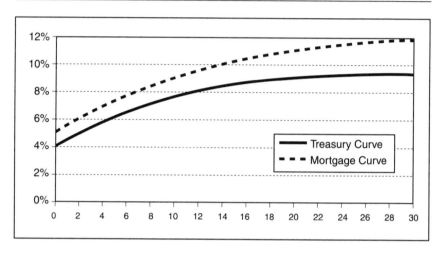

Once the average life of each tranche has been estimated, the appropriate coupon can also be assigned by pricing the bonds to a spread over the appropriate Treasury Security. Assuming the yield curve has its normal positive slope, tranches with longer expected lives will offer higher yields than tranches with shorter expected lives.

Naturally, as the speed of the underlying pool changes, so will the rate at which principal is returned, and thus, the expected lives of the sequential tranches.

In order to increase the marketability of sequent deals, SPCs will adjust the expected lives of the various tranches by changing both their

Figure 13-12
Maturity of Coupon Trade-off

Tranche	Size	Maturity	Coupon
A	$200,000	22 Months	6.25%
B	$200,000	45 Months	6.55%
C	$200,000	74 Months	7.35%
D	$200,000	117 Months	7.75%
E	$200,000	202 Months	8%

Figure 13-13
Various Maturity of Tranches

Tranche	Size	Expected Maturity @ 100% PSA	Expected Maturity @ 200% PSA	Expected Maturity @ 300% PSA
A	$200,000	31 Months	22 Months	18 Months
B	$200,000	72 Months	45 Months	35 Months
C	$200,000	124 Months	74 Months	54 Months
D	$200,000	193 Months	117 Months	83 Months
E	$200,000	291 Months	202 Months	144 Months

respective sizes and by selecting mortgages with different expected prepayment speeds as collateral.

While this sequential structure certainly provides investors with some control over the maturity of their investments, for many investors, the remaining uncertainty regarding the maturity of the bonds makes them unsuitable. For investors who require a greater degree of certainty regarding the maturity of their investments, another CMO structure called a planned amortization certificate (PAC) is more appropriate.

PACs and Companions

A planned amortization certificate is designed to have the same life regardless of whether the prepayment rate of the underlying mortgage collateral rises or falls—within certain limits. Consider first what happens to the amount of principal returned by the mortgage pool in this example if the prepayment speed rises to 300% PSA and falls to 100% PSA. (See Figure 13-14.)

Note that in Figure 13-14 the area that is under all three curves represents principal that will be received regardless of whether the prepayment speed of the underlying pool increases or decreases. If this principal was dedicated to paying off a specific set of bonds, the life of those bonds would remain unchanged, provided that the speed of the pool remained

Figure 13-14
Affect of Speed on Principal Repayment Schedule

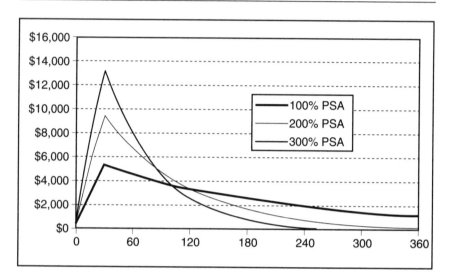

between 100% and 300% PSA. These bonds, whose life is predetermined provided that the prepayment speed stays within certain bands are referred to as planned amortization certificates or PACs for the simple reason that their life is planned. In this deal, approximately 50% of the principal that is received over the life of the deal is used to call in the PAC bonds.

The principal that is not set aside to call the PACs is used to call the other class of bonds in the deal. These bonds, referred to as "companion bonds," have a very uncertain life. In fact, it is their uncertainty that allows the life of the PACs to be certain. The principal that is received from the pool of mortgages that is not needed to redeem the PACs on schedule is used to call in the companions.

- If interest rates decline and the mortgage pool prepays faster than expected, the life of the companions will be very short.

- If interest rates rise and the mortgage pool prepays slower than expected, then the life of the companions will be very long.

Figures 13-15, 13-16, and 13-17 illustrate the principal that is used to pay the companions, as well as the average life of the companions.

Figure 13-15
100% PSA Speed

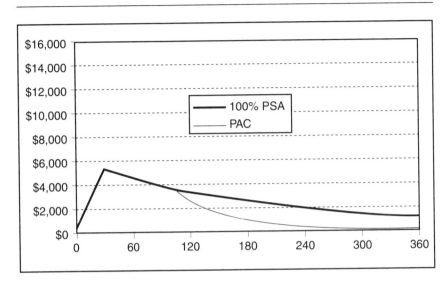

The life of the companions changes the opposite way that investors want it to change. When interest rates decline, investors do not want the life of their investments to get shorter, because they have

Figure 13-16
200% PSA Speed

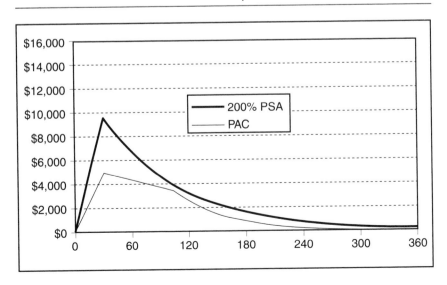

Figure 13-17
300% PSA Speed

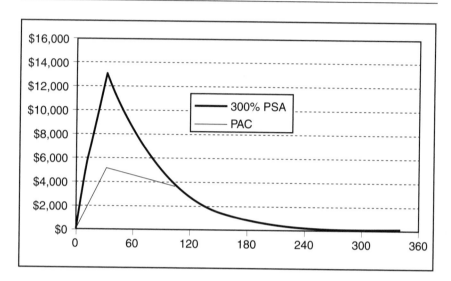

to reinvest at a lower rate. Likewise, when interest rates rise, investors do not want the life of their investments to be longer, because they would rather receive their money and reinvest it at a higher rate. In order for companion bonds to be attractive to investors, they have to offer a higher yield than the PACs.

Floaters and Inverse Floaters

Any pool, sequential, PAC, or companion bond can be subdivided into a floater and inverse floater. Consider what happens if a $200,000 7% sequential tranche is divided into a floater and an inverse floater.

Suppose the index for the floater and inverse floater is the 6-month T-bill rate and that the T-bill rate is currently 5%. Given this information, a floater and inverse floater could be designed as shown in Figure 13-18.

- The floater could have a coupon equal to T-bills + 2%.

- The inverse floater could have a coupon equal to 14% − (T-bills + 2%).

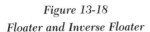

Figure 13-18
Floater and Inverse Floater

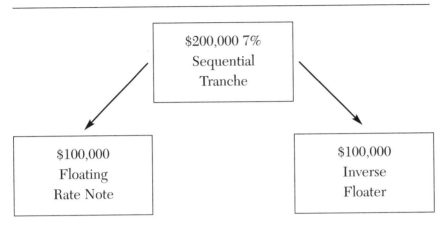

Given these formulas, both the floater and inverse floater would initially yield 7%. As the T-bill rate rose, the return of the floater would rise and the return of the inverse floater would decline. The opposite would happen if interest rates declined. In every case, the average interest expense remains 7%. (See Figure 13-19.)

Strip Securities

Mortgage pools can also be reengineered into principal only (PO) and interest only (IO) strips. If a pool is divided into strips, then the

Figure 13-19
Floater vs. Inverse Floater

T-bills	Floater	Inverse	Average
3%	5%	9%	7%
4%	6%	8%	7%
5%	7%	7%	7%
6%	8%	6%	7%
7%	9%	5%	7%

investor(s) who buys the PO receives all, or almost all, of the principal generated by the pool. The investor(s) who buys the IOs receives all, or almost all, of the interest generated by the pool. Suppose the example mortgage pool was divided into one PO and one IO and that the PO was sold for $600,000 and the IO was sold for $400,000. (See Figure 13-20.)

The owner of the PO receives all of the principal generated by the mortgage pool. Since the pool is insured, the owner of the PO will receive $1,000,000. Thus, the investor who buys the PO is guaranteed that the $600,000 invested will return $1,000,000. What the PO owner doesn't know is how long it will take to receive the $1,000,000. Naturally, the faster the PO owner receives the money, the higher the annualized return from the PO. A decline in interest rates will increase the prepayment speed, decrease the average time until the principal is received, and increase the annualized return.

The owner of the IO will receive all of the interest that is received from the mortgage pool. Initially, this results in a very high return for the IO holder. The investor receives 8% interest on $1,000,000 of principal—despite investing only $400,000. Thus, initially the IO will generate $80,000 of interest on a $400,000 investment. This equals approximately a 20% annualized return. In the case of an IO, however, the return

Figure 13-20
Dividing Pool into Floater and Inverse Floater

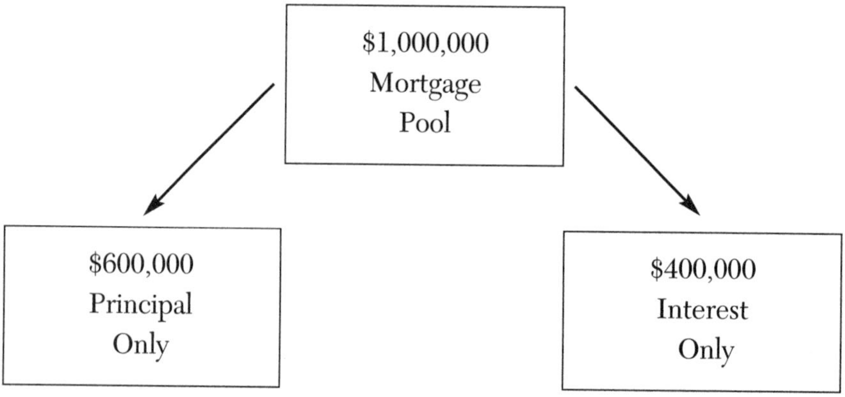

immediately starts to decline. Each month, the amount of interest the IO owner receives declines, because the amount of outstanding principal on which the homeowners pay interest declines. The big question for the IO owner is, "How long will the interest payments last?"

Investors who buy IOs want interest rates to rise slightly so that the prepayment speed of the mortgages in the pool slows down. As the prepayment speed declines, the size of the future interest payments also increases.

New Developments

The CMOs discussed in this chapter represent only a partial list of the various types of structures that can be created out of a pool of mortgages. There are also hybrids, such as sequential PACs, partial strips, floating rate companions, and so on. In addition, pools of other types of loans, including car loans, credit card debt, boat loans, and so on, can also serve as collateral for both pools and structured deals. When a transaction is backed by a type of loan other than mortgages, the transaction is referred to as an "Asset-Backed Security" (ABS).

FORWARD CONTRACTS

$\mathbf{A}$ forward contract is a private contract between a buyer and a seller in which the buyer agrees to buy and the seller agrees to sell a certain quantity of a certain security or commodity (referred to as the underlying instrument) at the price specified in the contract. The difference between a forward contract and most other sales contracts is that in the case of a forward contract, the delivery of and payment for the underlying instrument occurs at some specified date in the future, instead of immediately. Consider the following examples.

Before a corn farmer even plants his crop, he and a cereal company might sign a contract that would require the farmer to sell and the cereal company to buy 50,000 bushels of the farmer's crop at a price of $1 per bushel. The actual exchange of corn and money will not take place until after the crop is harvested in the fall. By entering into this forward contract, both parties reduce their respective risks. By pre-selling his crop at a $1 per bushel, the farmer protects himself against the risk that in the fall, the spot price will be lower than $1 per bushel. By pre-purchasing the corn at $1 per bushel, the cereal company protects itself against the risk that in the fall, the spot price will be higher than $1 per bushel.

Thus, both parties to the transaction are willing to sacrifice the possibility of getting a "better price" in exchange for eliminating the possibility that they will get a "worse price."

During the harvest, the spot price of corn will either be higher or lower than $1—depending upon the relative supply and demand for corn. If, in the fall, the spot price is $1.35 a bushel, the farmer will undoubtedly wish he hadn't entered into the forward contract. On the other hand, the cereal company will be ecstatic that it will be paying only $1 for corn that otherwise would cost $1.35. However, if the spot price in the fall is $0.80 per bushel, the farmer will be ecstatic, while the cereal company will wish it hadn't signed the forward delivery contract.°

In this forward contract, like all forward contracts, the buyer is happy if the contract price is below the spot price and the seller is happy if the contract price is above the spot price.

Terms of a Forward Contract

The primary goal when entering into a forward contract is to ensure that all of the terms and contingencies are clear so that there is no ambiguity. Some of the parameters that would need to be defined in the forward contract include:

- Delivery terms and location—In the above example, where is the corn to be delivered—the farmer's location, the cereal company's plant, or some location in between? Can the corn be delivered by the truckload or in railroad cars, or does it have to be in bushel baskets? Does the corn have to be delivered on a specific date or within a certain range of dates? Which of the parties pays for shipping?

- Quality specifications—In the example, does the corn have to be within a certain color range? Does it have to have a certain sugar or starch content? Do the ears need to be a certain minimum

°Trading futures and options on futures is not appropriate for all persons as the risk of loss is substantial. Therefore, only risk or hedge capital should be used in futures trading.

weight or size? Because this is a private contract, any terms that are agreeable to both parties can be included in the contract. It is the ability of these contracts to be customized to meet the specific needs of the parties that makes them so attractive for solving business problems.

- Payment and credit terms—Because a forward contract is a private contract between two parties, both parties are exposed to credit risk. Either party could fail to honor its commitment, leaving the other party with a problem. What if the price of corn drops to $.50 a bushel and the cereal company doesn't show up to buy? What if corn rises to $3 per bushel and the farmer sells his corn to another party before the cereal company can pick it up?

   Both parties need to protect themselves. Is the corn to be paid for upon delivery, prior to delivery, or within a certain number of days after delivery? Is payment by certified check, bank wire, credit card, purchase order, or invoice? Does either party have to post any credit enhances such as guarantees, letters of credit, or collateral to insure performance? The answers will depend upon the credit quality of the respective parties.

- Dispute resolution procedure—Under what country's law or state's law is the contract to be enforced? If either party believes that the contract is breached, what is the dispute resolution procedure—mandatory arbitration or lawsuit? Who pays the costs?

- Cancellation provisions—Does the contract include any cancellation provisions? The vast majority of contracts do not.

- Liquidity—Because these contracts include no cancellation provision, how can market participants change their market exposures after they have entered into forward contracts. The most common way is to enter into a second contract with an offsetting exposure. If a market participant has a contract in which the participant is obligated to buy 5,000 bushels of corn, that exposure can be mitigated by entering into a second contract to sell 5,000 bushels of corn. The price difference between the two contracts would determine the gain or loss on the position.

- Price transparency—Price transparency is the dissemination of timely and accurate price information to interested parties. Some forward markets, such as FX, interest rate, and precious metals, have very good price dissemination and, therefore, both parties know what a "fair" price is before they enter the contract. In other markets, such as unusual agricultural products (kiwifruit), there is little or no price transparency. In markets without price transparency, the party with more market knowledge will usually be in a position to cut a better deal. As with every market, the dealers who make a market for forward contracts impose a spread between their bid and ask prices.

Now that forward contracts have been defined, let's examine how they are priced.

Pricing Forward Contracts

In order to discuss the pricing of forward contracts, let's consider a forward contract for 10,000 ounces of gold to be delivered in one year. The question becomes, "What is the fair price to agree to today for gold that is to be delivered and paid for in one year?"

Suppose that gold is selling for $250 per ounce today. The price today is referred to as the "spot price." As of today, no one can know what the price of gold will be in a year. It could be selling for $1,000 if a major war should break out or $100 if a major new source of gold is discovered. The price of gold fluctuates based upon thousands of variables. Clearly basing the forward price on some sort of "price forecast" is not practical.

Instead, the price of gold for forward delivery is equal to the cost of buying gold today and storing it until the delivery date. For example, if a jewelry manufacturer wants to lock in the price that its gold will cost in a year, the company can simply buy gold today at the spot price and incur the expenses associated with storing the gold for a year. In one year's time, the company's cost of the gold will equal the spot price plus the cost of carrying the gold in inventory—usually abbreviated as the "cost of carry" or simply "carry."

The various costs associated with buying and storing gold include:

- Transaction charges—These would include any dealer commissions, mark-ups, spreads, administrative charges, and assay fees.

- Transportation charges—The cost of transporting the metal from the dealer's vault to the company's storage facility (or rented storage facility) and then to the company's manufacturing facility in a year's time.

- Vault space and insurance—The cost associated with renting a secure space to store the gold and the cost of insuring it against theft.

- The cost of money—In order to have the $2,500,000 necessary to purchase the 10,000 ounces today, the jewelry manufacturer must either borrow the money and incur interest expense or remove money from an interest-bearing investment and incur an opportunity cost. Either way, there is a cost of money that is the largest component of the cost of storage.

- Rental income—While the gold is being stored, it can be "lent" to a third party who wants to sell gold short and needs to borrow gold in order to make delivery. Lending gold to a short seller generates a rental income for the lender that reduces the cost of storage. The drawback of lending gold, like any other loan, is the credit risk.

Suppose, in the previous example, the "all in" cost of storage was $35 per ounce per year. The jewelry manufacturer could lock in the price of 1-year gold at $285.

$$\text{Spot} + \text{Storage} = \text{Price in 1 year}$$
$$\$250 + \$35 = \$285$$

Note that nowhere in this calculation did the jewelry company's expectations regarding the price of gold affect the forward price. The forward price in this example is $285, regardless of whether the jewelry manager believes that the price of gold will rise or fall over the next year.

For some underlying instruments, like gold, silver, and so on, calculating the cost of carry is fairly straightforward and exact. For others, like agricultural commodities, determining the cost of carry is very difficult and inexact. This is because the amount of "spoilage" in storage, the timing and size of new crops, and the impact of trade barriers on agricultural prices will all affect the cost of carry and are all hard to estimate.

Advantages of Forward Contracts

Since the jewelry manufacturer can lock in a forward price of $285 by buying and storing the gold, the next question becomes, "What's the advantage for the jewelry company of entering into a forward contract with a dealer, instead of simply buying and storing the gold itself?"

There are several possible reasons:

1. The company may not want to tie up its capital for a year in gold. By entering into a forward contract, the company doesn't have to spend (or borrow) $2,500,000 today.

2. The dealer may be able to offer the jewelry manufacturer a price that is lower than $285 and still make a profit if its cost of carry is substantially lower than the jewelry company's. The dealer may have a substantially lower cost of carry because it can either borrow money or metal at a lower rate, and/or may have more cost-effective transport and storage, and/or may be self-insuring. Suppose a dealer's cost of carry for gold is $25. In this case, the dealer could buy gold today for $250, agree to sell it in one year to the jewelry company for $280, and still make a profit of $5 per ounce. Because the dealer's cost of carry is $10 lower than the client's cost of carry, the client can save $5, and the dealer can still make $5.

Spot + Storage = Price in 1 year + Mark-up = Price to Client
$250 + $25 = $275 + $5 = $280

Interest Rate Forwards

In addition to buying and selling commodities for forward delivery, money can also be lent or borrowed forward. When one party agrees to lend and another party agrees to borrow money in a loan transaction that won't start until some time in the future, the transaction is referred to as an interest rate forward. Consider the following example.

Suppose on January 3, 2000, a business owner walks into her bank and makes two requests of her loan officer. Specifically, she would like:

1. To borrow $1,000,000 for 1 year with the loan to start on August 15, 2000 and to mature on August 15, 2001.

2. The bank to tell her today what rate it will charge on the loan when it begins.

The question becomes, "How can the client and the bank agree on the interest rate to charge for the loan that won't start for months?" Neither the bank nor the business owner can know on January 3, 2000, what 1-year interest rates will be in August. Fortunately, there is no need to be able to successfully forecast rates in order to price an interest rate forward. Instead, like other forwards, interest rate forwards are priced at whatever rate will eliminate the possibility of arbitrage.

The rate that eliminates the possibility of arbitrage is the rate that allows the same present value to grow to be the same future value over the same time frame. Consider Figure 14-1.

Figure 14-1
Relationship between Spot and Forward Rates

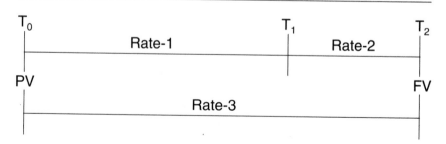

Both Rate-1 and Rate-3 are spot rates—rates on loans/investments that start today and run until some point in the future. Rate-2 is a forward rate in that it starts and ends at some time forward. If Rate-2 is set correctly, it should make no difference if an investor chooses to invest:

- At Rate-1 from T_0 until T_1 and then roll over the investment at Rate-2 from T_1 to T_2.
- At Rate-3 from T_0 until T_2.

The future value that will be accumulated will be the same. Banks use the same arbitrage relationship to price forward loans. Consider the example above. The first step is for a bank to determine how much money it will have to set aside *today* in order to have the money necessary to make the forward loan when the business owner comes to claim her loan on August 15, 2000. The bank has to decide how much money to store in inventory in order to fund the forward loan.

Fortunately, while a bank is storing the money it will need to fund the loan, it can invest the money to earn interest. Thus, if the bank needs $1,000,000 on August 15, 2000, today the bank just needs to set aside the present value of $1,000,000. The present value that must be set aside today is determined by the rate the bank can earn on the money while it is being stored. (See Figure 14-2.)

Figure 14-2
Calculating the Present Value

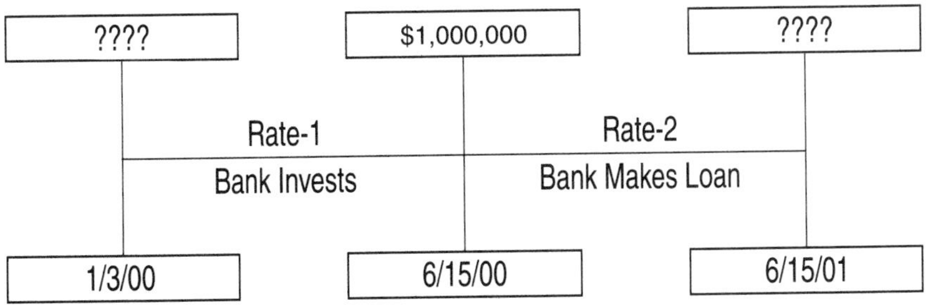

Figure 14-3
Calculating the Bank's Cost

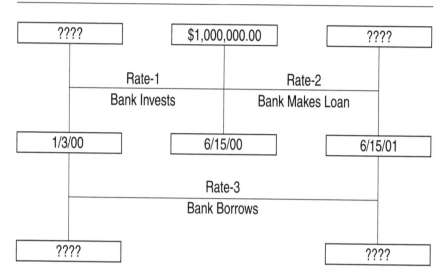

This begs the question, "Where does the bank get the money that it stores until the start of the forward loan and then lends to the client?" The bank obtains the money it needs by borrowing it in the marketplace. The rate at which the bank can borrow will determine how much the bank will have to pay back when its loan matures on August 15, 2001. (See Figure 14-3.)

When the client pays off her loan to the bank, the bank can pay off its loan to the depositors. In order for the bank to "break even" on the transaction, the future value of the client's loan on the day it comes due must equal the future value of the bank's loan. By knowing the present value of the client's loan ($1,000,000) and its future value (the amount required to pay off the bank's loan), the forward loan rate can be determined.

Consider the following numerical example. Suppose the bank:

- Can invest from 1/3/00 to 6/15/00 in an instrument that pays 6%, simple interest on a 30/360 calendar.

- Can borrow from 1/3/00 to 6/15/01 at a rate of 9% cc on an A/360 calendar.

- Wants to quote the client's break-even loan rate on a monthly rate expressed annually on a 30/360 calendar.

The first step is to determine how much money the bank will need to store in order to accumulate the $1,000,000 it needs to make the loan. Discounting $1,000,000 from 6/15/00 to 1/3/00 at a 6% simple interest rate on a 30/360 calendar results in a PV of:

$$PV = FV / [1 + (R \times T)]$$
$$PV = 1,000,000 / [1 + (.06 \times 162/360)]$$
$$PV = \$973,709.83$$

Once the bank determines that it needs to set aside $973,709.83 on 1/3/00 in order to have the $1,000,000 it needs on 8/15/00, the bank knows that it needs to borrow $973,709.83. (See Figure 14-4.) It borrows this money until 8/15/01, paying a 9% continuously compounded rate on an actual 360 calendar. Thus the amount the bank would have to repay is:

$$FV = PVe^{rt}$$
$$FV = \$973,709.83e^{(.09)(529/360)}$$
$$FV = \$1,111,386.20$$

Figure 14-4
Calculating the Forward Rate

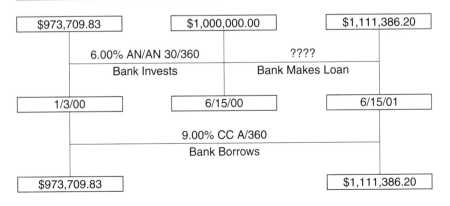

Finally, the bank knows that it will have to come up with $1,111,386.20 on 8/15/01 to pay off its loan. The money to pay off the bank's loan comes from the client. The question then becomes, "What rate, quoted M/AN 30/360, will the bank have to charge the client on a 1-year $1,000,000 loan to accumulate $1,111,386.20?"

$$FV = PV(1 + r)^n$$
$$\$1,111,386.20 = \$1,000,000 \, (1 + r)^{12}$$
$$1.11138620 = (1 + r)^{12}$$
$$1.00883951 = (1 + r)$$
$$r = 10.61\% \text{ M/AN 30/360}$$

If the bank and the client enter into a forward loan agreement today, the break-even rate for the bank is 10.61%. Naturally, to this rate the bank would have to add whatever spread it needed to cover its overhead and generate its desired profit margin. If the bank needed to make .50% on this transaction, the loan rate the bank would quote the client would be 11.11%.

If the rate is acceptable to the client, the bank and client will sign a contract and both parties will be obligated to perform. The bank will be obligated to make the loan and the client will be obligated to accept the loan.

If the client signs the contract, the client is protected against the risk that on August 15, 2000 the rate on one-year loans will be higher than 11.11%. If the one-year loan rate on August 15 is higher than 11.11%, the client will be very happy to have signed the forward contract. If, on August 15, 2000, the one-year loan rate is less than 11.11%, the client will be unhappy about having the forward.

Foreign Exchange Forwards

Another type of forward transaction is a foreign exchange (FX) or currency forward. In an FX forward, two parties agree to exchange a set amount of one currency for a set amount of another currency at some point in the future. Like all forward contracts, the forward price or "exchange rate" is set at a price that eliminates the possibility of arbitrage. In the case of currency forwards, eliminating arbitrage means that the return from investing currency A should not be higher or lower than the net return that can be obtained from:

- Converting currency A into currency B.
- Entering into a forward contract to reconvert currency B into A at a forward date.
- Investing the currency B until the forward date.

For example, suppose that on February 3, 2000, the spot FX rate between the US Dollar ($) and the Pound Sterling (£) is "1.4125." This means that £1.0000 buys $1.4125 or conversely that $1.0000 buys £0.7080 (1.0000 / 1.4125). Suppose further, that the six-month risk-free rate in the U.S. is 4% simple interest expressed on a 30/360 calendar and that the six-month risk-free rate in the U.K. is 6% cc on an A/360 calendar.

An investor with $1,000,000 can either invest the $1,000,000 for six months at 4% or:

- Convert the dollars into pounds.
- Enter into a forward agreement to reconvert the pounds into dollars in six months.
- Invest the pounds at 6% for six months.

If the forward exchange rate is set correctly, both investment alternatives result in the same net return to the investor.

To determine the correct forward FX rate:

- Start with the current spot rate.
- Invest the equivalent amount of both currencies at the prevailing rate in each country until the same forward date in order to determine how much of each currency can be accumulated on the forward date.

- Divide the resulting amounts of currencies by each other in order to determine the implied forward exchange rate.

In the previous example:

- $1,000,000 invested at 4% AN/AN 30/360 for 6 months:

$$FV = PV + (P \times R \times T)$$
$$FV = (\$1 \text{ million}) + (\$1 \text{ million} \times .04 \times 180/360)$$
$$FV = \$1,020,000$$

- $1,000,000 converted in pounds at the spot rate results in:

$$\$1,000,000 / 1.4125 = £707,964.60$$

- £707,964.60 invested at 6% cc A/360 for 6 months:

$$FV = PVe^{rt}$$
$$FV = £707,964.60e^{(.06)(182/360)}$$
$$FV = £729,768.55$$

- The forward exchange rate is then:

$$\$1,020,000 / £729,768.55 = (\$/£ = 1.3977)$$
$$\text{or}$$
$$£729,768.55 / \$1,020,000 = (£/\$ = .7155)$$

Expressed in chart format, the complete relationship between spot and forward FX rates is shown in Figure 14-5.

Figure 14-5
Determining Forward FX Rates

2/3/00		8/3/00
$1,000,000	4.00% AN/AN 30/360	$1,020,000
$/£ = 1.4125 £/$ = 0.7080		$/£ = 1.3977 £/$ = 0.7155
£707,964.60	6.00% cc A/360	£729,768.55

Given this forward rate, anyone who had a need to lock in a forward £/$ or $/£ exchange rate today would have to do it at this rate. If the forward rate was any rate other than the one just calculated, and/or if the dollar was either too weak or too strong in the forward market, arbitrageurs could make a risk-free profit.

Suppose, for example, that the pound was too strong in the forward market. Specifically, assume that the spot rate and the forward rate were exactly the same at $/£ = 1.4125. Since interest rates are higher in the U.K., an arbitrageur could:

- Borrow dollars in the U.S. at 4%.
- Convert the dollars into pounds at a rate of $/£ = 1.4125.
- Simultaneously enter into an agreement to re-exchange the pounds into dollars at the same rate in 6 months.
- Invest the pounds at 6% for 6 months.
- Use the forward agreement to reconvert the pounds into dollars in 6 months.
- Pay off the dollar loan plus the 4% dollar interest.
- Keep a profit of approximately 2%—the difference between the 6% interest earned and the 4% interest spent.

If the dollar is too strong in the forward market, arbitrageurs would do the reverse and sell pounds in order to buy and invest in dollars. It is the actions of arbitrageurs that keep the forward markets in equilibrium.

It should be clear that the currency that offers the higher interest rate must weaken in the forward market, since it is the interest rate differential that determines the forward FX rate.

Once again, note that the forward rate is not a forecast of the spot rate. In the previous example, U.K. rates are higher so the pound is weaker in the forward market. All of the fundamentals may suggest that the pound will get stronger. (The factors that cause spot FX rates to change over time are discussed in Chapter 21.)

Summary of Forward Contracts

As detailed in this chapter, the following table summarizes the characteristics of forward contracts.

Overview of Forward Contracts

	FORWARDS
Private vs. Public	Private
Credit	Yes
Customized	Yes
Marked to Market	No
Cash Settlement	No
Liquidity	No
Price Transparency	No
Choice	No

FUTURES CONTRACTS

A futures contract is a publicly traded forward contract. Like a forward contract, each contract is for the purchase or sale of a loan, currency, or commodity with delivery to occur at some time in the future. While the concept behind both forwards and futures contracts is the same—namely, providing a way for buyers and sellers to lock in the price today for transactions that will occur in the future—the way in which they implement the concept is almost exactly opposite.

While forward contracts are private contracts executed directly between two parties who know each other, futures contracts trade on the floor of a futures exchange. Futures are traded on the floor of an exchange, so the transactions are always handled by brokers who are members of the exchange, not by the parties themselves. Because the transactions are handled by brokers, the actual counter party to any particular contract is always anonymous. Thus, when someone buys gold via a futures contract, the party does not know from whom the gold is being purchased.

The only reason people are willing to buy and sell futures contracts with anonymous counter parties is that the exchange guarantees all trades. So, unlike forwards, where each party is exposed to the credit risk of its counter party, in the case of futures, the exchange assumes the credit risk if a counter party defaults on its obligations. The exchanges are, in turn, backed by lines of credit, insurance policies, and the financial backing of their members, making them free of credit risk for all practical purposes.

The exchanges dramatically reduce the amount of credit risk to which they are exposed by:

- Requiring customers who buy or sell futures contracts to post a security deposit, referred to as "margin," against their position.
- Requiring customers to cover their losses on a daily basis—commonly referred to as being "marked to the market."
- Having delivery of the underlying instrument at expiration occur at the then-current spot price.

Figure 15-1
List of Actively Traded Futures Contracts

Underlying Instrument	Contract Size	Exchange Traded
Cotton	50,000 lbs.	NYBT
U.S. T-bills	$1,000,000	CME
Eurodollars	$1,000,000	CME
Fed Funds	$5,000,000	CBOT
2 Yr. Treas	$200,000	CBOT
5 Yr. Treas	$100,000	CBOT
10 Yr. Treas	$100,000	CBOT
30 Yr. Treas	$100,000	CBOT
Cocoa	10 tons	NYBT
Coffee	37,500 lbs.	NYBT
Orange Juice	15,000 lbs.	NYBT
Sugar	112,000 lbs.	NYBT
Heating Oil	42,000 gallons	NYMX
Crude Oil	1,000 barrels	NYMX
Natural Gas	10,000 mm BTUs	NYMX

Figure 15-1 (continued)

Underlying Instrument	Contract Size	Exchange Traded
Unleaded Gas	42,000 gallons	NYMX
Corn	5,000 bushels	CBOT
Oats	5,000 bushels	CBOT
Soybeans	5,000 bushels	CBOT
Wheat	5,000 bushels	CBOT
Cattle	40,000 lbs.	CME
Hogs	40,000 lbs.	CME
Pork Bellies	40,000 lbs.	CME
Lumber	80,000 sq. ft.	CME
Gold	100 troy oz.	COMX
Silver	5,000 troy oz.	COMX
Copper	25,000 lbs.	COMX
British Pound	62,500	CME
Canadian Dollar	100,000	CME
Japanese Yen	12,500,000	CME
Mexican Peso	500,000	CME
Dow Industrials	$10 × Dow Index	CBOT
NASDAQ 100	$100 × Index	CME
NIKKEI 225	$5 × NSA	CME
U.S. Dollar	1,000 × Index	NYBT
S&P Composite	250 × Index	CME
Value Line	250 × Index	KCBOT
CRB Index	500 × Index	NYBT
RUSSEL 2000	500 × Index	CME

NYBT = New York Board of Trade

CME = Chicago Mercantile Exchange

KCBOT = Kansas City Board of Trade

CBOT = Chicago Board of Trade

NYME = New York Mercantile Exchange

Margin Requirements

When a client wants to open a futures account, the client contacts a firm that is a member of the exchange where the desired futures contract trades. The major securities firms are members of all the major futures exchanges. The firm then generally runs a credit check on prospective clients to make sure they have good credit rating before accepting them as clients.

Assuming the client has an acceptable credit rating, the firm will then ask the client to put up a security deposit, called a "margin," that can be used to cover any losses they may incur. Note that the term "margin" has different meaning in the futures market than it does in the equity market. In the futures market, "margin" means a security deposit, whereas in the equity market, the term "margin" means the client has purchased securities with borrowed money.

Naturally, the greater the number of futures contracts the client wishes to buy or sell, the greater the potential loss, and the larger the required security deposit. The futures exchanges set the minimum margin requirements that clients must meet, called the initial margin. This is usually 10 to 20 percent of the face value of the contract. Most securities firms require that their clients put up more than the minimum percentage required by the exchange, especially new clients. The initial margin requirements are lower for market participants who are hedgers than they are for speculators.

To illustrate how margin works in futures accounts, consider the following example.

On January 18, 2000, a small South African gold mining company is concerned that the price of gold will decline and so decides to pre-sell some of its future production. Simultaneously, a speculator in Denver, who believes that the price of gold will rise sharply, decides to buy gold. Both parties execute their transactions through brokerage firms that are members of the exchange.

The South African Gold Mining Company elects to use Prudential. The company informs Prudential that it wishes to sell 10,000 ounces of gold, and it will have them ready for delivery by late November. The company's broker at Prudential then sends an order on the floor of the future's exchange to sell 100 December gold contracts. By selling these contracts, the broker obligates the mining company to deliver and accept payment for the 10,000 ounces of gold (100 contracts at 100 ounces per contract) to one of the exchange-approved warehouses on or before the date specified in the gold contract in December.

The speculator also calls her broker. Her broker happens to be with Merrill Lynch. The speculator's broker at Merrill Lynch sends an order to the floor of the exchange to buy 100 December gold contracts. This obligates the speculator to pay for and accept delivery of 10,000 ounces of gold in December.

The two floor brokers, each representing their respective clients, then execute the transactions. The gold company posts a margin of $275,000 at Prudential, while the speculator posts a margin of $550,000 at Merrill Lynch.

The first question is, "At what price will the transaction between the buyer and the seller occur?" The answer is at the spot price today, plus the cost of carry until the delivery date—or at the forward/future price.

$$\text{Spot Price} + \text{Cost of Carry} = \text{Future Price}$$
$$\$250 + \$25 = \$275$$

The forward price has to equal the futures price or there would be the possibility of arbitrage. (If it was possible to buy gold for December delivery at $265 an ounce in the forward market, and it was selling for $275 in the futures market, arbitrageurs would buy gold forward and sell it in the futures market—and continue doing so until the prices were equal.) Thus, the starting position for the two counter parties is shown in Figure 15-2.

Figure 15-2
Initial Position

Time	Mining Company Margin Balance	Future Price	Speculator's Margin Balance
START	$275,000	$275	$550,000

As time passes, the future price will change. It will change because the spot price and/or the cost of carry changes.

- The spot price can change for any of a hundred reasons, including changes in central bank gold sales, changes in mine production, actions of speculators.

- The cost of carry will change either as interest rates change or as time passes. The cost of carry rises and falls with interest rates, while the passage of time lowers the cost of carry because it lowers the time that the gold must be stored.

Let's assume that at the end of the first day after the two parties have established their positions that the future price falls from $275 to $273. At this price, the mining company that sold at $275 has a $2 per ounce profit, while the speculator that bought at $275 has a $2 per ounce loss.

Because futures positions are "marked to the market" on a daily basis, the loser must pay the winner each day. In this case, the buyer has to pay the seller $2 per ounce or $20,000. Merrill Lynch would subtract the $20,000 from the speculator's margin account and pay the money to the exchange. The exchange would pass the $20,000 on to Prudential, which would credit the mining company's margin account. Thus, at the end of business the first day, the current position of the counter parties would be as shown in Figure 15-3.

Figure 15-3
Position After One Day

Time	Mining Company Margin Balance	Future Price	Speculator's Margin Balance
START	$275,000	$275	$550,000
Day 1	$295,000	$273	$530,000

If, the next day, an economic number is released that leads people to worry about inflation, the spot price of gold and interest rates might both rise. As a result, the future price rises by $7, making the forward price \$280. Because the forward price rose by \$7, the shorts must pay the longs \$7 per ounce. Thus, at the end of the second day, the current positions of the counter parties would be as shown in Figure 15-4.

Figure 15-4
Position After Two Days

Time	Mining Company Margin Balance	Future Price	Speculator's Margin Balance
START	\$275,000	\$275	\$550,000
Day 1	\$295,000	\$273	\$530,000
Day 2	\$225,000	\$280	\$600,000

Each day, as the futures price continues to fluctuate, each account is marked to the market. If either party loses more than 50 percent of its security deposit, the firm with whom it is doing business will issue a "margin call." A margin call is a demand for the client to deposit additional money into the client's security account.

In this first example, let's assume that both parties hold their positions until the futures contract expires and that, on the expiration date, the spot price of gold is \$260 per ounce. Thus, at the end of the last day, the current positions of the counter parties would be as shown in Figure 15-5.

Figure 15-5
Position After the Last Day

Time	Mining Company Margin Balance	Future Price	Speculator's Margin Balance
START	\$275,000	\$275	\$550,000
Day 1	\$295,000	\$273	\$530,000
Day 2	\$225,000	\$280	\$600,000
...	...	...	...
...	...	...	...
...	...	...	...
LAST	\$425,000	\$260	\$400,000

If the future is about to expire, the spot price and the forward price are equal. The reason they are equal is that, on expiration day, the cost of carry goes to zero. The mining company must deliver the 10,000 ounces of gold. The speculator must buy 10,000 ounces of gold. When the mining company delivers the gold, and the speculator accepts delivery of the gold, the speculator has to pay the mining company. Payment does not occur directly, since both parties are anonymous. Instead, the buyer pays the exchange and the exchange pays the seller.

The price that the buyer pays and the seller receives is $260 per ounce—*even though both parties entered into the futures market at $275 per ounce.* The reason that both delivery and payment occur at the spot price is that each party already has its respective gain and/or loss reflected in its margin account.

- The mining company originally sold its gold forward at $275 per ounce. It receives $260 from the actual sale and has a profit of $15 per ounce in its margin account for a net of $275.

- The speculator originally bought her gold forward at $275 per ounce. The speculator pays $260 per ounce on delivery and has a loss of $15 per ounce in her margin account for a net of $275.

The fact that delivery occurs at the spot price has two very important implications for the futures market.

1. Neither party has any incentive to default on the contract when it comes time to deliver. The spot price and price the exchange pays are the same, so neither buyer nor seller can gain an advantage by buying or selling from a source other than the exchange.

2. Neither party has any financial incentive to actually go through the exchange delivery procedure. Suppose on the last day, both parties close out their positions by taking offsetting positions. The mining company was short 100 contracts, so it buys 100 contracts to close out its position. The speculator was long 100 contracts, so she sells 100 contracts to close out her position.

Both parties entered the market at $275 and left the market at $260. The mining company has a $15 per ounce profit in its margin account. The speculator has a $15 per ounce loss. If both parties then buy or sell in the spot market at $260, their financial results will be the same as buying or selling from the exchange. For this reason, only a very small percentage of futures contracts actually go to delivery. Most are closed out in advance.

Of course, one of the advantages of futures is that neither party has to hold on to a position until expiration. Consider another futures example, this one based upon the T-bond futures contract.

The T-Bond Futures Contract

The T-bond futures contract is based upon the price of a hypothetical 8-percent 20-year U.S. Treasury bond. (Yes, this contract is based on the forward price of a bond that does not really exist. Its price is whatever the bond would be selling for if it actually did exist.) The forward price of a bond is equal to the spot price plus the cost of carry. If short-term interest rates are low, an investor makes money by storing the bond in inventory. To store the bond, an investor borrows money at, say, 5 percent, and invests it in a bond yielding 8 percent. Thus, the investor makes 3 percent per year storing the bond. Because an investor can make money storing the bond, the forward price of the bond tends to get lower the further out into the future the forward value is calculated.

Suppose the forward price of this hypothetical bond in nine months is 109.31. The futures contract is priced just like a Treasury bond, so this price quote equals a price of 109 + 31/32 points per bond. Each contract is for 100 bonds.

A fixed-income portfolio manager who is worried that interest rates will rise can hedge the risk by shorting T-bond futures. If rates rise, the gain in the value of these theoretical bonds will offset the loss in the manager's actual bond portfolio. Let's assume that, given the size, composition, and volatility of the portfolio the manager wants to hedge, that the manager needs to sell 10 contracts. The other side of the transaction happens to be taken by a speculator who believes that interest rates will decline and so goes long the T-bond contracts. Both sides post $25,000 of margin with their respective brokers. Thus, at the start of the transaction, the positions of the counter parties would be as shown in Figure 15-6.

Figure 15-6
Initial Position

Time	Hedger (Short Contract)	Future Price	Speculator (Long Contract)
START	$25,000	109.31	$25,000

At the end of the first day, the price of the futures contract rises five ticks to 110.04. Since the price rose, the "longs" profit. The amount of money that is transferred from one account to another is equal to:

10 Contracts × 100 Bonds Per Contract ×
5 Ticks × $.3125 Per Tick = $1,562.50

Thus, at the end of the first day, the current position of the counter parties will be as shown in Figure 15-7.

Figure 15-7
Position After One Day

Time	Hedger (Short Contract)	Future Price	Speculator (Long Contract)
START	$25,000	109.31	$25,000
Day 1	$23,437.50	110.04	$26,562.50

At the end of second day, the price of the futures contract rises to 111. The amount of money that is transferred is equal to:

10 Contracts × 100 Bonds Per Contract ×
28 Ticks × $.3125 Per Tick = $8,750

Thus, at the end of the second day, the current position of the counter parties will be as shown in Figure 15-8.

Figure 15-8
Position After Two Days

Time	Hedger (Short Contract)	Future Price	Speculator (Long Contract)
START	$25,000	109.31	$25,000
Day 1	$23,437.50	110.04	$26,562.50
Day 2	$14,687.50	111	$35,312.50

At this point, the speculator decides to close out his position and take his profit. He originally went long 10 contracts at a price of 109.31, and to close out his position, all he needs to do is to sell 10 contracts, which he does at a price of 111. Because the speculator bought low and sold high, he has a profit of $10,312.50, which is already in his margin account. The 10 contracts the speculator sold could have been sold to a buyer who was either looking to establish a "new" long position or to close out an "existing" short position.

In this example, the speculator closed out his position prior to the expiration of the contract. Suppose, however, that the speculator held on to the contracts and actually wanted to go through the delivery process. The question becomes, "How can the short deliver to the long 100 8-percent 20-year T-bonds per contract when these bonds do not actually exist?" The answer, of course, is that the long can't.

Instead, according to the terms of the T-bond contract, the short can deliver 100 of any single actual T-bond that has at least 15 years of life left. That means that there are 20 or more different T-bonds the short can choose to deliver in fulfillment of its delivery obligation. These 20 alternative bonds all have different coupons and maturates and, therefore, different values. The exchange compensates for this by assigning different delivery prices to different bonds.

Thus, if the short chooses to deliver a T-bond with a higher coupon and a longer life, it will receive a higher price than if the short delivers a low-coupon, shorter-term bond. (The various delivery prices are set by the exchange, based upon the bond's relative attractiveness.)

According to the terms of the T-bond futures contract, the short gets to choose which T-bond to deliver, when during the delivery month to deliver it, and can deliver bonds even after the cash market for bonds is closed. This flexibility regarding delivery is referred to as the contract's "delivery options." Because these options favor the short, they reduce the value that the longs will pay for the futures contract. After all, the long would only be willing to buy the contract at a price equal to spot plus the cost of carry if the contract treated both sides fairly. Because it doesn't, the actual price of the futures contract will be:

Spot + Cost of Carry − Value of Delivery Options

Even those parties that don't plan on holding on to their contracts until delivery need to be aware of the delivery process and the value of the delivery options, because it affects the fair value of the futures contract. Like any contract, in a futures contract, the Devil is in the details.

Eurodollar Futures

Of all the interest rate futures, the most important contract is the Eurodollar (ED) future. The underlying instrument for the ED future is a three-month $1,000,000 deposit in a London Bank. These deposits start and mature on the second business day before the third Wednesday of the month in March, June, September, and December. (See Figure 15-9.)

Figure 15-9
Contracts and Expiration Dates

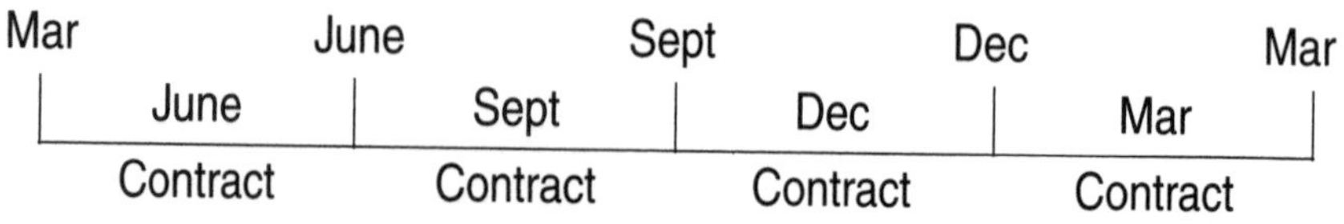

Mar		June		Sept		Dec		Mar
	June		Sept		Dec		Mar	
	Contract		Contract		Contract		Contract	

Eurodollar contracts are available with expirations up to nine years into the future. Thus, today, a hedger or speculator can take a position on what three-month rates will be as far as nine years into the future.

- Going long, the ED contract is the equivalent of agreeing to make a deposit in a London Bank on the day the contract expires and receiving whatever interest rate is "locked in" when the contract is purchased. The "longs" profit when interest rates decline to a rate lower than the one locked in when the contract is purchased.

- Going short, the ED contract is the equivalent of agreeing to accept a deposit in a London Bank on the day the contract expires and paying whatever interest rate is "locked in" when the contract is sold. The "shorts" profit when interest rates rise to a rate higher than the one locked in when the contract is sold.

The implied forward three-month ED rate can be determined by calculating the forward LIBOR rate for the same time period. For example, the yield of the June 2002 ED contract is the same as the forward rate from June 2002 to Sept. 2002. (See Figure 15-10.)

To convert the forward rate into an ED price, the resulting forward rate is then rounded to two decimal places and subtracted from 100. Because the price is rounded to two decimal places, the minimum price change is a basis point. The dollar value of a basis point on a $1 million deposit for three months is $25.

Figure 15-10
Determining Future Rates

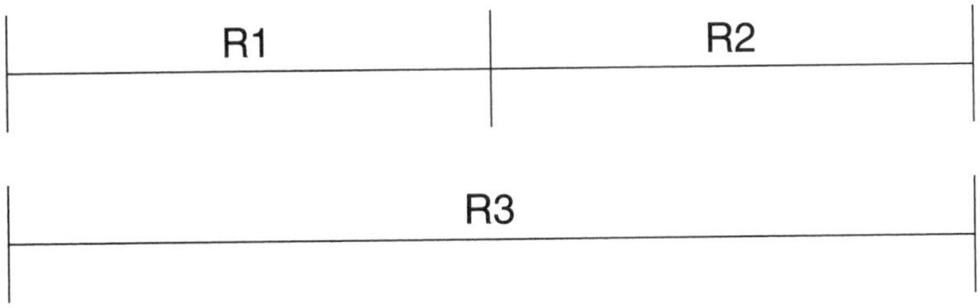

R1	R2

R3

Because a basis point is 1% of 1%:
1% of $1,000,000 = $10,000
1% of $10,000 = $100
For 1/4 of a year $100/4 = $25

For example, if the forward rate is 7.848954 percent, it would be rounded to 7.85 percent. The 7.85 percent is then subtracted from 100 in order to price the ED future—92.15 percent. The reason the yield is subtracted from 100 is that as the price of the ED rises, the long makes money. This makes the ED contract consistent with other futures contracts. If two counter parties traded this contract, the current position of the counter parties will be as shown in Figure 15-11.

Figure 15-11
Initial Position

Time	Long's Margin Balance	Future Price	Short's Margin Balance
START	$5,000	92.15	$5,000

If, the next day, the forward rate changed from 7.85 to 7.68 percent, then the price of the ED contract would change from 92.15 to 92.32. This represents a change of 17 basis points or 17 ticks. Since each tick in this contract is worth $25, the resulting price change is:

17 Ticks × $25 per Tick = $425

Thus, after the price move, the position of both counter parties would be as shown in Figure 15-12.

Figure 15-12
Position After One Day

Time	Long's Margin Balance	Future Price	Short's Margin Balance
START	$5,000	92.15	$5,000
Day 1	$5,425	92.32	$4,575

Each day, as the forward price changes, the positions are marked to the market. As time passes, the time until the 3-month period covered by the futures contract gets closer and closer. When the contract expires, the implied forward rate is no longer forward and is instead the three-month ED spot rate.

This raises the problem of delivery. The ED contract has no physical delivery. By definition, a deposit in a London Bank can't be delivered in the United States. Instead, on the expiration day, the contract is marked to the market just like any other day. This is referred to as cash settlement.

Even though the ED contract uses cash settlement, its expiration price still needs to be tied to the cash market. The procedure for determining the final price of the ED contract traded on the Chicago Mercantile Exchange (CME) is as follows. On the last day of trading the CME takes two surveys of 12 banks randomly selected from a master list of qualifying banks. The first survey occurs at 9:00 AM Chicago time (2:00 PM London) and the second survey at 10:30 AM Chicago time (3:30 PM London). The two highest and the two lowest values of each survey are thrown out. The remaining 16 values (8 per survey) are averaged and then rounded to the nearest two decimal places.

Applications of These Contracts

As with all futures contracts, the ED contract can be used both to speculate and to hedge. Speculators use these contracts for four principal types of trades.

1. Spot rate plays
2. Forward rate plays
3. Yield curve plays
4. Basis rate plays

SPOT RATE PLAYS

The most obvious application of ED futures is to speculate on how the yields at the various points along the LIBOR spot curve will change. By buying or selling a series of ED futures starting with the "next to expire ED contract," it is possible to create a synthetic cash market instrument. For example, by going long the four three-month ED contracts listed below (assuming the June contract is the next to expire), it is possible to create a synthetic one-year cash market instrument. This one-year synthetic instrument will behave like a long position in a one-year LIBOR zero coupon bond. A series of ED contracts that are purchased or sold together are referred to as an "ED strip." (See Figure 15-13.)

Likewise, by shorting a series of 12 ED futures—starting with the next to expire—an investor creates a synthetic three-year short position. This position will behave like a short position at the three-year point along the LIBOR zero coupon bond.

The advantages that using ED contracts offer speculators over simply buying and shorting the equivalent cash market instruments are the:

- High speed of execution for futures
- Low transaction costs of futures
- High degree of leverage inherent in futures
- Eliminating the need to borrow securities to deliver on short sales

FORWARD RATE PLAYS

The ED contract also allows investors to speculate on how a forward rate will change. To replicate a forward rate exposure, investors take

Figure 15-13
Synthetic One Year

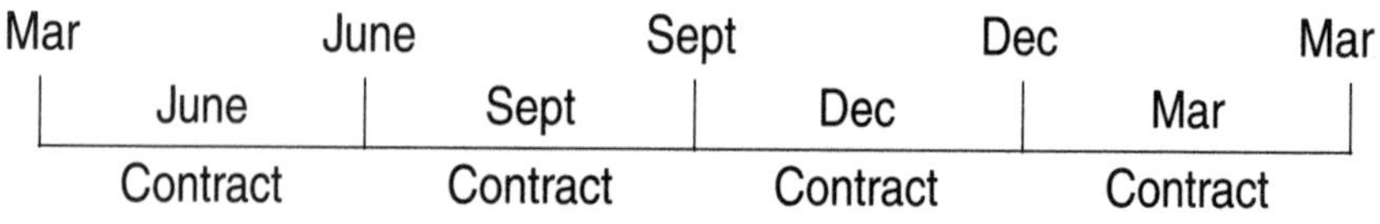

Mar	June	Sept	Dec	Mar
June Contract	Sept Contract	Dec Contract	Mar Contract	

Figure 15-14
Creating Synthetic Positions

M					M			M
2-Year Spot Rate					1-Year Rate - 2 Years Forward			
3-Year Spot Rate								

M	J	S	D	M	J	S	D	M	J	S	D	M
3M	3M	3M	3M	3M	3M	3M	3M	3M	3M	3M	3M
1	2	3	4	5	6	7	8	9	10	11	12

either long or short position in the ED contracts that mimic the forward rate. If, for example, an investor wanted to speculate on how the one-year ED rate, two years from now, will change, the investor can use a one-year ED strip that starts in two years. Thus, the investor would go long or short ED contracts 9, 10, 11, 12. (See Figure 15-14.)

YIELD CURVE PLAYS

ED contracts also make it possible for investors to speculate on the shape of the yield curve without taking any general interest rate risk. For example, a speculator might expect the shape of the yield curve to flatten, because either the short-term spot rate was expected to rise or the long-term spot rate was expected to decline. At the same time, the speculator might not want to take any general interest rate risk that eliminates the possibility of the speculator simply shorting the short-term ED strip or going long the long-term ED strip. Instead, the speculator needs to establish a position that profits if the curve flattens but is not exposed to general rate risk. This implies having offsetting short and long positions.

Specifically, suppose an investor expected the yield curve to flatten between the 3-month and 18-month points along the yield curve. To profit from this expected shift, the investor would go long the three-month ED contract and short an 18-month ED strip. However, in order to avoid any net interest rate exposure, the volatility of both the long position (L) and the short position (S) must be equal. In order for the volatility of the two positions to be equal, a speculator would have to go long six of the three-month contracts in order to offset the volatility of the six contracts that make up the ED strip that mirrors the 18-month rate. For the sake of efficiency, the two positions can be netted out. Consider Figure 15-15.

Figure 15-15
Steepening Play

Establishing a Yield Curve Play that Profits from a Steepening of the Curve

Long	Short	Net
6 3-Month (L)	1 3-Month (S)	5 3-Month (L)
	1 3-Month (S)	1 3-Month (S)
	1 3-Month (S)	1 3-Month (S)
	1 3-Month (S)	1 3-Month (S)
	1 3-Month (S)	1 3-Month (S)
	1 3-Month (S)	1 3-Month (S)
Vol = $150	Vol = $150	Vol = $0

BASIS RATE PLAYS

In a basis rate play, an investor speculates that the spread between two interest rates will either increase or decrease. One of the spreads that investors focus on most closely is the spread between the U.S. Treasury yield curve and the LIBOR yield curve. This spread tends to widen when:

- Interest rates rise.
- There is a "flight to quality" during periods of political or economic instability.

If a speculator expected the spread to widen, the investor would go long the TED (T-bill over ED) spread by going long T-bills and T-notes and short the ED contracts. If the speculator expected the spread to narrow, the investor would go short the TED spread by going short T-bills and notes and long the ED contract.

Hedgers

Hedgers take positions that are designed to protect themselves against the adverse affect of a change in interest rates. An adverse change can either be a rise or a decline in rates, depending upon the client's situation.

A rise in rates would adversely affect:

- A borrower with floating rate liabilities
- An investor with fixed rate assets

A decline in rates would adversely affect:

- A borrower with fixed rate liabilities
- An investor with floating rate assets

The objective when hedging is to match both the size and the timing of the exposure. For example, suppose an investor owned $10,000,000 of floating rate notes (FRNs) that paid LIBOR plus 25 bp. While the notes mature in two years, the interest rate they pay resets every quarter. Because the interest rate on this investment floats, the investor is exposed to the risk that rates will decline.

The investor could hedge this risk by taking a short position in a $10,000,000 two-year ED strip. If interest rates decline, the lower income from the FRNs will be offset by a rise in the value of the ED strip. Of course, a futures hedge is a double-edged sword. If rates rise, the higher income earned on the FRNs will be offset by an equal loss on the futures position. (See Figure 15-16.)

Figure 15-16
Comparison of Forwards and Futures

	Forwards	Futures
Credit Risk	Yes	No
Public vs. Private	Private	Public
Customized	Yes	No
Marked to Market	No	Yes
Cash Settlement	No	Sometimes
Liquidity	No	Yes
Price Transparency	No	Yes
Choice	No	No

Structure and Operation of a Futures Exchange

At first glance, there are few sights that appear to be as chaotic as a futures exchange. The sight of 300 to 400 people crushed shoulder to shoulder, all yelling at the top of their lungs and waving their hands violently is hardly the picture of an orderly market. Yet below the surface, the futures market is extremely orderly and efficient—with a definitive pecking order and structure.

Futures exchanges are often called "futures pits" for a reason. Futures exchanges are often three-dimensional hexagon or heptagon shaped floors with various tiers leading up from the recessed center. Booths that are rented by the various securities firms surround the hexagonal floor. It is to these booths that client orders are sent when they are received. The orders are then relayed via notes, electronic communications devices, and paper notes to the floor brokers. (See Figure 15-17.)

All along the top tier of the pit are the floor brokers, who work for the major securities firms. They usually stand sideways, so that they can have one eye on their clerk's booths and the other on what's happening in the pit.

When an order to buy or sell a certain number of futures contracts comes in from a client, it is relayed electronically or by phone to the firm's floor clerk. The firm's floor clerk uses either hand signs or paper

Figure 15-17
Top View of Futures Pit

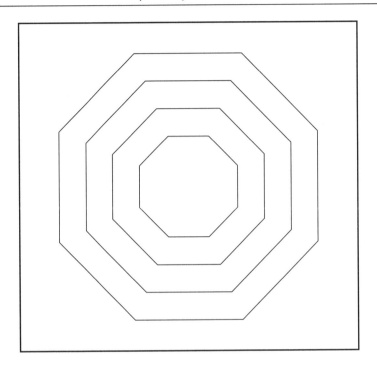

notes to pass the order on to the floor broker. The floor broker then tries to immediately execute the order by "open outcry" and "hand signal." The floor broker will both yell out the number of contracts that the firm's client wants to buy/sell and the price the client wants to pay/receive, and will also use hand signals to announce the order to the rest of the brokers in the pit.

From the floor broker's point of view, the best situation is for a client at a different firm to want to do the opposite transaction at the exact same time. For example, if the Prudential floor broker wants to buy 40 contracts, ideally the J.P. Morgan floor broker wants to sell 40 contracts. As soon as the Prudential broker announces his order, the J.P. Morgan can yell back "sold 40 to you" and complete the transaction. Both parties will note with which firm they did the transaction.

Of course, the order does not have to be filled with one counter party; it can be filled with many counter parties. The Prudential broker might buy 20 contracts from J.P. Morgan and 10 from Merrill Lynch. Because the floor broker's first choice is to transact business with another firm that is executing client business, a floor broker will first scan the top rung of the pit when looking for a counter party.

If, as is often the case, there is no firm that wants to be the counter party on the trade, the floor broker's next alternative is to deal with a "local broker." Local brokers are brokers who do not transact business for clients. Instead, they buy and sell for their own accounts. By standing ready to buy or sell, they provide liquidity to the market—for a price. When a floor broker does business with a local, the local always tries to sell the contract for a price slightly higher than the current forward price and when the local buys, the local tries to buy at a price slightly lower than the current forward price. By buying contracts at a slight discount and selling them at a slight premium, floor brokers hope to make a living out of providing liquidity. Since the profit they make on each transaction is usually quite small, floor brokers try to do a lot of trades per day.

Local brokers are located on the lower rungs in the pit. The largest locals—those who stand ready to buy or sell the largest numbers of futures—stand on the higher rungs. Brand new locals and trainees stand on the bottom rung.

The rules concerning trading are exacting, with high fines for those who violate them. Some of the rules include:

- Transactions can only occur in the pit. There is no trading outside the pit.
- Every order has to be announced to the entire pit in order to find the best price.

Proposals are always circulating about electronic markets replacing the open outcry system. Undoubtedly, this will happen some day, but of all the markets, the futures market may be the last to become fully automated.

Figure 15-18

Futures Prices reprinted from The **Wall Street Journal**

FUTURES PRICES

PLATINUM (NYM)-50 troy oz.; $ per troy oz.

	Open	High	Low	Settle	Change	Lifetime High	Lifetime Low	Open Interest
Apr	478.50	481.50	475.20	478.30	+ 0.20	555.00	343.50	7,314
July	470.00	475.00	469.50	471.80	+ 0.20	538.00	352.00	1,482

Est vol 619; vol Tue 791; open int 8,739, +136.

SILVER (Cmx.Div.NYM)-5,000 troy oz.;cnts per troy oz.

	Open	High	Low	Settle	Change	Lifetime High	Lifetime Low	Open Interest
Mar	512.0	514.5	511.0	512.7	+ 3.5	595.0	491.0	203
May	513.0	520.0	510.0	516.5	+ 3.3	577.0	500.0	54,285
July	516.5	524.0	515.0	520.0	+ 3.3	590.0	500.0	7,730
Sept	526.0	528.0	523.0	523.2	+ 3.3	580.0	500.0	2,165
Dec	524.5	530.0	524.5	525.5	+ 3.3	685.0	490.0	5,980
Mr01	....	....	....	528.0	+ 3.3	552.0	511.0	434
May	....	....	....	529.5	+ 3.3	527.0	525.0	130
July	....	....	....	530.5	+ 3.3	574.0	510.0	955
Dec	....	....	....	534.5	+ 3.3	680.0	498.0	1,197
Dc02	....	....	....	538.7	+ 3.3	613.0	495.0	545
Dc03	....	....	....	545.6	+ 3.3	565.0	510.0	377

Est vol 7,500; vol Tue 5,104; open int 74,268, +293.

CRUDE OIL, Light Sweet (NYM) 1,000 bbls.; $ per bbl.

	Open	High	Low	Settle	Change	Lifetime High	Lifetime Low	Open Interest
Apr	31.71	31.92	30.60	30.72	– 0.97	34.37	13.03	95,301
May	29.85	29.95	28.90	29.03	– 0.69	32.57	13.65	114,820
June	28.25	28.45	27.70	27.78	– 0.54	31.18	13.26	63,740
July	27.32	27.32	26.75	26.88	– 0.44	29.35	13.70	42,839
Aug	26.27	26.40	26.06	26.23	– 0.37	28.60	13.78	24,046
Sept	25.50	25.75	25.50	25.66	– 0.32	27.60	14.40	18,956
Oct	25.15	25.25	25.10	25.14	– 0.27	26.71	14.22	17,679
Nov	....	....	....	24.71	– 0.25	26.16	15.60	14,049
Dec	24.23	24.40	24.23	24.30	– 0.23	25.90	13.85	38,620
Ja01	23.85	24.06	23.85	23.92	– 0.21	25.35	14.25	16,444
Feb	....	....	....	23.56	– 0.19	24.78	14.30	5,578
Mar	....	....	....	23.22	– 0.16	24.30	14.44	4,729
Apr	....	....	....	22.88	– 0.13	23.31	15.80	1,999
May	....	....	....	22.55	– 0.11	23.55	15.80	2,385
June	22.20	22.25	22.20	22.27	– 0.07	23.30	14.56	18,714
July	....	....	....	22.02	– 0.05	22.55	19.05	3,350
Aug	....	....	....	21.79	– 0.03	22.30	18.40	1,521
Sept	....	....	....	21.58	– 0.02	22.02	17.96	2,489
Oct	....	....	....	21.39	....	21.90	19.80	730
Nov	....	....	....	21.21	+ 0.02	19.05	18.20	672
Dec	21.00	21.10	21.00	21.04	+ 0.04	21.60	14.90	23,381
Ja02	....	....	....	20.87	+ 0.06	20.42	18.90	1,119
Feb	....	....	....	20.72	+ 0.08	20.08	19.94	337
Mar	....	....	....	20.59	+ 0.10	18.65	18.45	2,075
June	....	....	....	20.25	+ 0.13	20.05	17.35	3,074
July	....	....	....	20.14	+ 0.13	19.85	19.85	100
Dec	19.60	19.60	19.60	19.69	+ 0.17	21.38	15.50	9,483
Dc03	....	....	....	19.01	+ 0.19	22.00	15.92	6,401
Dc04	....	....	....	18.83	+ 0.21	19.27	16.35	4,919
Dc05	....	....	....	18.77	+ 0.21	19.20	17.00	899

Est vol 169,221; vol Tue 155,036; open int 538,476, +2,609.

HEATING OIL NO. 2 (NYM) 42,000 gal; $ per gal.

	Open	High	Low	Settle	Change	Lifetime High	Lifetime Low	Open Interest
Apr	.7410	.7475	.7110	.7171	– .0197	.8260	.3760	25,418
May	.7050	.7050	.6810	.6890	– .0157	.7895	.3800	22,487
June	.6770	.6800	.6660	.6710	– .0122	.7540	.3790	10,722
July	.6540	.6640	.6540	.6600	– .0107	.7305	.3890	13,302
Aug	.6500	.6610	.6500	.6580	– .0092	.7210	.3970	6,402
Sept	.6525	.6630	.6525	.6595	– .0082	.7185	.4260	5,632
Oct	.6650	.6650	.6650	.6615	– .0077	.7150	.4717	2,769
Nov	.6690	.6690	.6670	.6640	– .0067	.7185	.4792	2,641
Dec	.6670	.6715	.6610	.6660	– .0062	.7150	.5110	15,674
Ja01	.6690	.6690	.6690	.6660	– .0052	.7165	.5254	3,680
Feb	....	....	....	.6540	– .0042	.6995	.5360	1,590
Mar	.6350	.6350	.6350	.6295	– .0032	.6640	.5250	954
Apr	....	....	....	.6060	– .0022	.6400	.5140	768
May	....	....	....	.5855	– .0012	.6169	.5075	362
June	....	....	....	.5695	– .0002	.5984	.5685	443

Est vol 25,087; vol Tue 28,934; open int 112,319, –17.

GASOLINE-NY Unleaded (NYM) 42,000; $ per gal.

	Open	High	Low	Settle	Change	Lifetime High	Lifetime Low	Open Interest
Apr	.9689	.9750	.9305	.9328	– .0351	1.9995	.5050	31,771
May	.9050	.9070	.8710	.8734	– .0291	.9730	.5170	26,113
June	.8600	.8600	.8350	.8349	– .0216	.9210	.5510	17,827
July	.8150	.8160	.8050	.8034	– .0161	.8800	.5980	9,158
Aug	.7750	.7820	.7700	.7744	– .0101	.8480	.5965	6,877
Sept	.7400	.7470	.7385	.7484	– .0056	.8150	.5980	8,749
Oct	....	....	....	.7114	– .0026	.7570	.6300	2,165
Nov	....	....	....	.6914	– .0006	.7400	.6630	892
Dec	.6650	.6760	.6650	.6784	+ .0014	.7260	.6275	1,073

Est vol 32,990; vol Tue 36,922; open int 104,236, –481.

NATURAL GAS, (NYM) 10,000 MMBtu.; $ per MMBtu's

	Open	High	Low	Settle	Change	Lifetime High	Lifetime Low	Open Interest
Apr	2.815	2.885	2.750	2.866	+ .057	2.880	2.015	53,236
May	2.821	2.910	2.775	2.881	+ .047	2.910	1.960	33,578
June	2.860	2.915	2.800	2.896	+ .044	2.920	2.001	22,369
July	2.865	2.925	2.825	2.910	+ .040	2.930	2.005	17,435
Aug	2.850	2.935	2.840	2.921	+ .034	2.930	2.005	15,037
Sept	2.860	2.930	2.845	2.922	+ .032	2.935	2.100	18,625
Oct	2.880	2.945	2.870	2.942	+ .029	2.955	2.100	17,058
Nov	3.000	3.060	2.990	3.055	+ .025	3.070	2.240	12,305
Dec	3.140	3.170	3.110	3.167	+ .022	3.190	2.380	16,004
Ja01	3.135	3.190	3.130	3.187	+ .021	3.210	2.400	11,350
Feb	....	....	....	3.033	+ .018	3.050	2.305	7,229
Mar	....	....	....	2.878	+ .018	2.900	2.210	7,103
Apr	2.720	2.755	2.720	2.753	+ .018	2.770	2.120	5,080
May	2.675	2.700	2.675	2.702	+ .022	2.710	2.119	4,691
June	2.675	2.700	2.665	2.703	+ .022	2.710	2.095	7,501
July	2.690	2.690	2.686	2.718	+ .022	2.725	2.095	5,468
Aug	2.695	2.700	2.695	2.727	+ .022	2.740	2.102	3,355
Sept	2.705	2.705	2.700	2.732	+ .022	2.745	2.137	2,464
Oct	2.730	2.730	2.730	2.755	+ .022	2.765	2.133	3,115
Nov	....	....	....	2.867	+ .022	2.885	2.275	3,215
Dec	2.960	2.960	2.958	2.984	+ .022	3.015	2.415	4,932
Ja02	2.983	2.985	2.980	3.007	+ .022	3.045	2.450	3,433
Feb	....	....	....	2.885	+ .026	2.920	2.440	2,630
Mar	....	....	....	2.753	+ .027	2.785	2.360	2,297

EUROYEN (CME) -Yen 100,000,000; pts. of 100%

	Open	High	Low	Settle	Change	Lifetime High	Lifetime Low	Open Interest
June	99.81	99.81	99.80	99.81	– .01	99.84	98.09	19,888
Sept	99.69	99.69	99.69	99.69	– .01	99.74	98.00	14,319
Dec	99.52	99.52	99.52	99.52	– .01	99.60	97.92	10,057
Mr01	99.39	99.39	99.38	99.39	– .01	99.54	98.07	16,923
June	99.25	99.25	99.25	99.25	– .02	99.41	98.20	4,717
Sept	....	....	....	99.09	– .02	99.30	98.05	10,374
Dec	....	....	....	98.94	– .02	99.15	97.89	1,154
Mr02	98.80	98.80	98.80	98.80	– .02	98.87	97.97	379

Est vol 5,663; vol Tue 3,982; open int 91,375, –1,808.

SHORT STERLING (LIFFE)-£500,000; pts of 100%

	Open	High	Low	Settle	Change	Lifetime High	Lifetime Low	Open Interest
Mar	93.78	....	93.77	93.80	+ .02	95.17	91.96	160,167
Apr	93.65	93.65	93.64	93.64	– .02	93.67	93.38	2,266
May	....	....	....	93.54	– .02	93.59	93.47	406
June	93.44	93.44	93.39	93.41	– .02	95.17	92.47	185,821
Sept	93.27	93.27	93.21	93.24	– .01	95.13	92.80	180,019
Dec	93.14	93.15	93.09	93.12	....	98.80	92.61	92,397
Mr01	93.11	93.11	93.06	93.09	....	95.08	92.55	68,002
June	93.07	93.09	93.03	93.06	....	95.08	92.49	62,032
Sept	93.04	93.04	93.00	93.03	+ .01	95.09	92.41	46,290
Dec	92.98	92.99	92.95	92.98	+ .01	95.07	92.31	26,752
Mr02	93.01	93.01	92.99	93.02	+ .01	95.13	92.34	21,421
June	93.03	93.04	93.02	93.05	....	95.10	92.39	12,224
Sept	93.10	93.10	93.10	93.11	....	95.11	92.38	9,453
Dec	93.17	93.17	93.15	93.17	+ .02	95.11	92.45	4,880
Mr03	93.26	93.26	93.24	93.25	+ .01	94.69	92.49	1,892
June	93.34	93.34	93.34	93.35	+ .01	93.88	92.77	488
Sept	93.42	93.42	93.42	93.43	+ .01	93.56	92.90	546
Dec	93.48	93.48	93.48	93.49	+ .01	93.48	92.92	591
Mr04	....	....	....	93.57	+ .01	93.41	93.01	672
June	....	....	....	93.62	+ .01	93.16	93.04	326

Est vol 139,553; vol Tue 87,877; open int 876,650, –2,722.

LONG GILT (LIFFE) (Decimal)-£50,000; pts of 100%

	Open	High	Low	Settle	Change	Lifetime High	Lifetime Low	Open Interest
Mar	113.44	113.50	113.17	113.39	+ .20	115.66	108.00	10,014
June	113.21	113.23	112.52	113.03	+ .22	113.92	109.97	64,635

Est vol 21,619; vol Tue 18,366; open int 74,649, –2,708.

3 MONTH EURIBOR (LIFFE) Euro 1,000,000; pts of 100%

	Open	High	Low	Settle	Change	Lifetime High	Lifetime Low	Open Interest
Apr	96.07	96.10	96.05	96.07	....	96.27	96.05	31,960
June	95.80	95.83	95.80	95.83	+ .02	97.27	95.80	328,035
Sept	95.52	95.56	95.51	95.55	+ .02	97.16	95.51	292,494
Dec	95.30	95.33	95.29	95.32	+ .01	97.00	93.36	152,476
Mr01	95.18	95.21	95.18	95.20	+ .01	96.96	95.05	123,273
June	95.06	95.09	95.05	95.07	+ .01	96.85	94.87	84,150
Sept	94.95	94.97	94.93	94.95	+ .01	96.75	94.70	65,988
Dec	94.80	94.82	94.78	94.81	+ .02	96.58	92.57	38,504
Mr02	94.76	94.79	94.74	94.76	+ .01	96.48	94.42	30,237
June	94.71	94.71	94.66	94.68	+ .01	96.37	94.32	21,056
Sept	94.62	94.62	94.58	94.61	+ .01	96.25	94.24	12,738
Dec	94.52	94.52	94.49	94.51	+ .01	96.06	94.06	9,996
Mr03	94.50	94.50	94.48	94.49	+ .01	96.01	94.05	5,179
June	94.46	94.46	94.42	94.43	+ .01	95.45	93.99	3,705
Sept	94.38	94.38	94.38	94.38	+ .01	95.15	93.91	4,772
Dec	....	....	....	94.28	+ .01	95.07	93.80	1,919
Mr04	....	....	....	94.30	+ .01	94.50	93.83	846
June	....	....	....	94.26	+ .01	94.43	93.79	538
Sept	....	....	....	94.14	+ .01	94.40	93.73	691

Est vol 195,323; vol Tue 235,394; open int 1,208,592, +50,551.

3-MONTH EUROSWISS (LIFFE)

SFr 1,000,000; pts of 100%

	Open	High	Low	Settle	Change	Lifetime High	Lifetime Low	Open Interest
June	96.85	96.89	96.85	96.87	+ .02	98.51	96.82	85,246
Sept	96.58	96.59	96.56	96.57	+ .02	98.36	96.52	30,580
Dec	96.37	96.37	96.32	96.34	+ .02	98.12	96.27	20,699
Mr01	96.28	96.37	96.28	96.34	+ .02	98.04	96.20	10,964
June	....	....	....	96.30	+ .01	97.47	96.19	3,088
Sept	96.26	96.26	96.25	96.26	+ .01	96.76	95.88	4,909
Dec	96.14	96.14	96.14	96.14	+ .01	96.46	96.02	6,473

Est vol 8,906; vol Tue 13,123; open int 161,959, +2,204.

EURO BTP ITALIAN GOVT. BOND (LIFFE)

Euro 100,000; pts of 100%

	Open	High	Low	Settle	Change	Lifetime High	Lifetime Low	Open Interest
June	103.05	103.35	102.99	103.14	+ .14	103.58	101.41	433

Est vol 96; vol Tue 108; open int 433, –37.

CANADIAN BANKERS ACCEPTANCE (ME)-C$1,000,000

	Open	High	Low	Settle	Change	Lifetime High	Lifetime Low	Open Interest
Apr	....	....	....	94.47	– 0.03	94.49	94.43	950
June	94.30	94.31	94.25	94.26	– 0.04	95.33	93.73	109,395
Sept	93.95	94.00	93.92	93.95	– 0.03	95.24	93.50	55,382
Dec	93.71	93.76	93.71	93.73	– 0.02	95.13	93.34	25,938
Mr01	93.59	93.63	93.59	93.61	– 0.02	95.10	93.16	12,043
June	93.55	93.55	93.55	93.53	– 0.02	95.07	93.07	7,111
Sept	93.47	93.48	93.47	93.49	– 0.01	93.73	93.06	4,209
Dec	93.45	93.50	93.45	93.46	– 0.01	94.74	92.97	1,245
Mr02	93.40	93.40	93.40	93.41	– 0.01	94.73	93.30	175
June	....	....	....	93.36	– 0.01	93.42	92.95	1,675
Sept	....	....	....	93.31	– 0.01	93.39	93.11	365

Est vol 19,527; vol Tue 19,757; open int 218,300, –3,700.

10 YR. CANADIAN GOVT. BONDS (ME)-C$100,000

	Open	High	Low	Settle	Change	Lifetime High	Lifetime Low	Open Interest
Mar	....	....	....	119.66	– 0.28	120.80	115.45	3,632
June	98.90	99.30	98.60	98.76	– 0.28	99.30	97.65	41,306

Est vol 5,044; vol Tue 3,401; open int 44,900, +1,300.

10 YR.EURO NOTIONAL BOND(MATIF)-Euros 100,000

	Open	High	Low	Settle	Change	Lifetime High	Lifetime Low	Open Interest
June	85.90	86.01	85.64	85.79	+ 0.13	86.16	83.76	154,638

Est vol 206,632; vol Tue 161,916; open int 154,638, +356.

3 MONTH EURIBOR (MATIF)-Euros 1,000,000

	Open	High	Low	Settle	Change	Lifetime High	Lifetime Low	Open Interest
June	95.81	95.82	95.81	95.82	+ 0.01	97.26	95.81	5,789
Sept	95.52	95.54	95.52	95.54	+ 0.01	97.14	95.52	5,117
Dec	95.30	95.30	95.29	95.31	....	97.00	95.21	7,471
Mr01	95.19	95.19	95.18	95.19	....	96.95	95.07	2,608
June	95.06	95.06	95.05	95.05	....	96.85	94.89	1,775
Sept	94.95	94.95	94.94	94.94	....	96.75	94.73	1,282
Dec	94.80	94.80	94.79	94.79	....	96.58	94.52	561
Mr02	94.76	94.76	94.75	94.75	....	96.48	94.45	596

..AP CONTRACTS

An interest rate swap is a private agreement between two parties, in which they agree to exchange one stream of interest payments for another stream of interest payments on a specific notional amount of principal for a specific period of time.

Investors use swaps to convert fixed-rate liabilities/assets into floating rate liabilities/assets and floating-rate liabilities/assets into fixed-rate liabilities/assets. For example, suppose:

- Company A currently has $100,000,000 of floating-rate non-callable debt outstanding on which it is paying LIBOR plus 150 bps computed on an A/360 calendar and paid quarterly. The company is worried, for whatever reason, that interest rates will rise. If rates rise, the company's interest expense will rise, and so the company decides to convert its debt from floating-rate debt into fixed-rate debt.

- Company B currently has $100,000,000 of fixed-rate noncallable debt outstanding on which it is paying 9% interest computed on a 30/360 basis and paid annually. The company believes, for whatever reason, that interest rates will fall. If rates fall, the company would like to have floating-rate debt instead of fixed-rate debt, so that its interest expense will decline. (See Figure 16-1.)

Figure 16-1
Initial Positions

By entering into an interest rate swap, both companies can effectively convert their existing liabilities into the liabilities they truly want. In this swap:

- Company A might agree to pay to Company B fixed-rate interest payments of 8% computed on a 30/360 calendar and paid annually. Thus, the payment at the end of each year would be:

$$\$100,000,000 \times .08 \times 30/360 = \$8,000,000$$
and

- Company B might agree to pay to Company A floating-rate interest payments of LIBOR computed on an A/360 basis and paid quarterly. Thus, if LIBOR was at 5%, and the quarter has 91 days, the payment at the end of the first quarter would be:

$$\$100,000,000 \times .05 \times 91/360 = \$1,263,888.89$$

Each quarter the amount will change depending upon the number of days in that particular calendar quarter and the LIBOR rate during that particular calendar quarter. (See Figure 16-2.)

Figure 16-2
Swap

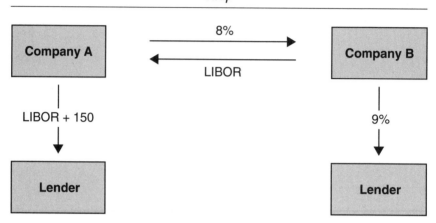

In this swap:

- Company A pays LIBOR+150 to its original lender and 8% in the swap. The total amount it pays out, therefore, is "LIBOR+950" bp or "LIBOR+9.50%." It receives LIBOR in the swap. The two LIBORs cancel each other leaving an "all in" cost of funds of 9.50%, a fixed rate.

- Company B pays 9% to its original lender and LIBOR in the swap. The total amount it pays is, therefore, "LIBOR+9%." It receives 8% in the swap for an "all in" cost of LIBOR+1%, a floating rate.

To implement this transaction, the two companies in the example can simply sign a contract that specifies each party's obligations. Since this is a private contract between two parties, it is very much like a forward contract and has the same advantages (customization, privacy, and so on) and disadvantages (credit risk, illiquidity, and so on) as forward contracts.

Applications of Swaps

Interest rate swaps are often used to either:

- Lower a borrower's interest expense.

- Increase an investor's interest income.

Let's consider some examples. Suppose Figure 16-3 represents the best loan rates that are available in the marketplace on a particular day.

Figure 16-3
Market Rates

	AA	BBB+
3-Year Fixed	7%	8%
3-Year Floating	LIBOR+10	LIBOR+60

The CFO of a "AA rated" company wants to borrow $100,000,000 for three years. The CFO also wants to borrow at a floating rate, because he believes that interest rates will decline. The CFO could simply borrow at the floating rate available for companies with a AA credit rating—namely LIBOR+10 bp. Unfortunately, that would be a mistake because the CFO would not be borrowing in away that his company would have a "competitive advantage."

The AA company has a high credit rating. A high credit rating should entitle the company to borrow at a lower rate than a company with a lower credit rating. On the floating-rate side of the market, the AA-rated company's "reward" for having a higher credit rating is being able to save 50 basis points in interest expense relative to the BBB+ company. However, on the fixed-rate side of the market, the AA-rated company saves 100 bp relative to a BBB+ company. (See Figure 16-4.)

Figure 16-4
Difference

	AA	BBB+	Difference
3-Year Fixed	7%	8%	100 bp
3-Year Floating	LIBOR+10	LIBOR+60	50 bp

The AA-rated company enjoys a greater relative savings on the fixed side of the market than it does on the floating-rate side. In the jargon of the trade, the AA-rated company is "stronger on the fixed-rate side of the market" and has a "competitive advantage" on the fixed-rate side of the market. Companies should *always, always, always* borrow on the side of the market where they are the strongest.

The treasurer of the BBB+ company also wants to borrow $100,000,000 for three years. However, the treasurer wants to borrow money at a fixed rate because her company cannot afford the risk of having floating rate financing. The treasurer of the BBB+ company knows that her company will have to pay a higher interest rate to borrow money than a AA-rated company has to pay. The question is, however, "How much more will the BBB+ company have to pay because of its lower credit rating?"

If the BBB+ company borrows at a fixed rate, it will have to pay a premium of 100 basis points relative to the AA-rated company. However, if the company borrows at a floating rate, the company has to pay only 40 basis points more than the AA-rated company. Thus, the lower-rated company is stronger and has its competitive advantage on the floating-rate side of the market.

Unfortunately for the CFO and the treasurer, they both have valid business reasons for wanting to borrow on what for their respective companies is the "weak side" of the market. The CFO of the AA-rated company believes rates will decline and wants to save his company money. The treasurer of the BBB+ company wants to protect her company from the risk of higher rates.

However, instead of both companies borrowing on the weak side of the market, both companies could instead borrow on what for them is the strong side of the market and then use a swap to convert their respective financing to the type of financing that they really want. By doing so, both companies can reduce their respective financing costs. By borrowing on the strong side instead of the weak side, the combined savings in interest expense can be used to create a "slush fund" that equals the "difference of the differences in the yields." In this example, the difference of the differences is 50 basis points (100 bps – 50 bps). This slush fund can be used to reduce the total borrowing cost of both parties. Assuming, just for the moment, that the parties agree to benefit evenly from this swap, then each party will benefit by 25 basis points. (See Figure 16-5.)

Figure 16-5
Difference in Rates

	AA	BBB+	Difference
3-Year Fixed	7%	8%	100 bp
3-Year Floating	LIBOR+10	LIBOR+60	50 bp

The Difference of the Differences is 50 Basis Points

By simply borrowing at a floating rate, the AA-rated company could lock in a cost of LIBOR+10. Thus, in order to benefit by 25 basis points, the AA-rated company's "all in" cost of financing would have to be LIBOR – 15 bps.

By simply borrowing at a fixed rate, the BBB+ company could lock in a cost of 8%. Thus, in order to benefit by 25 basis points, the BBB+ – rated company's "all in" cost of borrowing must be 7.75%.

When determining which rates to exchange in the swap so that both companies benefit, the convention is to start with the floating-rate side and set it equal to LIBOR flat. The fixed rate is then set at whatever rate is necessary for both parties to have their desired "all in" cost of financing.

In this example, there is only one fixed rate that will allow both parties to benefit by 25 basis points. That rate is 7.15%. If the fixed rate is set to 7.15%:

- The AA-rated company pays LIBOR and receives a net "15 basis points" from the difference between the two fixed rates for a net cost of L-15.

- The BBB+-rated company offsets the two LIBORs and is left paying 7.15% + .60% = 7.75%. (See Figure 16-6.)

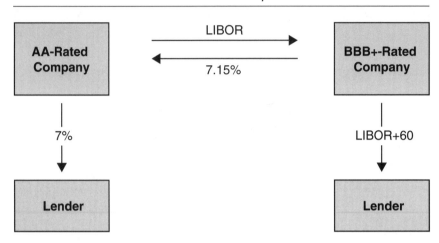

Figure 16-6
Interest Rate Swap

In reality, both parties to the swap will not benefit evenly. A strip of Eurodollar futures can also be used to convert floating-rate liabilities to a fixed rate liabilities and vice versa. Because both swaps and Eurodollar strips can be used to accomplish the same goal, they can be arbitraged against each other. Thus, the fixed rate in the swap will be equal the rate that can be locked in with an equivalent Eurodollar strip. (See Chapter 15.)

In the previous example, a swap allowed both parties to lower their cost of financing. Using the same data, two investors can exploit the same concepts to increase their returns. When investors use swaps to increase their returns, they are referred to as "asset swaps."

Asset Swaps

If the data in the previous example is the rate at which borrowers can borrow, it is also the rate at which investors can invest—after all, borrowers borrow from investors. Suppose there are two investors:

- Investor 1 is adverse to credit risk and believes that interest rates over the next few years will decline.

- Investor 2 is willing to accept credit risk and believes that interest rates will rise.

Figure 16-7
Difference in Rates

	AA	BBB+	Difference
3-Year Fixed	7%	8%	100 bp
3-Year Floating	LIBOR+10	LIBOR+60	50 bp

Investor 1 could simply buy the AA-rated 3-year 7% fixed-rate note and Investor 2 could simply buy the 3-year BBB+-rated 3-year floating rate note yielding LIBOR+60. Unfortunately, if both parties simply invest directly in the cash market instrument that matches their objectives, they will both be leaving money on the table. This is because both investors will be investing on what for them is the weak side of the market.

Investor 1 wants an investment with high credit quality. Unfortunately, credit quality has to be "purchased" by sacrificing yield. Higher credit quality instruments offer a lower yield than lower credit quality instruments. The question becomes, "How much yield will the investor have to sacrifice in order to buy credit quality?" On the fixed-rate side of the market, it costs 100 bps to buy credit quality. On the floating-rate side of the market, it costs only 50 basis points to buy the same increase in credit quality. Thus, since Investor 1 wants to buy credit quality, Investor 1 should buy it on the side of the market where it is cheap, instead of where it is expensive. Investor 1 should initially invest on the floating-rate side of the market, where it has its competitive advantage.

Investor 2 wants a higher return and is willing to assume some additional credit risk in order to get it. There is nothing wrong with an investor accepting additional risk as long as the investor is adequately paid for the additional risk. On the floating-rate side of the market, the yield premium for accepting credit risk is 50 bps. However, on the fixed-rate side of the market, the premium for accepting the same amount of additional credit risk is 100 bps. Thus, Investor 2 should invest where the premium for accepting credit risk is high—on the fixed-rate side of the market. It has a competitive advantage on the fixed-rate side of the market.

After both investors have invested in what for them is the strong side of the market instead of the weak side, they can use a swap to convert their investments to the type they really want. As with the previous example, the advantage that's available is equal to the difference of the differences, or 50 bps. If both parties benefit by 25 basis points, then the resulting swap will look like Figure 16-8. Note that in this case, the arrows are pointing up since these are investors.

After investing on the respective strong side of the market and executing the swap, the net returns of the investors will be:

- Investor 1 has LIBOR+10 and 7.15% coming in, for an overall income of LIBOR+7.25%. The investor has an outflow of LIBOR, for a "net income" of 7.25%.

- Investor-2 has LIBOR+8% coming in and 7.15% going out, for a net income of LIBOR+0.85%.

Figure 16-8
Asset Swap

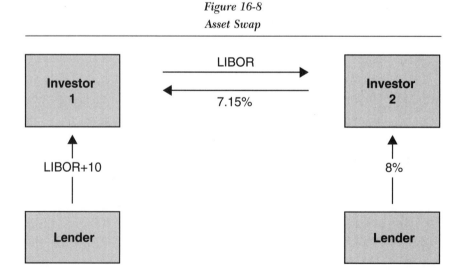

Index Swaps

In the previous example of interest rate and asset swap, a stream of fixed-rate interest payments is swapped for a stream of floating-rate interest payments. However, a swap can just as easily swap one floating rate for another. Consider the following example and again assume that the rates are the best rates available in the market.

A AA-rated company wants LIBOR-based financing, because it has LIBOR-based liabilities and it wants to match its assets against its liabilities. A BBB+-rated company believes that commercial paper (CP) rates will decline relative to other rates and so wants its financing tied to the CP rate. However, if both companies were to simply borrow money tied to their desired index rates, both companies would be borrowing on the weak side of the market. (See Figure 16-9.)

Figure 16-9
Floating Rates

	AA	BBB+
90-Day US Dollar LIBOR	L	L+80
90-Day Commercial Paper	CP	CP+100

The AA-rated company's strong credit rating saves it only 80 bps if it borrows at a rate tied to the LIBOR rate, while it would save 100 bps if the company borrows at a rate tied to the commercial paper rate. The BBB+ company would be paying a penalty of 100 basis points for its lower credit quality if it borrows tied to the CP rate. However, if the BBB+ company borrowed on the LIBOR side of the market, its penalty would be only 80 basis points.

The answer is for both companies to initially borrow on what for them is the strong side of the market and then enter in a swap to obtain financing tied to the indices they desire. (See Figure 16-10.)

Figure 16-10
Swap Tied to Indices

	AA	BBB+	Difference
3-M Libor	L	L+80	80 bp
3-M CP	CP	CP+100	100 bp
Difference of the Differences			20 bp

In this example, the difference of the differences is 20 basis points. If both parties benefit evenly as a result of the swap, each party should end up with a cost of financing that is 10 basis points lower than what it obtains by borrowing directly on the weak side of the market.

- For the AA-rated borrower, the overall transaction that would result in a total financing cost of L–10 bps is if the company borrows at CP, pays LIBOR flat in the swap, and receives CP+10 in the swap.

- For the BBB+-rated borrower, the overall transaction that would result in a total financing cost of CP+90 bps is if the company borrows at L+80 bps, receives LIBOR flat in the swap, and pays CP+10 bps in the swap. (See Figure 16-11.)

Figure 16-11
Floating Swap

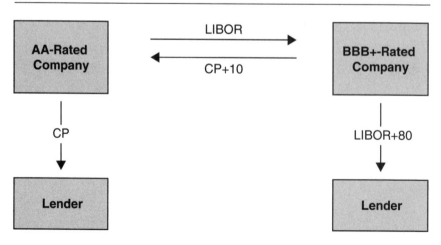

Role of the Dealer

When the swap market first started, it started as an investment banking product. Investment banking firms would match up two customers who entered into a swap contract directly with each other. The banking firm charged a fee for arranging the deal and providing the documentation. This proved to be incredibly inefficient. Banks found it very hard to find two counter parties who wanted to take opposite sides of a swap on the same notional amount on principal at the same time and for the same time frame. For example (See figure 16-11.)

- One company might want to swap on $50,000,000, while the counter party wants to swap $75,000,000.

- One company might want to swap for 18 months, while the counter party wants to swap for 24 months.

- One company may not be willing to sign a contract with a proposed counter party because of moral reasons or because it is concerned about the counter party's credit quality.

To solve these problems, swap dealers started making a market in swaps. By making a market, dealers were able to offer clients immediate executions without the problem of finding a specific counter party for a specific transaction. If, for example, the fair rate to exchange for LIBOR in a 3-year swap is 8% (as determined by the equivalent ED strip), a dealer might make a market as shown in Figure 16-12.

The dealer stands ready to pay 7.95% in exchange for receiving LIBOR in a 3-year swap and to pay LIBOR in exchange for receiving 8.05% in a 3-year swap. Ideally, the dealer would like to attract an equal

Figure 16-12
Dealer Swap Spread

amount of business on both sides of the market. If the dealer executed $1,000,000,000 (notional) of swaps on which it received floating and $1,000,000,000 (notional) of swaps on which it paid floating, the dealer would be hedged and would have revenue of 10 basis points on the billion.

If the dealer attracted more business on one side of the market than it did on the other, it would simply raise or lower rates in order to adjust the amount of business it attracts. The dealer can hedge any temporary mismatches in its swap book (its collection of swap transactions) by using Eurodollar futures and by taking offsetting positions in U.S. Treasuries.

Quoting Swaps

Instead of dealers quoting swaps on an absolute yield basis, the fixed rate that will be exchanged for LIBOR is typically quoted as the spread over a Treasury bond with the same maturity. For example, a dealer might quote a 3-year swap at "45 by 55," meaning that the dealer is willing to:

- Pay a fixed rate equal to the yield on the 3-year T-bond plus 45 bps in exchange for receiving LIBOR.

- Receive a fixed rate equal to the yield on the 3-year T-bond plus 55 bps in exchange for paying LIBOR.

The reason swaps are quoted this way is so that the quote is good for a longer period of time. The Treasury bond yield and swap yield tend to move in tandem over fairly short periods of time.

Credit Risk of Interest Rate Swaps

The credit risk of any investment is the loss the participant may suffer if the other party defaults on its obligations. In an interest rate swap, the credit risk is real, but usually quite manageable and much lower than the transaction's notional value. Consider the $100,000,000 two-year swap in Figure 16-13.

Figure 16-13
Example Swap

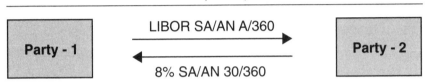

Even though the notional amount of the swap is $100,000,000, the principal is never exchanged. It would make no sense for both parties to pay each other $100,000,000 at the start of the swap. Since there is no initial exchange of principal, there is no re-exchange of principal at the conclusion of the swap. The only credit exposure, therefore, comes from the interest payments on the notional amount.

Suppose, as time passes and as interest rates change, the resulting interest payments on both sides of the swap are as indicated in Figure 16-14.

Figure 16-14
Swap Calculation

Period Number	# Days	Fixed Rate	Fixed Payment	Floating Rate	Floating Payment
1	181	8%	$4,000,000	7.78%	$3,911,611.11
2	184	8%	$4,000,000	8.43%	$4,308,666.67
3	182	8%	$4,000,000	7.93%	$4,009,055.56
4	183	8%	$4,000,000	8.88%	$4,473,333.33

Because both sides of the swap pay interest semi-annually and on the same dates, it would make no sense for both parties to make full interest payments to their counter parties. Instead, in most swaps, the two payments would be netted out and only the net cash flow is exchanged. In the event one party files for bankruptcy, the other is normally relieved of its obligations to pay. Thus, the total credit risk inherent in this $100,000,000 swap is not $100,000,000, not even the interest on the $100,000,000, but just the difference between the two streams of interest payments.

If the two sides of the swap had different payment dates, then the magnitude of the credit risk is larger, because the payments do not offset each other. Although the credit risk of a swap can be substantial, it is always much lower than a loan of equal notional size, because the principal is not at risk.

OPTION CONTRACTS

The last type of derivative instrument to be presented is the option. As the name implies, "options" are different from other derivatives in that they give their owners the choice of whether or not to use them. While options are not that difficult to understand, the option market is replete with jargon, much of which is defined and discussed below.

The definition of an option is "a contract that gives its owner (the long) the right, though not the obligation, to buy (in the case of a call option) or to sell (in the case of a put option) a certain quantity of a certain underlying at a certain price (referred to as the strike price) either during a certain time period (in the case of an American option) or on a certain date (in the case of a European option)." The seller of an option contract (the short) must stand ready to sell (in the case of a call option) or to buy (in the case of a put option) the underlying at the strike price if asked to do so (if the option is "exercised") by the long. (See Figure 17-1.)

As stated in the previous definition, investors who are long either call or put options have the choice of whether or not to use their options and, therefore, will only do so when it is to their benefit. If the party who is long the option insists that the counter party meet its obligation under the terms of the contract, the long is said to have "exercised its option." The short has a "contingent obligation" to either sell (call) or buy (put) if demanded to do so by the long. In exchange for assuming this contingent obligation, the short receives an up-front fee from the long, referred to as the option's price or "premium."

Figure 17-1
Option Basics

	Long	Short
Calls	Right to buy	Contingent obligation to sell
Puts	Right to Sell	Contingent obligation to buy

For example, suppose that today XYZ, Inc., common is selling for $98 per share and that two investors enter into the following transaction:

> Investor-A agrees to pay Investor-B $5 in exchange for the right to buy XYZ, Inc., from Investor-B for $100 anytime during the next six months.

In this example, the option type is a call, the strike price is $100, the premium is $5, the option type is American, and the expiration date is six months.

If, in six months, the price of the stock is:

- $130, then Investor-A will force Investor-B to sell it for $100. After all, who wouldn't want to pay $100 to buy something that could be immediately sold for $130? Investor-A will make a profit of $25 ($130 – $100) minus the initial premium paid. Investor-B will lose the same $25.

- $105, then Investor-A will force Investor-B to sell it for $100. While Investor-A will not make a profit, at least it will recoup the premium it paid to buy the option ($105 – $100) minus the initial premium paid. Investor-B is also flat.

- $90, then Investor-A will simply let the option expire. After all, why would Investor-A want to buy the stock from Investor-B for $100 when it can be purchased in the open market for $90? Investor-B gets to keep the $5 premium.

In, At, and Out of the Money Options

Options that would be valuable if they were exercised immediately are said to be "in the money." For example, a call option that allowed an investor to buy a stock for $30 when the stock was selling in the open market for $40 would be in the money. If the option was exercised, the long could buy the stock for $30 and immediately resell it for $40 for a $10 per share profit. If the market price of the stock was $25, a call option with a strike price of $30 would be out of the money, because exercising the option would make no sense. After all, why would anyone use an option to buy the stock at $30 when they could buy it for $25 in the open market? (See Figure 17-2.)

Likewise, a put option with a strike price of $50 would be in the money if the stock's market value was $40, and out of the money if the stock's market value was $60. Why would a long use an option to sell a stock at $50 when the same stock could be sold for $60 in the open market?

If the option's strike price and the market value of the underlying are either the same or very close, the option is said to be at the money.

Figure 17-2
Strike vs. Market

	In the Money	At the Money	Out of the Money
Calls	Strike < Market	Strike = Market	Strike > Market
Puts	Strike > Market	Strike = Market	Strike < Market

Option Premium

An option's premium is divided into two portions: the intrinsic value and the time value.

Premium = Intrinsic Value + Time Value

The "intrinsic value" is the portion of the premium that can be immediately realized by exercising the option. Any premium above the intrinsic value is referred to as "time value." Consider the following examples:

- A call option with a strike price of $40 is selling for $9 when the market value of the underlying is $45. In this case, the intrinsic value is $5 and the time value is $4. The intrinsic value is $5 since the option can be used to buy the stock worth $45 for only $40. The time value is $4 because $9 − $5 = $4.

- A call option with a strike price of $50 is selling for $2 when the market value of the underlying is $45. In this case, the intrinsic value is $0, so the entire premium is time value.

- A put option with a strike price of $100 is selling for $12 when the price of the stock is $96. In this case, the intrinsic value is $4 because the option enables stock that can be purchased for $96 to be sold for $100. The time value is $8.

Option Markets

Options trade in two different markets: the listed market and the over-the-counter market. Option Clearing Corporation (OCC) issued standardized options can only trade on a registered securities exchange.

As with any exchange traded transaction:

- The counter parties to the transactions are anonymous and transact business through brokers.

- The brokers who are members of the exchange assume the credit risk for their clients, and the exchange assumes the credit risk of the brokers. The options are issued and guaranteed by the options clearing corporation.

- The contracts are public with immediate and widespread price dissemination.

- The contract terms are established by the exchange and are non-negotiable. The contracts are offered with a limited number of strike prices and expiration dates.

- The contracts are less liquid than futures contracts. The lower liquidity is a result of both lower trading volume on each underlying and the fact that trading volume is distributed across a number of different option contracts with different strike prices and expiration dates. A ready market may not always be available.

- Parties that go long option contracts are required to pay the premium in full and in cash. Parties that go short options are required to deposit substantial margin balances with their brokers in order to cover their potential loses.

Unlike listed futures contracts, however, listed options are not traded in a pit by open outcry. Instead, they are sometimes traded by a "specialist" in a manner very similar to the way in which listed stocks are traded on the NYSE or via designated primary market makers. (See figure 17-3.)

Listed option contracts exist for the following types of underlying instruments:

- Stocks.
- Stock Indices.
- Futures Contracts.
- Commodities.
- Currencies.

Over-the-Counter Options

Over-the-counter (OTC) options are private contracts between two parties, usually an option's dealer and a client. Over-the-counter options offer the advantage of being highly customizable. As such, the contract terms can be set to meet the specific needs of specific clients.

Figure 17-3

Options Listing. Reprinted from The Wall Street Journal.

MOST ACTIVE CONTRACTS

Option/Strike			Vol	Exch	Last	Net Chg	a-Close	Open Int
Mc Don	Jul	30	p 22,400	XC	1/8	− 7/16	31 13/16	91,096
Mc Don	Aug	30	p 16,865	XC	3/4	− 3/16	31 13/16	1,980
EricTel	Jul	20	p 13,791	XC	1 1/8	+ 3/8	19 7/8	26,445
Micsft	Jul	80	12,293	XC	1 15/16	− 11/16	78 1/2	215,980
Cisco	Jul	55	11,469	XC	7 7/8	− 2 3/8	61 7/8	152,192
Terdyn	Jul	85	11,463	XC	1 3/4	− 1 1/4	73 1/8	35,112
EricTel	Aug	20	p 11,275	XC	1 1/2	+ 1/4	19 7/8	28,524
GenMotH	Sep	43 3/8	p 9,675	XC	14 3/8	...	28 13/16	26,850
QwestCom	Jul	50	9,071	XC	8 1/4	+ 4 3/8	56 3/4	149,868
I B M	Jul	115	9,006	XC	1	− 1 1/8	104	69,648
QwestCom	Jul	55	7,948	XC	3 1/2	+ 1 3/4	56 3/4	127,344
Oracle	Jul	85	7,725	XC	1/2	− 1 3/16	72 3/8	76,048
GenMotH	Sep	43 3/8	7,705	XC	7/16	...	28 13/16	28,350
QLT	Sep	60	p 7,585	XC	4 3/4	+ 3/4	68 7/8	292
QLT	Sep	45	p 7,580	XC	1	− 1/2	68 7/8	202
Oracle	Jul	80	7,064	XC	1 1/8	− 2 3/4	72 3/8	48,732
Palm	Aug	50	7,025	XC	1/2	+ 1/8	32 7/16	100,228
Cisco	Jul	65	6,951	XC	1 1/4	− 1	61 7/8	154,904
NortelNwk	Jul	70	p 5,664	XC	2 7/16	+ 11/16	70 11/16	9,288
Palm	Aug	50	p 5,619	XC	19 3/4	− 1/4	32 7/16	110,072

Option/Strike			Vol	Exch	Last	Net Chg	a-Close	Open Int
Xerox	Jan 02	20	5,513	XC	5 1/2	− 3/8	20 1/4	22,20
USWest	Jul	95	5,380	XC	7 3/4	+ 5 1/2		..
I B M	Jul	100	p 5,123	XC	2 9/16	+ 1 9/16	104	42,83
DellCptr	Aug	35	p 5,103	XC	3/16	...	47 7/16	21,53
DellCptr	Aug	45	p 5,100	XC	2 1/16	+ 1/2	47 7/16	54,29
DellCptr	Aug	50	p 5,054	XC	4 1/2	+ 1	47 7/16	17,84
I B M	Jul	105	4,968	XC	4	− 3 1/4	104	21,84
Cisco	Aug	65	4,676	XC	3 1/4	− 1 1/2	61 7/8	40,42
Cisco	Aug	60	4,668	XC	6 1/8	− 1 5/8	61 7/8	4,22
AT&T	Jul	35	p 4,405	XC	2 1/8	− 7/8	33 1/2	108,75
AmOnline	Jul	55	4,339	XC	2 1/8	+ 3/8	55	251,43
Micsft	Jul	85	p 4,187	XC	6 3/8	+ 5/8	78 1/2	55,61
Intel	Jul	140	4,139	XC	1 7/8	− 1 5/8	131 5/8	94,13
TelMex	Jul	60	4,086	XC	4 7/8	+ 1/4	63 7/8	59,20
Oracle	Jul	80	p 4,019	XC	8 1/2	+ 5 1/4	72 3/8	35,98
Oracle	Jul	70	4,018	XC	5 1/4	− 5 5/8	72 3/8	40,86
DelhaizeA	Oct	17 1/2	p 4,006	AM	1 7/16	...	17 5/16	2,17
NortelNwk	Sep	62 1/2	p 4,004	XC	3	− 7/8	70 11/16	3,70
Sap AG	Jul	55	p 4,000	XC	7 7/8	− 1/2	46 5/16	5,82
Nasd100Tr	Sep	67 1/2	p 3,852	AM	15/16	− 1/8	91 3/8	1,30

Complete equity option listings and data are available in the online Journal at **WSJ.com.**

Option/Strike		Exp.	Call Vol.	Call Last	Put Vol.	Put Last
ADC Tel	75	Jul	331	6 1/8	78	2 3/4
77 9/16	80	Jul	215	3 1/2	792	5 1/8
77 9/16	85	Jul	582	1 13/16	44	8 3/8
77 9/16	90	Jul	481	7/8	10	9 1/2
A M R	25	Jul	1027	3 7/8	10	5/16
28 3/8	30	Jul	306	1	10	2 1/8
ASM Litho	45	Jul	300	3/8	...	...
ATT Wrls	30	Aug	40	11/16	800	4
AT&T	30	Jul	1019	3 1/2	405	3/16
33 1/2	30	Aug	370	4 3/8	306	3/4
33 1/2	35	Jul	2358	5/8	4405	2 1/8
33 1/2	35	Aug	2332	1 9/16	59	3
33 1/2	40	Jul	913	1/8	567	6 7/8
33 1/2	40	Aug	482	7/16	40	6 3/4
Abbt L	40	Aug	264	5 3/8	2	9/16
44 9/16	45	Aug	506	2	5	2 5/16
Adelph	50	Jul	760	1 3/16	...	...
AdvFibCm	45	Jul	357	3 3/8	21	5 1/4
42 15/16	55	Jul	576	7/8	...	...
A M D	60	Jul	313	16 1/8	66	1 1/4
74 1/2	65	Aug	6	14	328	5 3/8
74 1/2	70	Jul	844	7 3/4	319	4 1/8
74 1/2	70	Aug	562	11 3/4	278	7 1/2
74 1/2	70	Oct	320	16 3/8	139	10 1/2
74 1/2	75	Jul	1481	6 1/2	885	6 1/2
74 1/2	75	Aug	566	9 3/4	73	8 5/8
74 1/2	75	Oct	390	14 1/4	297	12 5/8
74 1/2	80	Jul	2817	4 1/4	2198	10
74 1/2	80	Aug	1128	7 3/4	8	12 5/8
74 1/2	85	Jul	1313	3	5	11 1/2
74 1/2	85	Aug	335	6 1/8	5	14 3/4
74 1/2	90	Jul	2567	1 13/16	35	15 3/8
74 1/2	90	Aug	1173	4 7/8	20	18
74 1/2	90	Jan	598	13 1/2	10	26 1/8
74 1/2	95	Jul	850	1 3/8	...	...
74 1/2	100	Aug	304	2 1/2	...	...
74 1/2	105	Jan	536	9 5/8	...	...
74 1/2	110	Jul	493	7/16	...	...
74 1/2	115	Jul	306	3/16	...	...
Aetna	65	Jul	630	3	50	2 1/8
65 5/16	70	Jul	971	1 1/4	...	...
65 5/16	75	Jul	914	5/8	...	...
Alcatl	55	Sep	...	...	310	1 3/8
66 1/8	60	Sep	6	9 1/2	316	2 5/8
66 1/8	65	Jul	211	3 1/4	758	1 5/8
66 1/8	65	Aug	7	5	1000	3 5/8
Altera	100	Jul	341	3 5/8	22	8 5/8
92 7/16	105	Jul	833	2	20	10 7/8
Amazon	40	Jan	279	8 1/2	23	10 3/4
36 1/2	45	Oct	345	4 3/8	...	...
36 1/2	60	Jul	42	1/8	2015	21 3/4
36 1/2	65	Jul	1	1/8	2000	26 3/4
36 1/2	120	Jan	...	...	400	83 1/2
AmOnline	45	Jul	83	10	542	1/8

Option/Strike		Exp.	Call Vol.	Call Last	Put Vol.	Put Last
45 1/8	50	Aug	310	1 15/16	100	5 3/4
Analog	75	Jul	401	3 1/8	51	7 1/2
70 7/16	80	Jul	1041	2 1/8	14	10
answthink	17 1/2	Oct	...	...	850	4 1/4
15 5/8	20	Jul	3	5/16	500	4 1/2
15 5/8	22 1/2	Jul	...	...	300	6 7/8
Apache	60	Jul	17	1	477	5 3/4
AppleC	42 1/2	Jan	300	17 1/4	5	4 7/8
51 5/8	45	Jan	271	15 7/8	...	...
51 5/8	50	Jul	334	4 3/8	275	2 7/16
51 5/8	55	Jul	358	2	12	4 5/8
51 5/8	55	Aug	322	3 7/8	...	...
51 5/8	60	Jul	664	7/8	12	8 3/4
ApiMat o	75	Jul	330	10 3/8	558	1 5/8
83 7/16	77 1/2	Jul	10	8 1/8	380	2 3/16
83 7/16	80	Jul	336	6 1/2	740	3
83 7/16	80	Aug	105	9 3/4	272	6
83 7/16	80	Oct	138	13 3/4	1022	9 1/2
83 7/16	85	Jul	838	4	240	5 1/2
83 7/16	85	Aug	271	7 1/2	659	8 3/8
83 7/16	87 1/2	Jul	307	2 7/8	270	7
83 7/16	90	Jul	1451	2 1/8	236	8 1/2
83 7/16	90	Aug	343	5 3/8	20	11 1/4
83 7/16	90	Jan	261	14 3/4	...	...
83 7/16	92 1/2	Jul	275	1 1/2	46	9 1/2
83 7/16	95	Jul	1405	1 1/16	32	11 7/8
83 7/16	97 1/2	Jul	358	3/4	...	...
83 7/16	100	Jul	1584	1/2	10	16 5/8
Ariba	75	Jul	7	23 5/8	311	9/16
97 1/4	100	Jul	312	5	58	7 1/8
97 1/4	150	Aug	404	1 1/8	...	...
AstraA	70	Jul	503	4 1/4	101	3 7/8
...	80	Jul	262	1 1/8	51	9 1/8
...	85	Jul	371	1/2	...	...
...	90	Jul	30	1/2	500	19 1/4
AtHome	20	Jul	339	15/16	72	1 7/16
19 3/16	25	Oct	271	1 15/16	9	7
19 3/16	40	Jul	8	1/16	1000	21
19 3/16	55	Jul	...	...	1000	36
Atmel	35	Jul	192	3	376	3 1/8
34 1/2	40	Jul	933	1 1/4	23	5 3/4
34 1/2	45	Jul	405	9/16	10	9 5/8
BCE g	25	Aug	275	1 1/16	...	...
BEA Sys	50	Jul	436	1 1/4	40	4
BJ Svc	65	Jul	9	1 1/4	2030	7
59 3/4	75	Jul	5	1/4	1500	15 3/4
59 3/4	75	Aug	2500	1 1/8	...	...
BMC Sft	30	Aug	1321	9/16	39	8 5/8
21 5/16	30	Nov	1214	2	389	9 5/8
21 5/16	35	Aug	223	1/4	552	13 5/8
21 5/16	40	Nov	1097	13/16	...	...
BP Amoco	55	Jul	557	1 3/16	70	1 3/4
53 7/8	55	Oct	676	3 3/8	25	3 1/2
53 7/8	60	Jul	285	3/16	...	...

Option/Strike		Exp.	Call Vol.	Call Last	Put Vol.	Put Last
54 9/16	55	Aug	627	7 1/4	10	5 7/
54 9/16	60	Jul	695	1 15/16	31	5 9/
54 9/16	65	Jul	289	3/4	1	11 1/
BrdbsSft	35	Jul	5	1 3/8	300	5 1/
Broadcom	155	Jul	3	65 1/2	290	1/
221 11/16	160	Jul	10	62	420	7/
221 11/16	215	Nov	...	...	316	3 1/
221 11/16	230	Jul	415	11 3/8	62	20
221 11/16	240	Jul	597	7	12	27
221 11/16	250	Jul	989	5	...	...
BrcdeCo	170	Jul	21	12 3/4	553	3 1/
178 15/16	180	Jul	404	6	116	9 1/
178 15/16	180	Aug	372	14	2	18
BurlRs	37 1/2	Aug	...	...	365	3 1/
CMGI Inc	50	Jul	267	1 7/16	30	6 1/
44 3/8	50	Aug	519	3 1/4	24	8 3/
44 3/8	55	Jul	380	1/2	...	...
44 3/8	55	Sep	387	3 7/8	2	12 1/
CblWre	60	Jul	421	1 15/16	...	...
55 9/16	65	Aug	514	1 7/8	...	...
Cabltrn	25	Jul	493	1 1/8	18	1 1/
24 1/4	25	Aug	18	2 3/4	332	2 5/
24 1/4	27 1/2	Jul	427	1/4	...	...
CapRck	17 1/2	Jul	...	...	1000	2
Carnvl	25	Jan	414	1 1/16	2	6
19 3/4	30	Oct	400	1/4	...	...
Casella	15	Dec	265	1 1/16	...	...
Caterp	35	Nov	4	3 1/4	335	3
Celgene	55	Jul	50	4 1/4	300	2 1/
CellPath	25	Jul	379	2	13	2 1/1
24 11/16	30	Jul	714	9/16	...	...
Cendant	12 1/2	Jul	412	2 1/8	50	3/1
ChaseM	45	Aug	13	5 3/4	536	1 5/
47 3/4	50	Jul	347	13/16	192	3 1/8
CienaCp	160	Jul	294	13 1/8	137	8 3/8
164 13/16	170	Jul	306	8 1/8	196	14
164 13/16	175	Jul	306	5 1/2	23	12
164 13/16	180	Jul	270	3 7/8	...	...
Cisco	55	Jul	11469	7 7/8	258	5/8
61 7/8	60	Jul	1068	3 7/8	1244	1 11/16
61 7/8	60	Aug	4668	6 1/8	836	3 1/4
61 7/8	60	Jan	47	11 5/8	429	7 1/8
61 7/8	62 1/2	Jul	837	2 1/8	457	2 11/16
61 7/8	65	Jul	6951	1 1/4	904	3 3/4
61 7/8	65	Aug	4676	3 1/4	180	5 7/8
61 7/8	67 1/2	Jul	525	9/16	10	4 1/4
61 7/8	70	Jul	1605	3/8	221	7 5/8
61 7/8	70	Aug	860	1 5/8	30	8 3/8
61 7/8	70	Oct	313	3 5/8	20	9 1/2
61 7/8	75	Jul	296	1/8	38	12 7/8
61 7/8	75	Oct	995	2 5/16	4	14
Citigrp	60	Jul	427	3 3/4	85	11/16
63 1/4	65	Jul	729	1 1/4	17	2 7/16
63 1/4	65	Aug	1442	2 7/16	8	3 7/8

One of the reasons clients need OTC options is that they want an option whose size and/or expiration date doesn't align with the schedule of strike prices and/or expiration dates available in the listed market. For example, suppose a U.S. client, who is negotiating a contract with a U.K. supplier, needs an option to buy £1,234,666 at a price of $1.3447 per pound for 43 days. This option can only be "approximated" with combining listed options, while it can be created exactly with an OTC option.

Another reason clients need OTC options is to deal with underlying instruments for which there are no listed options. For example, a central bank that has as part of its gold reserves bars that are only 90% gold will need to use the OTC market, since these bars cannot be delivered in fulfillment of short positions in the listed market. Good delivery in the listed market is bars with 99.99% gold content.

OTC option dealers enter into thousands of OTC contracts with different customers. In some of the contracts, the clients are the buyers. In others, the clients are the sellers. Thus, some of the risk the dealer assumes by entering into these contracts is offset by being "on both sides of the market"—albeit with different customers. The dealer's

Figure 17-4
Summary Comparison of Derivatives

	Forward Contracts	Futures Contracts	Swap Contracts	Listed Options	OTC Options
	COMPARISON OF DERIVATIVE CONTRACTS				
Counter party	Known	Anonymous	Known	Anonymous	Known
Credit Risk	Yes	No	Yes	No	Yes
Public/Private	Private	Public	Private	Public	Private
Customized	Yes	No	Yes	No	Yes
Marked Market	No	Yes	No	No	No
Liquidity	No	Yes	No	Yes	No
Transparency	No	Yes	No	Yes	No
Choice	No	No	No	Yes	Yes

remaining net risk exposure, if any, is hedged by using other derivatives, including forwards, futures, swaps, and listed options.

Option Pricing

One of the first questions many investors ask when they first become familiar with options is, "How can options be priced?" If a stock is currently selling for $70, how is it possible to determine what "the right to buy the stock at $80 anytime over the next six months" should be worth? The answer is not immediately apparent.

Other derivative instruments, such as forwards, futures, and swaps, are all priced "quantitatively" by determining the price at which there would be no possibility for arbitrage between the cash market instrument and the derivative. Ideally, options should be priced the same way. The question is, "Does the same type of arbitrage relationship exist between options and the underlying instruments?" The somewhat surprising answer is "yes." The price of options can be calculated by a quantitative approach that determines what price the option would have to be selling for in order to eliminate the possibility of arbitrage.

To illustrate this quantitative approach, consider first how lottery tickets are priced in a fair lottery. Suppose a lottery ticket offers a one in a million chance of winning $1,000,000, and that the winning lottery ticket is chosen immediately. What would this ticket be worth? The answer obviously is $1. A dollar has the same economic value as a "one in a million" chance of having $1,000,000. Likewise, a lottery ticket that offers a one in a 100,000 chance of winning $1,000,000 would be worth $10—again, assuming the winning ticket is chosen immediately.

Suppose in these two examples that instead of the winning ticket being chosen immediately, the winning ticket wasn't picked for a year. In this case, the value of the two lottery tickets wouldn't be $1 and $10, respectively. Instead, their true values would be the present values of $1 and $10, respectively. (The present value of $1 and $10 is equal $1 and $10 discounted for a year at the prevailing 1-year rate.) The price of the lottery tickets have to be present valued or the possibility of a risk-free profit is created. Consider the following example.

Today, an entrepreneur sells one million lottery tickets for $1 each. Under the terms of the lottery, the winning ticket will be picked in a year and the winner will receive $1,000,000. In this case, the entrepreneur can invest the $1,000,000 raised from selling the tickets today, earn a year's worth of interest, pay off the winner, and keep the year's worth of interest as a risk-free profit. Therefore, in a fair lottery, if there is a substantial time difference between when the tickets are sold and the winner is picked, the ticket price has to be present valued.

In general form, the value of a lottery ticket in a fair lottery is equal to:

Lottery Ticket = PV (Probability of Winning × Size of the Prize)

An option is also priced based on probability theory, so its value is also equal to:

Option Value = PV (Probability of Winning × Size of the Prize)

In the case of an option, the:

- Probability of "winning" is equal to the probability that the option will be "in the money" on the day the option expires.
- Size of the prize is equal to the difference between the exercise price and the value of the underlying on the day an option expires.

Thus, if the probability of the option being in the money and the difference between the expiration price and market value can be estimated, so can the value of the option. Therefore, in order to value an option, a way needs to be found to estimate these two values.

Fortunately, it is possible to estimate these values, provided the following information is known:

- The price of the underlying instrument today.
- The risk-free interest rate.

• The historic price volatility of the underlying's price, as measured by the standard deviation of its historic returns.

Given this information, it is possible to create a probability distribution of the underlying's possible prices at some point in the future. (The mathematics required to do this are beyond the scope of this text, but can be found in any book on option pricing models. This text will limit its discussion of option pricing to a "conceptual" approach.)

For example, suppose a stock is currently selling for $100. As time passes, the stock's price will change and its price will either rise or fall. The greater the volatility of the stock's price, the greater the possible price change over a given time change. For example, Figures 17-5 and 17-6 compare the future price distributions of two $100 stocks over the same one-year time frame. The first stock has a 10% historic volatility, while the second stock has a 40% historic volatility. (Both assume a 5% risk-free interest rate.)

Figure 17-5 shows the future price distribution of a low-volatility and a high volatily stock. Note that for the high-volatility stock, there is

Figure 17-5
Low vs. High Probability

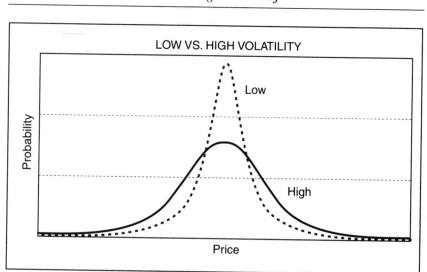

a much greater probability of a relatively large gain and large loss. It is these distributions that are used to price options.

Consider 1-year call options with $100 strike prices on both stocks. These call options will be in the money if, in one year, the value of the stocks is above $120. For both options, the probability of the stock's price being greater than $120 in one year is equal to the percentage of the area under the curve that is above the $120 strike price relative to the total area under the curve.

In this example, the probability of the:

- Low-volatility stock being above $120 in one year is 15%.
- High-volatility stock being above $120 in one year is 30%.

This answers the first question that needs to be answered in order to value the options, namely, "What is the probability that the option will be a winner?"

Figure 17-6
Low Vs. High Volatility

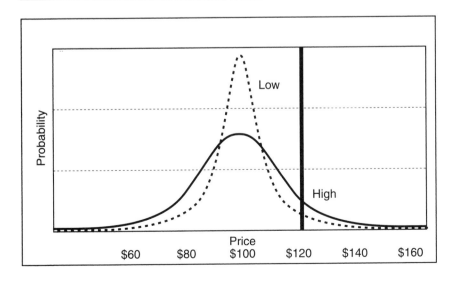

Of course, the second question, "What will the stock be worth when the option expires?" cannot be known exactly. At least, not without a call to a psychic hot line. What can be calculated is the weighted average of all of the prices higher than $120. There is some probability that the stock will be $120, some probability it will be $121, some probability it will be $122, and so on. By calculating the weighted average of these prices, it is possible to calculate what the average win will be—assuming the option is a winner. Sometimes the investor will win more, sometimes less, but since it's impossible to know how large the win will be today, the option valuation has to be based on the average win.

In this example, the weighted average of all the prices higher than $120 is:

- $130 for the low-volatility stock.
- $150 for the high-volatility stock.

Thus, if an investor buys the option on the low-volatility stock, the investor has a 15% chance of "winning," on average, $10 ($130 − $120). However, if an investor buys the option on the high-volatility stock, the investor has a 30% chance of "winning," on average, $30 ($150 − $120).

This means that the value of the options, when valued as lottery tickets, would be:

Option Value = PV(Probability of Winning × Size of the Prize)
Option Value for Option on the Low-Volatility Stock = PV(.15 × $10)
Present Value of $1.50 = $1.50 / (1+r) = $1.50 / (1 + .1) = $1.36
Option Value for Option on the High-Volatility Stock = PV(.30 × $30)
Present Value of $9 = $9 / (1+r) = $9 / (1 + .1) = $8.18

If an investor paid these prices for these options, then the investor would not, on average, do better or worse than if the investor simply bought the underlying stocks directly.

This has to be the case. If buying the options generated a higher return than buying the underlying, investors would short the underlying and invest the sales proceeds in options. If owning the underlying generated a higher return, investors would sell the options and invest in the underlying. The two alternatives must offer the same return in order to avoid the probability of this type of riskless arbitrage. Today, there are numerous publicly available software packages that price options on various types of underlying instruments.

Option Sensitivities

The option sensitivities measure how much the value of an option changes in response to a change in one of the variables that determines an option's price—assuming all of the other variables remain constant. From the previous discussion on pricing, it is obvious that three of the major variables that determine an option's value are the time until the option matures, the volatility of the stock, and the value of the stock. Other variables such as interest rates also impact option values.

The sensitivity that measures how the value of the option changes in response to the passage of time is referred to as an option's theta. As time passes, the probability distribution becomes steeper and narrower. As a result, as time passes, the probability of a large price change declines, and with it, the value of an option. (See Figure 17-7.)

Figure 17-7
Long Vs. Short Time Frame Distribution

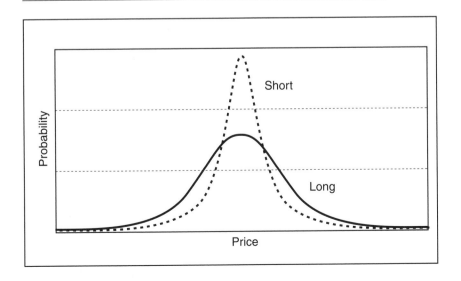

Note that the passage of time becomes more significant as the option's remaining life gets shorter. The passage of one day's time is not very significant for an option with six months until expiration. It is significant for an option with five days until expiration. Figure 17-8 illustrates the value of an at the money option as time passes. It shows that the option's value declines in an ever-increasing manner as the life of the option gets shorter.

The option sensitivity that measures how the price of the option changes in response to a change in the underlying's price volatility changes is vega. As volatility rises, the probability distribution becomes wider and the value of the option rises—all other factors being equal.

The sensitivity that measures how the value of an option will change in response to a change in the value of the underlying is referred to as an option's delta (also called the *hedge ratio*). Simply put, the delta of an option is the amount by which the call will increase or decrease in price if the underlying stock moves by one point. Consider the proba-

Figure 17-8
Effect of Time on Option Price

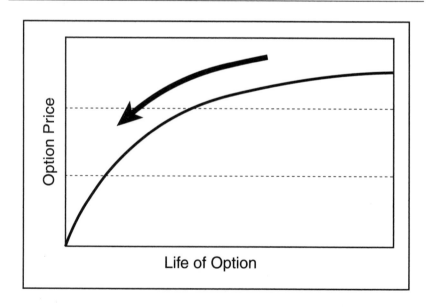

bility distribution and a call option with a strike price of $110. The probability of this option being in the money when the option expires is 40%. If there is a 40% probability of this option being in the money when it expires, then if the price of the underlying rises by $1, there is a 40% chance that the owner of the option will receive that $1. A 40% chance of having $1 is, of course, worth $.40.

Thus, if the price of the underlying moves up or down by $1, the price of this option changes by $.40. The ratio of how the price of an option changes in response to a change in the value of the underlying is very important when using options to hedge a cash market position.

A copy of the option disclosure document can be obtained by calling your local Prudential Securities Office or the options strategy desk at (212) 778-1000.

EXOTIC OPTIONS

$\mathbf{E}$xotic options are options with unusual strike price or pay-off features. These highly customized options are usually created by the over-the-counter desks of major derivatives dealers in order to help their clients solve some very specific types of business problems. Exotic options are becoming quite common and are the fastest-growing segment of the options market. There are numerous types of exotic options in existence today and new ones are being created all the time. This chapter discusses several types of exotic options and how they are used to solve specific business problems.

Look-back Options

Look-back options are options that grant their owners the right to buy or sell the underlying at the most attractive price at which it actually trades in the cash market over a specified time horizon. This time horizon is usually the same time frame as the option's life. For look-back options, the value at expiration is:
- Look-back call = Max [0, Price at Expiration − Minimum Price at Which the Underlying Trades Over the Specified Horizon]
- Look-back put = Max [0, Maximum Price at Which the Underlying Trades Over the Specified Horizon − Price at Expiration]

Since look-back options allow their owners to buy or sell at the most attractive price at which the underlying actually trades in the cash market over a specified time horizon, the strike prices of these options can, and do, change. When a look-back option is first created, the strike price equals the then-current market value. As the price of the underlying changes, the strike price is reset to whatever the lowest value is at which the underlying trades in the case of a call and whatever the highest value is at which the underlying trades in the case of a put.

Figures 18-1 through 18-3 illustrate how the strike price of both a look-back call and a look-back put change as the price of the underlying instrument changes. The examples also illustrate the option's value.

Figure 18-1
Affect of Price on Strike Price of Look-backs

Price of Underlying	$100	$110	$120	$110	$100	$90	$80	$70	$80
Strike Price of Call	$100	$100	$100	$100	$100	$90	$80	$70	$70
Strike Price of Put	$100	$110	$120	$120	$120	$120	$120	$120	$120

- The value of a look-back call = expiration price ($80) – minimum price ($70) = $10
- The value of a look-back put = maximum price ($120) – expiration price ($80) = $40

Figure 18-2
Affect of Price on Strike Price of Look-backs

Price of Underlying	$100	$90	$80	$70	$60	$50	$60	$70	$80
Strike Price of Call	$100	$90	$80	$70	$60	$50	$50	$50	$50
Strike Price of Put	$100	$100	$100	$100	$100	$100	$100	$100	$100

- The value of a look-back call = expiration price ($80) – minimum price ($50) = $30
- The value of a look-back put = maximum price ($100) – expiration price ($80) = $20

Note that in these two examples, even though the price of the underlying at expiration was the same, the look-back calls and puts had different values because of the price path the underlying instrument followed.

Figure 18-3
Affect of Price on Strike Price of Look-backs

Price of Underlying	$100	$90	$90	$80	$80	$70	$70	$60	$60
Strike Price of Call	$100	$90	$90	$80	$80	$70	$70	$60	$60
Strike Price of Put	$100	$100	$100	$100	$100	$100	$100	$100	$100

- The value of a look-back call = expiration price ($60) − minimum price ($60) = $0

- The value of a look-back put = maximum price ($100) − expiration price ($60) = $40

Look-backs are also called "reset options," because the strike price is constantly reset to the most attractive strike over a time horizon. By their very nature, look-backs are always either at the money or in the money.

The primary business application of look-back options is to allow portfolio managers to smooth out their results. In years when they have sharply outperformed their index, they buy look-back calls and puts that expire the next year. By doing so they take some of the return from the current year and use it to stack the deck in their favor for the following year. Of course, to take advantage of look-backs, portfolio managers must be authorized to take naked option positions.

Binaries (AKA Digitals)

Binary options are options that have a fixed payoff if the option ends up being in the money at expiration, regardless of how little or how far it is in the money at expiration. Consider the following example.

Suppose a binary option is written that pays $1,000,000 if the price of XYZ, Inc.'s, stock is above $80 per share in one year's time. It does not matter if the stock is at 80 1/8th or $165 when the option expires, the payoff is still $1,000,000. The value of a binary option is simply the payoff times the probability that the option will be in the money at expiration, discounted back to today.

$$\text{Value} = \frac{\text{Payoff} \times \text{Probability the Option Will Be in the Money at Expiration}}{\text{Discount Factor}}$$

If the previous option expired in a year, had a 10-percent probability of being in the money at expiration, and market interest rates were 8 percent, the option's value would be:

$$\text{Value} = \frac{\$1,000,000 \times .10}{108} = \$92,593$$

Binary options have several business applications. Consider a company that has an executive bonus program that awards its senior management $4,000,000 if the stock rises by 40 percent over the next three years. The company could hedge the cost of its compensation program by buying a binary option with a $4,000,000 payoff. For this option, the payoff will either be $4,000,000—if the option ends up being in the money—or $0 if the option does not.

Binary options come in a number of varieties. Some of the more common ones include:

- Cash or nothing binaries—Payoff is either a fixed sum or nothing (as previously described).
- Asset or nothing binaries—Payoff is fixed number of shares or a fixed face value of bonds instead of a fixed sum of cash. The big difference is that the market value of the shares or bonds can fluctuate between the day the option is created and the option expires.
- Range binaries—Pays off either a fixed sum or a fixed number of shares if the underlying is between two values upon expiration.

The most common business application of binaries is to allow portfolio managers to buy insurance policies when they underweight an asset class in their portfolio. For example, a portfolio manager might elect to underweight blue chip stocks in his or her portfolio, betting that blue chips will underperform. However, just in case the manager is wrong, he or she might also buy a binary call on the S&P 500 or DJIA that offers a high payoff if these market sectors soar.

Bermuda Options

Bermuda options are a hybrid between an American and a European option. Unlike American options, which can be exercised anytime, and European options, which can be exercised only upon expiration, Bermuda options can be exercised prior to maturity, but only on certain dates. The most common application of Bermuda options is to hedge the embedded call options found in bonds. Since callable bonds can normally only be called on certain days, investors who own them only need to hedge the call risk on those specific call dates—not every day.

Barrier Options

Barrier options are options that are either activated or deactivated when the price of the underlying passes through some predefined value referred to as the barrier. Barrier options come in eight different varieties:

1. Up and in call—A call option that is activated if the price of the underlying rises above a certain price level.

2. Up and out call—A call option that is deactivated if the price of the underlying rises above a certain price level.

3. Down and in call—A call option that is activated if the price of the underlying falls below a certain price level.

4. Down and out call—A call option that is deactivated if the price of the underlying falls below a certain price level.

5. Up and in put—A put option that is activated if the price of the underlying rises above a certain price level.

6. Up and out put—A put option that is deactivated if the price of the underlying rises above a certain price level.

7. Down and in put—A put option that is activated if the price of the underlying falls below a certain price level.

8. Down and out put—A put option that is deactivated if the price of the underlying falls below a certain price level.

Like look-back options, the value of these options is dependent both upon the value of the underlying at expiration and the path that the underlying takes prior to expiration. Therefore they are "path dependent" options.

Consider the following examples that illustrate how the barriers are used to activate and deactivate the options.

Example 1—Consider how the following price path affects the value of a "down and in call"—a strike price of $100 and an "in price" of $85. Because the price of the underlying fell below $85, the option was activated and would have a $20 value at expiration. (See Figure 18-4.)

Figure 18-4
Price Path Over Time

								$180
							$170	
						$160		$160
					$150		$150	
				$140		$140		$140
			$130		$130		$130	
		$120		$120		$120		$120
	$110		$110		$110		$110	
$100		$100		$100		$100		$100
	$90		$90		$90		$90	
		$80		$80		$80		$80
			$70		$70		$70	
				$60		$60		$60
					$50		$50	
						$40		$40
							$30	
								$20

Example 2—A down and in call with a strike price of $100 and an in price of $80. This option would be worthless even though it is in the money because the underlying never went through the barrier. (See Figure 18-5.)

Example 3—A down and in call with a strike price of $120 and an in price of $90. This option would also expire worthless. Even though the option is activated, it is not in the money at expiration. (See Figure 18-6.)

Figure 18-5
Price Path Over Time

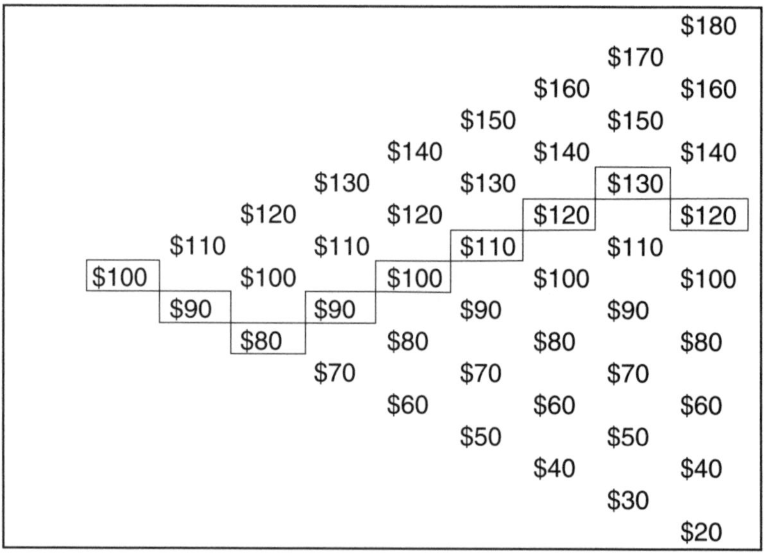

A common business application of barriers is to allow portfolio managers who are prohibited from having naked option positions to do covered writing. Consider the following example.

A portfolio manager likes a stock that is currently selling for $100 a share. The manager buys the stock and sets a long-term goal of $150 a share with a stop loss at $90. To increase the current income from the portfolio, the manager sells a short-term down and out call with a strike price of $110 and an out price of $90. If the stock:

Figure 18-6
Price Path Over Time

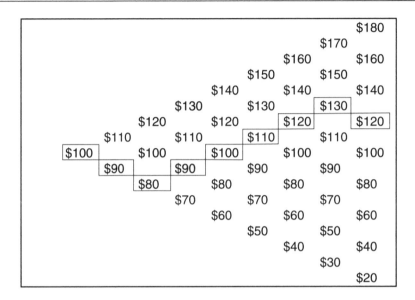

- Goes above $110, the down and out call will be exercised and the stock will be called away.

- Stays between $110 and $90, the option will be neither exercised nor canceled. Eventually it will expire.

- Declines below $90, the manager will sell the stock and the option will automatically be canceled so that the manager is not left with a naked option position.

Restrikes

A restrike option is an option whose strike price changes if the price of the underlying passes through a barrier price. These options are typically written so that the strike price of calls is lowered and the strike price of puts is raised. An example would be a call option with an initial strike price of $100 that would drop to $70 if the price of the underlying drops below $80. Consider Figure 18-7.

Figure 18-7
Price Path Over Time

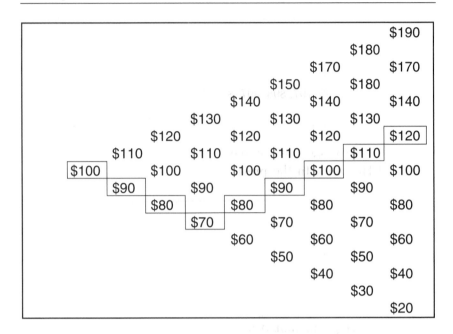

In this example, the value of the option would be $50 ($120 − $70) because the strike price changed to $70 when the price of the underlying dropped below $80.

Restrike options are combinations of knock out and knock in options. The previous example is really the combination of:

- A down and out call with a strike of $100 and an "out" at $80.
- A down and in call with a strike of $70 and an "in" at $80.

Asian Options

Asian options come in two categories: Asian strike options and Asian expiration options.

For an Asian strike option, the option's strike price is not a set price, but is instead the average of the prices at which the underlying trades over a specified period of time. For example, the formula for the strike price of an Asian strike call might be: "The average of all of the prices at which the underlying trades between the option's inception and its expiration." If the prices at which it traded were the ones listed here, the strike price would be the average of the prices, or $97:

$100, $99, $98, $97, $98, $97, $96, $95, $96, $95, $94, $96, $100

The value of the call at expiration would be = Max [0, Price at Expiration − Average Price at Which the Underlying Trades Over the Specified Horizon]. In the previous example, the value of the call at expiration would be $3, since the option would allow the investor to buy a stock selling for $100 for $97.

Likewise, the value at expiration of an Asian strike put = Max [0, Minimum Price at Which the Underlying Trades Over the Specified Horizon − Price at Expiration].

The second type of Asian option is an Asian expiration option, where the terminal value is not a single fixed value, but is instead the average of the prices at which the underlying trades over a specified period of time. For example, an option's expiration value might be: "the average of the closing prices over the last two weeks before the option expires."

- Asian price call = Max [0, Average of Price Over the Specified Horizon − Strike Price]

- Asian price put = Max [0, Strike Price − Average of Price Over the Specified Horizon]

Asian options are very similar to look-backs with the exception that while look-backs are based on the highest or the lowest price over a time horizon, Asians are based on the average price. Asians have many variables including:

- The term over which the price data to be average is gathered. This term can be longer than, shorter than, or equal to the life of the option.

- How frequently the price data is gathered (daily, weekly, monthly).
- Whether the average price is to be calculated on an arithmetic or geometric basis.

Compound Options

Compound options are options that provide their owners with the right to buy or sell another option. These options create positions with greater leverage than traditional options. There are four basic types of compound options:

1. Right to buy a call, called a "Ca-call."
2. Right to sell a call, called a "Pu-call."
3. Right to buy a put, called a "Ca-put."
4. Right to sell a put, called a "Pu-put."

There is only one common business application for compound options and that is to hedge bids for business that may or may not be accepted. Consider the following example.

On March 15, a U.S. company receives a request for proposals from a British company to perform some software development. The U.S. company must submit a binding bonded bid quoted in pounds on June 1. The contract will be awarded on July 10 with the work to be completed by and payment made on December 15. Given this time line, when does the company's FX risk begin and how can it hedge the risk? (See Figure 18-8.)

Figure 18-8
Business Schedule

MAR 15	JU 01	JY 10	DC 15
Request	Bids	Bid	Payment
Proposal	Submitted	Selected	Date

The company's risk actually begins when it decides it wants to bid on the project—provided its bid is accepted. If its bid is not accepted, it has no risk. If its bid is accepted, then it will have to perform the work specified for a fixed price in pounds, even though it will eventually want dollars. Thus, the company is exposed to rate changes retroactively if, and only if, its bid is accepted.

The company can hedge this risk by immediately buying a compound option that gives it the right to buy an option on July 10 that, in turn, allows it to convert pounds into dollars on December 15. The company would exercise its compound option on July 10 if its bid was approved; otherwise, it would allow the option to expire.

Perpetual Zero Options

Perpetual zero options are, as the name implies, options that:

- Have a strike price equal to zero.
- Never expire.

The perpetual right to buy an underlying at a price of zero has the same value as the underlying (unless the underlying pays interest or dividends). For example, the perpetual right to buy a growth stock that is currently selling for $30 for $0 is worth $30.

These options are often used to extract the value of stock positions that the owner does not wish to sell either for tax reasons or for corporate control reasons. For example, suppose the founder of a technology firm owns a million shares of a stock that is selling for $20 each. The owner's cost basis is zero, so any sale proceeds are 100% taxable. The owner wants to free up the wealth that is tied up in this stock position but doesn't want to actually sell the stock. Instead, the owner sells a perpetual zero strike call option against the position. By selling this option, the owner effectively transfers all future losses and gains to the owner purchaser.

Delay Options

Delay options are options where the strike price is not set when the option is created. Instead, the strike price is set to equal the current market price at some defined time in the future. They are used to hedge certain types of executive options.

For example, a one-year delay call option could have its strike price set in six months. Given the price history in Figure 18-9, the value of the option upon expiration would be $3. (Expiration – strike = $112 – $109)

Figure 18-9
Price History

Month	1	2	3	4	5	6	7	8	9	10	11	12
Price	$100	$95	$89	$97	$104	$109	$105	$100	$105	$114	$107	$112

Chooser Options

A chooser option is an option in which the long gets to decide whether the option is a call or a put some time after the option is purchased. The "choose date" can be any date after the option is created, up to and including the option's expiration date. They are used as volatility plays and are purchased when the buyers expect the volatility of the underlying to increase, but are uncertain as to the direction (elections/mergers). Because they are volatility plays, chooser options are similar to straddles and strangles.

Contingent Premium Option

A contingent premium option is an option in which the long does not initially pay for the option. Instead, the long pays only for the option if the option ends up being in the money. Any option, whether exotic or not, can become a contingent premium option by the mutual consent of the buyer and seller. Consider the following example.

Suppose that the fair price of a standard European call that expires in one year is currently $100. Normally, the buyer pays this $100

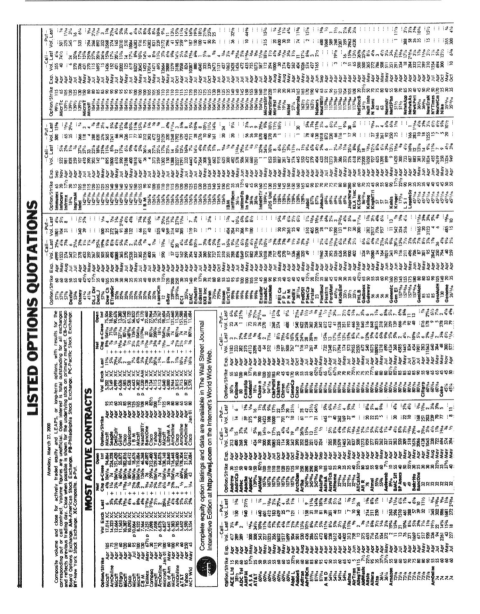

Figure 18-10
Listed Options Quotations from The Wall Street Journal

275

at the time the option is purchased. Alternatively, the buyer could offer to pay the seller a larger premium—but only if the option is in the money at expiration. The contingent premium that the buyer owes the seller if the option ends up in the money at expiration is:

$$\left[\frac{\text{Value of Regular Option}}{\text{Probability It Will Be in the Money}} \right] \times (1 + \text{Risk} = \text{Free Rate})$$

For example, if the value of the option is $100, and there is a 40-percent probability that the option will end up being in the money, and the risk-free rate is 7%, then the contingent premium would be:

$$\left[\frac{\$100}{.4} \right] \times (1 + .07) = \$267.50$$

Thus, the seller of the option has a choice of accepting $100 today or having a 40-percent chance of receiving $267.50 in a year. Both alternatives have the same current economic value.

Option buyers like contingent premium options, since they require no initial outlay of cash. However, the downside is that the option must end up at least $267.50 in the money in order for the buyer to break even overall, instead of $107 (the cost of the option plus financing). The $267.50 is payable even if the option ends up being only $1 in the money.

CHAPTER 19

EQUITY-RELATED INVESTMENTS

In the 1990s, there was an explosion of equity-related investments. These investments include indices, warrants, LEAPS, and convertible securities. Each has a role to play within a portfolio.

Index Securities

Index securities are designed to have returns that mirror the performance of some of the popular equity indexes. The issuers of these securities buy the actual stocks in the underlying index, place them in a trust account, and use the trust as collateral for the index securities. Some of the more popular index securities include *spiders*,™ *diamonds*,™ and iShares^{SM}.

Warrants

Equity warrants are long-term options that allow their owners to buy the company's common stock at a set price. Because they are options, they offer investors a leveraged way to play the underlying stocks. Companies issue warrants to raise capital. Warrants are sometimes issued by themselves and at other times are issued in conjunction with stock. For example, an investor might receive two warrants for every share of a new offering they purchase. When shares and warrants are sold together, they are referred to as "units."

Long Dated Equity Participation Securities

Long Dated Equity Participation Securities (LEAPS) are also longer term options on common stocks. The difference between warrants and LEAPS is that warrants are issued by the underlying company while LEAPS are derivative instruments.

Convertible Securities

A convertible security is a security that contains an embedded option that grants the investor the right to exchange the security for another type of security. While there are innumerable varieties of convertible securities, the most traditional and common types of convertible securities are bonds and preferred stocks that investors can exchange for a fixed number of shares of the company's common stock.

In this module, we will base the examples around a hypothetical bond issued by XYZ, Inc. This bond is issued at par with a 6% coupon and includes an option that allows the bond to be converted at any time into 100 shares of a company's common stock. At the time the bond is issued, the company's common is selling for $8 per share and pays no dividend.

No rational investor would buy the bond and immediately exchange it for the stock, since the $1,000 bond could be exchanged for only $800 (100 shares at $8 per share). However, if a year later the stock is selling for $16 per share, the bond can be converted into $1,600 worth of stock. If it was selling at any price below $1,600, an investor could make an immediate risk-free (that is, arbitrage) profit by buying the bond, exchanging it for stock, and selling the stock.

In reality, the bond would be worth more than $1600 since in addition to being convertible into $1600 worth of the company's common, it also generates $60 of income per year for its owner. The present value of those future interest payments would have to be added to the conversion value in order to determine the bond's fair current market value.

Convertible Vocabulary and Ratios

Before we discuss convertible securities in more detail, it is necessary to become familiar with several terms and ratios related to convertible securities.

CONVERSION VALUE

The conversion value is the current market value of the common stock into which the bond converts. It is calculated by multiplying the number of shares into which the bond converts by the current price of the common stock.

Conversion value = number shares × price of the shares

In this example, the initial conversion value would be:

Conversion value = 100 × $8 = $800

After the stock rose to $16 per share, the conversion value would be:

Conversion value = 100 × $16 = $1,600

Conversion Premium

The conversion premium is the difference between the market value and the conversion value of the bond, expressed on either an absolute or a percentage basis. In the previous example, the initial conversion premiums would be:

$$\text{Absolute premium} = \$1,000 - \$800 = \$200$$
$$\text{Percentage premium} = (\$1,000 - \$800) / \$800 = 25\%$$

In the U.S., the typical initial conversion premium for convertible bonds is 17 to 30%. The greater the perceived upside potential of the stock and the longer the period of call protection, the higher the conversion premium. As the bond approaches either its call date or its maturity date, the conversion premium contracts.

WORK-OUT PERIOD

One of the most useful ratios for analysis of convertible bonds is the "work-out period." The work-out period is a measure of how long it takes for the conversion premium to be amortized by the higher current income generated by the bond. In the previous example, the bond generates current income of $60 per year, while the stock generates no income since it pays no dividends. Since the bond has a $200 conversion premium, the work-out period would be:

$$\text{Work-out period} = \text{Conversion premium in dollars} / (\text{income from bond} - \text{income from an equivalent investment in stock})$$

$$\text{Work-out period} = \$200 / (\$60 - \$0) = 3.33 \text{ years}$$

If the stock generated a $.10 dividend per year, then the work-out period would be:

$$\text{Work-out period} = \$200 / (\$60 - \$12.50) = 4.21 \text{ years}$$

Note that in this example, the income from the stock is $12.50, since $1,000 would buy 125 shares of stock at $8 each. In order to have a fair comparison, it is necessary to compute the work-out period using the income from an equal investment in both the convertible bond and the underlying common.

The shorter the work-out period, the more attractive the convertible is when compared to the underlying stock. Conservative investors are often willing to buy convertibles with work-out periods as long as 3.5 years, while aggressive investors are often unwilling to accept work-out periods longer then 2.5 years.

Why Invest in Converts?

Investors always have to choose between the various ways to invest in a company. They can invest directly by buying the common stock or indirectly by buying a security that converts into the common. Convertibles offer investors numerous advantages relative to investing directly in common stock. Some of these advantages include:

- More senior security:

  In the event the company files for bankruptcy, the investors who own the convertible bonds become creditors of the company and, as such, have a senior claim on any remaining assets relative to both the common and preferred holders. Of course, in order for this seniority to have any value, the company has to have assets after the more senior creditors, including the government, employees, and senior debt holders, are all paid in full.

- Higher current income:

  Convertible bonds almost always offer a higher current income than the underlying common stocks. The cash flow from the bond's interest payments almost always exceeds the dividend payments from an equal size investment in the underlying common stock. For investors that require or desire current income, convertibles are often the more attractive investment alternative.

- Favorable risk-adjusted return:

  Because of the way the value of the embedded conversion option changes as the price of the underlying instrument changes, the price of the convertible rises more when the price of the underlying stock rises than the price of the convertible declines when the underlying stock declines. Thus, convertible securities exhibit a positive asymmetric risk reward pattern in response to a change in the value of the underlying common.

- Automatic tactical asset allocation:

  One of the most attractive advantages of convertible securities is that they automate one of the most basic and important tactical asset allocation decisions investors have to decide: the decision of how much to allocate to equity versus fixed income. Many market timers try to increase the weighting of stocks in their portfolio when the market is rising, and retreat to the higher income and relative safety of bonds when they expect the stock market to decline. Fortunately, for owners of convertible securities, these securities behave more like stocks when the market is rising and more like bonds when the market is either flat or declining. In effect, they automatically tactically reallocate in a way that benefits the investor.

Disadvantage of Convertible Securities

While convertible securities offer numerous advantages, they also have some disadvantages that investors need to consider.

- Underperforming the common:

  In a down, flat, or slowly rising market, convertible securities will outperform the underlying common. However, in a rapidly rising market, convertible securities will underperform the underlying common stocks.

- Call risk:

Almost every convertible bond is callable. Generally the bonds are callable either after a certain period of call protection is passed or after the stock price has risen to the point where the conversion option is deeply in the money. When the issuer calls the bond, the investor can lose any remaining conversion premium. Consider the following example:

Suppose the XYZ, Inc., bond previously introduced is purchased as a new issue and that subsequently the underlying stock price rises to $16 a share. Since the conversion value is $1,600 and the bond generates a higher current income, an investor might be willing to pay a $150 premium over conversion value—$1,750 in this example.

However, paying a premium over conversion value can be a disaster if the bond shortly becomes callable. If the bond is called at par (or par plus a small conversion premium), the investor would have little choice other than to convert the bond into the underlying common. After all, converting the bond that the investor paid $1,750 for into $1,600 worth of stock beats accepting $1,000 (or $1,030) in cash.

When the bond is called, the $150 conversion premium ($1,750 minus $1,600) is lost. Therefore, it is important for investors to research the call provisions of convertible securities prior to purchasing a convertible bond or preferred. Investors should not pay a conversion premium that is higher than the present value of the incremental cash flows the investor can expect to receive from the bond before the bond is called.

- Loss of accrued interest upon forced conversion:

When a convertible bond is called, and the investor is effectively forced to convert the bond into the underlying common in order to avoid receiving the call price for the bond, the investor also sacrifices any interest that the bond has accrued. Because they don't have to pay the accrued interest on bonds that are converted, many companies that have issued convertibles often force conversion by calling the securities just prior to an interest payment date.

Thus, in a forced call an investor can lose both the conversion premium and any accrued interest. Because accrued interest is lost when a convertible is called, it is not uncommon for bonds that are likely to be called to be trading at a price that is equal to their conversion value minus their accrued interest.

- Lower liquidity of convertibles:

  Convertible securities have lower liquidity than the underlying common. Investors should use limit orders and build orders over time in order to avoid disturbing the market.

Why Do Issuers Issue Convertibles?

There are two main reasons issuers elect to issue convertibles: either to borrow money at a lower rate or to delay the issuance of stock in the hope that it can be issued in the future at a higher price.

By embedding a conversion option into its debt, companies with high credit ratings can borrow money at a lower interest rate than they would ordinarily have to pay. For start up companies, or companies with low credit ratings, embedding a conversion option into its bond may be a necessary incentive to attract lenders even if the bonds offer a higher return.

When companies issue convertibles, they hope that the bonds will eventually be converted into stock. If the conversion occurs, it will occur at a price that is higher than the stock's current price.

MUTUAL FUNDS

Three of the most important rules investors need to follow are:

1. Diversify your investment portfolio.

2. Try to stack the deck in your favor.

3. Don't invest in anything you will not be able to monitor.

Diversification

No matter how carefully investors research potential investments, something unforeseen can always go wrong. For example, an impressive set of historic financials can suddenly turn out to be the fictitious invention of a crooked management team, causing the value of both the company's stock and debt to plunge. Because there is always some probability of an unforeseen disaster befalling any investment, investors should not risk all of their money in any one investment.

Portfolios should not only be diversified among different investment vehicles, but also within each asset class. For example, many experts recommend that investors hold a minimum of eight different stocks—each from a different industry—in order to reduce the risk of their portfolios.

Stacking the Deck

Investing is a game played on an uneven field. Those players with the most experience, most knowledge, most up-to-date information, and clearest insight have a clear advantage when playing on this field. While naïve or uninformed investors do occasionally get lucky, the deck is stacked against them over the long term.

Investors should always try to invest in markets where they have an advantage and avoid markets where they have clear disadvantages. For example, suppose a dentist in Paramus, N.J., buys a technical analysis software package at Software Discount Land, and based on the results of the package, decides to trade corn futures. The dentist should realize that he or she is competing against Kellogg's, Con-Agra, and other very sophisticated players. These competitors have access to substantially more information about the probable size of the next corn crop, possible changes in federal price support programs, changes in global tariff arrangements, and the hundreds of other factors that affect the price of corn. Clearly the dentist is at a disadvantage.

Investment Monitoring

Once an investment is made, an investor's work is not done. Markets are constantly moving and changing. News items and other events that affect the value and attractiveness of an investment occur 24 hours a day, 365 days per year. Breaking news often has to be responded to quickly, since the last to know often gets the worst price.

Most investments have to be monitored on an ongoing basis. In this rapidly changing world, an investment that is attractive today may not be attractive tomorrow. Monitoring an investment portfolio requires both expertise and a dedicated timely effort. Ignoring a portfolio even for a short period of time can be disastrous.

Why Mutual Funds?

Many investors, when considering the three rules, realize that they lack either:

- The resources required to create a properly diversified portfolio.
- The expertise necessary to separate attractive from unattractive investment opportunities.
- The time or interest required to monitor the portfolio on an ongoing basis.

Therefore, instead of making their own investment decisions, these investors prefer to hire professional money management firms to invest their money for them. There are two ways to do this:

1. Hire a money manager to manage the account on an individual basis. There are numerous professional money management firms that manage individual portfolios for investors. Unfortunately, most of these managers have a relatively large minimum account size (more than $1,000,000) and charge fairly large fees for their services.
2. Invest in a mutual fund.

What Is a Mutual Fund?

In simplest terms, a mutual fund is a collection of investors who pool their money and collectively hire a professional money manager to administer and invest their funds.

Suppose a money manager has a $150,000 minimum per account. Ten investors who otherwise wouldn't be able to hire the manager individually could each pool $20,000 in order to exceed the manager's minimum and be able to hire the manager. From the manager's point of view, the account is handled as one account—even though the gains, losses, and fees are shared evenly by the ten investors, since each investor has an equal interest in the account.

If one of the participants wanted to cash out, the manager would be instructed to liquidate 10% of the portfolio. If 10% of the portfolio was worth $56,278, then the investor would receive $56,278; if 10% of the portfolio was worth $3,453, the investor would receive $3,453.

This example is fairly straightforward, since there are only 10 investors pooling their resources and each investor has an equal interest in the account. Suppose, however, that several thousand investors wanted to pool their funds and each investor wanted to invest different amounts. The record-keeping and administrative challenges posed by this many investors would prohibit this structure from working.

Instead, in order to accommodate numerous investors, the structure that is most common is as follows.

Instead of investing directly in securities, investors buy shares in the fund and the fund buys the securities. Each share represents an equal proportional ownership in the underlying portfolio. Consider the following example.

A money manager raises $10,000,000 by selling one million shares at $10 each. The manager then invests the $10,000,000 in a portfolio of securities. The value of each share is then equal to 1/1 millionth of the portfolio. If the portfolio value rises to $18,650,000, then each share will be worth $18.65. If the value of the portfolio falls to $7,765,491, then each share would be worth $7.77. The value of the portfolio divided by the number of shares is referred to as the share's "net asset value," or NAV.

Mutual funds come in two broad categories: "open-end" and "closed-end" funds.

- Open-end funds sell and purchase shares in their own fund every business day at the fund's net asset value (NAV). Thus, an investor can buy shares any day at the then-current NAV and can sell shares any day at the then-current NAV. By selling and buying shares at the NAV, the selling of new shares or the redemption of existing shares does not affect the NAV of the existing shares.

Thus, investors in open-ended funds never trade shares with other investors. Instead, they buy from and sell to only the fund company itself. The fund company makes the market in the fund's shares. Running an open-ended fund poses the special challenge of not knowing from day to day how much money will be available to invest. If a few bad news stories occur, the managers of open-ended funds can find themselves flooded with requests for redemptions, while a few positive news stories can cause a flood of new money to pour into the fund.

A few open-ended funds with good performance histories have become so large that the managers have had trouble finding enough attractive investment opportunities to absorb all of the money they've attracted. As a result, sometimes these funds have resorted to ceasing to sell any fund shares to investors who did not already own fund shares.

- Closed-end funds do not make a market in their own shares. Instead, after the original offering, the shares trade either on an exchange or in the OTC market just like any other stock. Further, just like any other stock, the shares of closed-end funds trade at whatever price is determined by the law of supply and demand. Investors are free to buy and sell the shares at any price, not just the NAV. In practice, closed-end funds often trade at a discount to their NAV in the secondary market.

Closed-end funds offer the managers the freedom from untimely redemptions and cash inflows.

Advantages of Mutual Funds

Mutual funds are so popular with investors because they offer numerous advantages, including the following:

1. *Diversification.* Many professionals believe that diversification is one of the best ways to enhance a portfolio's risk-adjusted return. Mutual funds make it possible for investors with as little as $100 to own an undivided interest in a diversified portfolio.

2. *Low minimum investment.* Mutual funds put investment vehicles such as commercial mortgages and gold bullion within the reach of many investors for whom they would otherwise be unattainable.

3. *Professional management.* Mutual funds give investors access to the talents of managers whose required minimum account size would otherwise put their services out of reach.

4. *Wide range of risk reward trade-offs.* Mutual funds are available with risk levels ranging from the very conservative (insured money market funds) to the very speculative (emerging market growth funds).

5. *Convenience.* Perhaps one of the most important advantages that mutual funds offer is a number of conveniences. These conveniences can include 24-hour phone/Internet access to account information, check-writing privileges, and automatic investment plans that deduct a set amount each month from investors' bank accounts.

6. *Inexpensive tactical reallocation.* Most mutual funds are part of fund families—a series of funds with different investment objectives that are issued by the same parent company. Most fund families allow their shareholders a reasonable number of opportunities per year to switch their money among the various funds within the family, either at no cost or by paying a nominal service charge. Therefore, mutual fund investors can often reallocate their portfolios at a lower cost than investors who invest in the underlying securities directly.

7. *Asset allocation and retirement planning tools.* As a service to their shareholders, many mutual fund companies offer free services,

such as asset allocation optimization software or retirement planning analyzers, that are designed to help investors select the appropriate funds.

8. *Wide range of investment styles.* With more than 10,000 mutual funds in existence and more being created every week, it is not an exaggeration to say there is a mutual fund that specializes in investing in every investment vehicle, style, and approach that investors can imagine. For example, there are funds that invest exclusively in:

- Stocks from a single industry (finance, telecommunications, etc.).
- Stocks from a single market sector (utilities, technology, etc.).
- Small-cap growth stocks.
- Small-cap value stocks.
- Municipal bonds from a single state.
- Large-cap value stocks.
- Large-cap growth stocks.
- The securities from a single country.
- Sovereign debt.
- The securities from a single continent or region.
- The securities that mirror an index, such as the S&P 500.
- Short-term treasuries.
- Mortgages.
- Mining stocks.
- Stocks that also have listed options, so the managers can write options against the stocks.
- Stocks with high-dividend yields.
- Mortgage-backed securities.
- Preferred stocks.
- Floating-rate notes.

Disadvantages of Mutual Funds

While mutual funds offer many advantages, they also have some disadvantages that should not be overlooked. These disadvantages include:

- Management turnover—Many investors select mutual funds based on their past performance. Unfortunately, given the high rate of management turnover within the asset management industry, the managers who are primarily responsible for a fund's superior performance in the past may now be working for a different fund company. Therefore, investors need to examine not only what the past performance of a fund is, but also who was responsible for that performance, and whether or not the managers are still running the fund.

- Style drift—An investor who wants to maintain a certain asset allocation has to rely on the managers of the funds that the investor selects not to deviate from their stated investment styles. For example, if an investor wants to allocate 10% of his portfolio to growth stocks, and puts 10% of the portfolio into a growth stock fund, the investor wants that growth stock fund to remain completely invested in growth stocks. However, the manager of the fund may have a different priority. The manager of the fund naturally wants to outperform the managers of other growth stock funds. If the manager believes that large-cap stocks will outperform growth stocks over the near term, the manager may elect to shift a portion of the portfolio into large-cap stocks. This change, which often goes undetected, overrides and defeats the investor's asset allocation.

- Panic selling—During sharp market downturns, investors have an unfortunate tendency to panic. If they panic, they call their mutual fund companies and/or brokers and sell their fund shares. Since the fund managers must redeem the fund shares, they have no choice but to sell the underlying securities at a time when there are few, if any, buyers. If it wasn't for the flood of redemptions, the fund manager would not sell the underlying securities. Thus, the professional manager's expertise, judgment, and objectives are thwarted and overridden by the action of the fund's investors.

- Return dilution—Fund investors also run the risk of "return dilution." Consider the following example: The best time to buy bonds and, therefore, bond funds, is when interest rates are high. As interest rates decline, not only do the investors enjoy a high return but also the capital appreciation that accompanies a decline in rates. Bond funds, therefore, should generate strong "total return" numbers when interest rates decline.

  Unfortunately, the high total return numbers generated by these funds tend to attract a flood of new investors. As new investors pour money into the funds, the fund managers have to buy more bonds. Of course, the new bonds are purchased at a lower yield that, in turn, reduces the overall return of the fund. Thus, through no fault of the investor, any attempt to successfully time the bond market with mutual funds often proves to be unsuccessful due to the actions of other investors. The same problem occurs, albeit to a lesser degree, with stock funds.

- Investors in mutual funds can be liable for taxes on capital gains that don't benefit them. Consider the following, grossly oversimplified, example. Consider a mutual fund that issues only one fund share to Investor A for $10. The fund then invests the money in one share of XYZ, Inc., which is also selling for $10. The value of the stock, and thus the fund share's NAV, subsequently rises to $20. The fund then sells another fund share to Investor B at the then-current NAV of $20. The fund invests the $20 in another share of XYZ, Inc.

  Later the price of XYZ, Inc., falls to $18, and the fund manager sells both shares of XYZ in order to buy another stock. For tax purposes, the fund has an $8 capital gain on one share of XYZ, Inc., and a $2 capital loss on the other share of XYZ, Inc. As a result, the fund has a net capital gain of $6. The gain is assigned equally to both shareholders:

  - Investor A invested $10, has a fund share worth $18, and has to report a capital gain of $3.

- Investor B invested $20, has a fund share worth $18, and has to report a capital gain of $3.

Thus, even though Investor B has so far suffered a loss, for tax purposes the investor has to report a gain.

FEES AND EXPENSES

Mutual fund investors are subject to a number of fees and expenses. These expenses can affect performance and, therefore, the overall level of fees and expenses should be considered before making an investment. Some of these fees include:

1. *Marketing expenses*. Every mutual fund must market itself to the investing public. Different funds elect to use different marketing channels.

   - No-load funds rely on direct marketing. These funds solicit investors via print ads, direct mail, and an ever-increasing reliance on television advertisements.

   - Load funds instead rely on salespeople to market their funds. These salespeople can either be employees of the fund company itself or employees of brokerage firms, financial planning firms, banks, and insurance companies. These salespeople are normally paid on a commission basis. These commissions can be paid several different ways, including:

Shareholder Fees[1] (paid directly from your investment)	CLASS A	CLASS B	CLASS C	CLASS Z
Maximum sales charge (load) imposed on purchases (as a percentage of offering price)	5%	None	1%	None
Maximum deferred sales charge (load) (as a percentage of the lower of original purchase price or sale proceeds)	None	5%[2]	1%[3]	None
Maximum sales charge (load) imposed on reinvested dividends and other distributions	None	None	None	None
Redemption fees	None	None	None	None
Exchange fee	None	None	None	None

➤ Front-end load fees are fees that are subtracted from the investment at the time the investment is made. These fees range from 1 percent to as high as 8¼ percent, depending upon the fund. The size of these fees declines as the purchase size increases. A typical sales fee schedule is listed below:

➤ Back-end fees are fees that are charged if the investor withdraws money from the fund. The size of these fees declines as the investment horizon increases. They usually disappear completely in four to six years, depending upon the fund.

2. *Operating expenses/administration costs.* Every fund has to mail statements to its shareholders, answer phone calls, hire staff, and perform the other basic administrative functions associated with running a business. Like any business, the lower the administrative costs, the better the bottom line.

3. *Management/advisory fees.* Management or advisory fees are the fees paid to the managers who make the buy and sell decisions. Managers who have the knowledge, experience, and temperament to successfully manage portfolios over the long term are quite rare. It's not surprising then that, given the law of supply and demand, successful managers are very well paid. From an investor's perspective, fund managers should:

- Be paid on an incentive basis tied to the fund's performance.
- Have their own money invested in the fund.

The information on all risks, fees, and expenses can be found in the fund's prospectus.

Other Issues Mutual Fund Investors Need to Consider

The following section discusses some of the issues that investors should consider when they evaluate alternative mutual funds.

The Size of the Fund

The size of a mutual fund (that is, the number of dollars invested in the funds) can affect its performance. Small funds:

- Have the advantage of being nimble. While large funds have to find hundreds of attractive investment opportunities in order to spend all their money, small funds can be more selective. Small funds also find it easier to move in and out of positions without disturbing the market or competing against themselves.

- Have the disadvantage of having to amortize their fixed costs over a smaller asset base. Thus, the fees per dollar invested tend to be higher with small funds than they are with large funds.

Where Is the Asset Allocation Decision Made?

One of the first issues that fund buyers should consider is, "Do they want individual fund managers to make asset allocation decisions or not?" If they want to make the asset allocation decisions themselves, they should seek out funds where the fund managers are required to stay 100 percent invested in their stated investment vehicle. Otherwise, their asset allocation might be distorted.

Consider the following example. An investor decides to allocate 40% of his or her portfolio to cash and 60% to growth stocks, believing that this allocation offers the best risk-adjusted return over the long term. However, if the manager of the growth fund is permitted to retreat to cash and elects to hold 50% of the fund's assets in cash, then the investor's asset allocation becomes 70% cash and 30% growth stocks. The investor's allocation objectives are thwarted by the fund manager's decision to hold cash instead of growth stocks.

If the investor uses only funds that have to stay 100% invested in their respective market sectors, then the asset allocation decision made by the investor can't be thwarted by the fund managers. The investor alone makes the asset allocation decisions by increasing or decreasing the percentage of the portfolio invested in each fund. The performance of funds that are required to stay fully invested should not be compared with the performance of funds that are allowed to retreat to cash, since it would not be a fair "apples to apples" comparison.

In addition to affecting asset allocation decisions, managers who do not stay 100% invested in their asset classes also thwart dollar cost averaging strategies. Investors who dollar cost average believe it is impossible to time the market, and instead elect to invest a fixed number of dollars each month or each quarter. When the market is low, a fixed dollar investment buys more shares, and when the market is high, it buys fewer shares. Because more shares are purchased at the lower price, the average cost of shares is lower than the average price that the shares trade for over the same horizon. In order for dollar cost averaging to work, the money actually has to be invested each month. Thus, market timing and dollar cost averaging are inconsistent.

(Note: A periodic investment plan such as dollar cost averaging does not assure a profit or protect against a loss in declining markets.)

NON-DOLLAR MUTUAL FUNDS

U.S. investors who consider investing in non-dollar mutual funds have a special issue they need to consider. Non-dollar funds can be managed in an effort to maximize the return in either local currency terms or in U.S. dollar terms. Consider the following example. Suppose a fund that invests in European stocks is considering two alternative investments:

1. A British stock that is expected to rise by 20% in sterling terms.

2. A German stock that is expected to rise by 15% in Euro terms.

Suppose further that the fund manager expects sterling to decline by 10% against the dollar and the Euro to rise by 15% against the dollar. If the fund were managed to optimize the return in local currency, the manager would buy the British stock instead of the German stock (20% versus 15%). However, if the fund is managed to optimize the return in U.S. dollar terms, the manager would buy the German stock instead of the British stock (15% plus 15%) versus (20% minus 10%).

(Note: Investing in foreign securities presents certain unique risks not associated with domestic investments, such as currency fluctuation and political and economic changes. This may result in greater share price volatility.)

DOES THE FUND USE DERIVATIVES?

Many mutual funds try to enhance their performance with derivatives. The use of derivatives is controversial, partly because of the well-publicized and spectacular losses taken by Proctor & Gamble, Orange County, and so on. Investors should decide whether they want their funds to use derivatives, and how they want the derivatives to be used. There are three main alternatives:

1. *No derivatives.* Some funds have a blanket ban on the use of derivatives for any purpose whatsoever.

2. *Use of derivatives only for hedging purposes.* Some funds allow derivatives to be used only for hedging purposes. For example, if the manager of a growth stock fund wishes to reduce exposure to the markets, the fund manager can either sell stocks or use derivatives. Selling the actual stocks can be very expensive, especially if the stocks are "thinly traded." Just one fund selling a substantial position can severely depress the price. Derivatives can be a far more cost-effective way of reducing market exposure.

3. *Use of derivatives to enhance return potential.* Some funds use derivatives as an investment vehicle to enhance their portfolio's return potential. Derivatives provide leverage on both the upside and the downside. If the manager invests correctly, the fund's return can exceed the return of funds that do not use derivatives. If the manager invests wrong, the fund's performance will suffer. Only investors whose risk tolerance is high enough to accept the large potential losses should elect to invest in funds that use derivatives to seek to enhance performance.

GLOBAL INVESTING*

Most United States investors are surprised to learn that you have to look outside the U.S. to find:

- 9 out of 10 of the world's largest beverage companies.
- 9 out of 10 of the world's largest electronics companies.
- 8 out of 10 of the world's largest gas and electric companies.
- 7 out of 10 of the world's largest insurance companies.
- 6 out of 10 of the world's largest chemical companies.
- 6 out of 10 of the world's largest metal companies.
- 5 out of 10 of the world's largest banking companies.
- 5 out of 10 of the world's largest machinery companies.

United States citizens tend to be myopic when it comes to investment opportunities. Part of this is myopia is due to the fact that the United States is somewhat geographically isolated, part of it is due to the dominant position of the United States, both politically and eco-

*Foreign investing is subject to certain risks, such as currency fluctuation and social and political changes (as well as the lesser degree of public information required to be provided by non-U.S. companies), which may result in greater share price volatility.

nomically. The other reason for this myopia is that investors in the United States stock and bond markets have enjoyed terrific returns over the last 10 years, and often see little benefit of diversifying their portfolios globally. Most United States investors would be surprised to learn that over the last 15 years, the United States stock market has never offered the highest return.

There are a number of reasons non-dollar markets have outperformed, and will probably continue to outperform, the United States market.

Faster Rate of Economic Growth

The first reason overseas markets might offer investors a higher return potential is that many overseas economies are growing at a faster rate than the United States economy. The consensus of many of the world's leading economists is that while the United States should enjoy a long-term growth rate of approximately 2 to 2.5% per year, the average growth rate for the economies of the so-called "emerging nations" will be at least 5%. Naturally, the faster the rate of local economic growth, the greater the growth potential is for the companies that operate in those markets. The underlying reasons for this faster growth rate include:

- The faster rate of population growth in these markets relative to the United States market.

- The dramatic transformation of these often-backwards economies into more modern and productive economies.

- The widespread adoption of democracy, capitalism, and the rule of law among these nations.

As long as these trends continue, and as of this writing there was no reason to believe that they will not, the emerging markets should continue to enjoy a faster rate of economic growth than the United States. The United States is a mature market by comparison.

Less Government Regulation

Overseas companies are sometimes subject to less government regulation. United States-based companies face a daunting amount of government regulation. There are United States Government regulations that cover almost every aspect of creating and operating a business. Just a few of the many types of regulations to which United States businesses are subject include zoning rules, employment rules, packaging and labeling rules, tax rules, environmental rules, and antitrust rules. While no one would argue that many of these regulations are beneficial and even necessary, they do put United States businesses at a competitive disadvantage relative to their foreign competitors. Companies operating outside the United States often face far less government regulation and, therefore, lower operating costs.

Lower Labor Costs

One of the principal advantages that non-United States companies (as well as United States companies that operate overseas facilities) enjoy is sharply lower labor costs. These lower costs include both wages and benefit costs. In many emerging markets, there is no such thing as medical insurance, disability insurance, or unemployment insurance, much less dental insurance and company-sponsored retirement plans. Additionally, laws such as the United States Family Leave Act—which guarantees that United States workers who take time off to care for newborn children or sick family members will not lose their jobs—are unheard of in many overseas markets.

While the average total labor cost of a blue-collar worker in the United States is more than $17 an hour, the cost in China or India is only $.25 an hour. Likewise, a Ph.D. in physics will cost $90,000 a year in the United States, but only $3,000 a year in Russia. An experienced computer programmer can cost $110,000 a year in the United States, but only $9,000 a year in India. In the future, professionals and white-collar workers in the United States are clearly going to feel the pressure of wage competition—just as blue-collar workers have experienced in the past.

Better Educated Work Force

Low labor costs alone can be a false economy unless the work force is also well-educated and has a strong work ethic. In many countries, the school year is longer and the curriculum is more rigorous than it is in the United States. Many educators regard a European high school education as the equivalent of a United States high school education plus two years of college. In addition, the work ethic among blue-collar workers in many countries is either equal to or exceeds that of United States blue-collar workers.

Favorable Political Environment

In many countries, the government takes a very active role in promoting and protecting business—unlike the United States market, in which the relationship between government and business is often more antagonistic than cooperative. Additionally, one of the favorite tools of United States foreign policy-makers is the "trade embargo." While the government considers these embargoes to be an effective tool to promote United States national interests, these embargoes hurt United States companies. Since United States companies are prohibited from doing business with or in nations that are embargoed, non-United States companies are free to step in and fill the void. While there are many advantages to living in the world's only remaining superpower, it can place a severe burden on United States companies whose future is often sacrificed to further political goals.

Disadvantages of Overseas Markets

While non-dollar markets have many advantages—some of which were previously outlined—they also have disadvantages that should not be overlooked. Some of these disadvantages include:

- *Less well-regulated securities markets.* Many non-dollar securities markets are not so tightly regulated as the United States securities markets. While no one would suggest that the United States market is completely free of market manipulation, it is certainly less of a problem in the United States than it is in many other markets, where market manipulation is sometimes rampant.

- *Lower liquidity.* In the United States market, daily trading volume is extremely high. This high trading volume results in excellent liquidity, especially for the smaller investor. In other markets, volume can be so low that stocks seem to trade only by appointment. Low liquidity can force investors to accept a lower price when they sell or pay a premium when they buy.

- *Higher trading and transaction costs.* The lower liquidity and the lack of automation (particularly back office automation) in many overseas markets dramatically raises trading costs. In the United States, the cost of trading is only a few cents per share, while in other markets, the cost can be many times higher. This both reduces investment profits and limits investors' flexibility.

- *Less required financial disclosure.* United States companies that have publicly traded stocks have rigorous reporting requirements. Overseas companies often are subject to more flexible reporting requirements. These include the ability to maintain undisclosed reserve accounts and the ability to hide potential liabilities. As such, investors who buy non-dollar stocks may have a greater risk of unpleasant financial surprises.

- *Stockholders are a lower priority.* In the United States, CEOs of public companies know that their major (and sometimes only) priority is to enrich the shareholders to whom they report. In other markets, enriching shareholders is often just one of many priorities and not necessarily one of the highest priorities. Several Japanese managers, in particular, have been quite vocal about the fact that enriching shareholders is for them a very low priority. In other cases, some governments have made it clear that they expect shareholder returns to take a back seat to social progress and wealth redistribution.

- *Higher short-term volatility.* While non-dollar markets may offer a higher return, they also have higher short-term volatility. Large short-term price swings, both up and down, should be anticipated. These swings are the result of both changes in the valuation of the stocks in their native currencies, as well as swings in the US$/native currency FX rate. Investors who cannot tolerate high volatility should avoid these markets, even if it reduces their total return.

Thus, while non-dollar markets offer numerous advantages, those advantages always come with corresponding risks.

The Influence of Globalization on United States Companies

The global marketplace is no longer "coming"—it is here. No longer are corporate giants like Sony, Ford, Coca-Cola, and IBM the only global enterprises. Today, companies with just a few employees and a Web site can, and do, compete effectively on a global basis. Even investors who do not choose to invest in investment vehicles denominated in currencies other than their reference currency must still be aware of how the fluctuation of currency values will affect the performance of their investments. To illustrate, consider how United States investors who buy stock in United States companies are affected by FX risk if the companies in which they invest either import or export, have overseas operations, and/or have foreign competitors.

- United States companies that import—United States companies that import raw materials or components from overseas are exposed to the risk that the US$ will decline. If the US$ declines, then the cost of the imported goods rises in dollar terms. Consider the following example:

A United States computer company agrees to buy some specialized computer chips from a chip fabricator in Japan. The United States company agrees to pay ¥150,000,000 for the chips within 10 days of delivery, which is due to occur in 90 days. At the time the deal is struck, the exchange rate is ¥150/$1, so the United States company expects to pay the equivalent of $1,000,000 for the chips. Over the next hundred days, however, the dollar weakens to the point where each dollar buys only ¥130. Because of the change in the exchange rate, it will cost the United States company almost $1,154,000 to buy the yen it needs to pay the invoice (¥150,000,000/¥130). Of course, the United States company could hedge the risk by using derivatives, but this can be quite expensive.

- United States companies that export—United States companies that export raw materials or components from overseas are always exposed to the risk that the dollar will get stronger. If the dollar gets stronger, then the revenue that the company generates in other currencies will buy fewer dollars.

- United States companies that have overseas operations are exposed to the risk that either the dollar will strengthen or weaken, depending upon whether they are making overseas investments or are repatriating profits. If the company is investing overseas, it is exposed to the risk that the dollar will decline. If the company is repatriating profits, the company is exposed to the risk that the dollar will rise. Consider the following example:

A United States company enters into a contract to build a new plant in England. It will take three years to complete the plant, bring it fully online, and have it become profitable. For the three years it takes until the plant becomes profitable, the United States company will be converting dollars into pounds. During this phase, the company is exposed to the risk that the dollar will decline. After the plant becomes profitable, the company will be converting pounds into dollars and it will be exposed to the risk that the dollar will get stronger.

- United States companies that have foreign competitors—Even United States companies that do not import, export, or have overseas operations are often exposed to FX risk. Consider the following example:

  The Acme Trophy Manufacturing Company is located in Cincinnati, Ohio. The company has been manufacturing and wholesaling trophies and plaques (Little League, bowling, employee of the month, and so on) for more than a hundred years. The company buys all of its raw materials locally and sells only to dealers in Ohio and Kentucky. The company makes one million trophies per year and sells them for an average price of $10 each. It costs the company $9 million per year to make and sell its trophies, leaving the owner a pre-tax profit of $1 million per year. (See Figure 21-1.)

Figure 21-1
Financials of the Acme Trophy Manufacturing Company

Number of Trophies Sold Per Year	1,000,000
Average Sale Price	$10
Annual Sales	$10,000,000
Cost of Goods	$4,000,000
Cost of Sales	$5,000,000
Pre-tax Profits	$1,000,000

Because the company buys and sells only locally in dollars and has no overseas operations, the company's owners may be under the mistaken impression that the company has no exposure to FX risk. However, they would be wrong.

Consider the following scenario. While the United States company may not be interested in importing or exporting, other companies around the world are interested. Suppose, for example, that there is a Japanese company called the "Yagucki Company" that also makes trophies. It has the financials shown in Figure 21-2.

Figure 21-2
Financials of the Yagucki Company

Number of Trophies Sold Per Year	1,000,000
Average Sale Price	¥1,000
Annual Sales	¥1,000,000,000
Cost of Goods	¥400,000,000
Cost of Sales	¥500,000,000
Pre-tax Profits	¥100,000,000

The Japanese company needs to sell its trophies for ¥1,000 each in order to maintain its profit margin. If the current exchange rate is ¥100/$1, then the Japanese company would have to charge $10 for its trophies. Because this is the same price the Acme Trophy Company is charging for its trophies, the Japanese company would probably find it difficult to compete.

However, if the dollar was to rise sharply against the yen, to the point where the exchange rate became ¥200/$1, then the Japanese company could afford to sell its trophies in the United States for $5 each. The company could charge such a low price, because each dollar buys so many yen—which is both the Japanese company's reference company and the currency in which its expenses are denominated. Because the Japanese company can profitably afford to sell its trophies in the United States at half the price of its United States competitor, the viability of the United States company is threatened by the FX risk.

The changing value of the United States dollar affects almost every United States company to one degree or another, so even United States investors who restrict themselves to buying only United States investments need to be aware of how changing FX rates affect their portfolios. In order to do this, investors should understand some of the reasons FX rates change.

307

.it Cause FX Rates to Change

.ा every economic event has at least some indirect influence
⎦ relative value of different currencies, six major factors cause the
⎦ alue of currencies to either rise or fall relative to each other.

PURCHASING POWER PARITY

Perhaps the most important factor that causes the relative value of two currencies to change over the long term is their "Purchasing Power Parity" (PPP). Martin Navarro first presented this theory back in the 1500s. In an oversimplified form, the theory suggests that the same goods should cost the same amount of money in different countries, allowing for the then-current exchange rate. If this were not true, it would create the possibility of a riskless arbitrage. The resulting arbitrage would cause the value of the currency of the country in which the goods were cheaper to rise relative to the currency of the country in which the goods were more expensive. An example will illustrate.

Suppose that an ounce of silver can be bought or sold for ¥550 in Japan and for $5 in the United States at a time when the exchange was ¥100/$1. In this case, an investor could:

- Buy silver in the United States for $5 per ounce.

- Immediately sell the silver in Japan for ¥550 per ounce.

- Immediately use the yen received from the sale (¥550) to buy dollars at the then-current exchange rate (¥100/$1) for a net of $5.50— or a $.50 per ounce profit. Provided the transactions occurred nearly simultaneously, the transaction would be nearly riskless.

An investor would then repeat this series of transactions. Because the investor:

- Buys the silver in the United States, the price of silver in the United States would rise.

- Sells silver in Japan, the price of silver in Japan would decline.
- Sells yen to buy dollars, the value of the yen would decline against the dollar.

The prices of silver in Japan and the United States, as well as the yen/dollar exchange rate, will change until the transactions no longer generate a risk-free profit. Naturally, this example is an oversimplification, because transaction charges, import duties, shipping costs, and so on, are omitted from the calculation. Although the price differential would strengthen the yen against the dollar, the price differential of other products might result in the weakening of the yen. Whether PPP works to raise or lower the value of the yen relative to the dollar, therefore, depends on the net price difference of the price of all goods and services that are traded between the United States and Japan, always allowing for the then-current exchange rate.

RELATIVE REAL INTEREST RATES

The second factor that affects exchange rates is the size of the differential between the real interest rates available to investors in the respective countries. The "real" interest rate is the nominal interest rate available to an investor in a high-quality short-term investment minus the country's inflation rate. Suppose the real interest rates in Japan and the United States were those shown in Figure 21-3.

Figure 21-3
Nominal Versus Real Inflation Rate

	Hypothetical Nominal Rate	Inflation	Real Rate
United States	8%	3%	5%
Japan	3%	2%	1%

This hypothetical example is for illustrative purposes only and does not represent a specific investment. Individual investor results will vary.

Because the real investment return available in the United States is five times larger than the investment return available in Japan, some percentage of the Japanese investors will want to invest in the United States. Of course, in order to invest in the United States, the Japanese investors first have to sell their yen and buy dollars. Their exchanging of yen for dollars will cause the dollar to rise against the yen. Further, United States investors will have less incentive to invest in Japan and, consequently, will reduce their buying of yen with dollars.

TRADE IMBALANCE

The third factor that affects exchange rates is the size of the trade deficit, if any, between the two countries. Trade deficits affect exchange rates, because they result in an imbalance of currency reserves among trading partners. Consider the following example.

Throughout the 1980s and 90s, Japan consistently ran fairly large trade surpluses with the United States. Consequently, Japanese companies have accumulated a large amount of dollars, while United States companies have not accumulated nearly so much yen. Eventually, the Japanese companies have to convert the dollars they accumulated into yen and the United States companies have to convert the yen they accumulated into dollars. Given the mismatch in the amount of currencies to be exchanged between the two countries, the law of supply and demand will tend to distort the exchange rate. The United States companies are in a strong position to demand an ever-increasing number of dollars in exchange for their limited amount of yen. Thus, the United States trade deficit with Japan causes the yen to strengthen against the dollar. As the yen gets stronger against the dollar, Japan's ability to compete against the United States declines.

POLITICAL STABILITY

In the past, currencies were backed by, and interchangeable with, precious metals. Anyone who held a country's currency could present the currency to the country's central bank (or any major bank) and receive a fixed amount of gold or silver. Over the past 30 years, however, the tremendous increase in the size of the economy created a need for money that far outstripped the ability of the mining industry to produce gold. Therefore, the United States, like all other countries, had little choice other than to "close the gold window." This means that holders of paper dollars can no longer exchange them for gold.

Instead, today "confidence" backs the world's currencies. The only reason anyone is willing to accept paper money in exchange for their goods or labor is that they are confident that they will be able, in turn, to pass the paper on to someone else. Most countries require their citizens to accept their paper money as payment. In the United States, the paper money is printed with a legend that says "legal tender for all debts public and private." As long as people's confidence remains intact, this system works just fine.

However, if a country's government becomes politically unstable due to political gridlock, votes of no confidence, revolution, or civil war, confidence can be lost. People understandably become less willing to accept paper currency in exchange for their goods and services, primarily because they are unsure they will be able to pass the paper money along to someone else. In the late 1990s, the political stability of Indonesia and Malaysia declined and, as a result, the values of their currencies plunged.

GOVERNMENT INTERVENTION

The relative value of a country's currency is of great interest to its government. The relative value of the country's currency affects the wealth of its citizens, the competitiveness of domestically produced goods, the relative cost of the country's labor, and the country's ability to compete. As a result, governments often try to influence the relative value of their currencies. Governments have numerous ways in which they can influence the value of their currencies, including altering its monetary policy, fiscal policy, and by directly intervening in the currency markets.

- The term "monetary policy" refers to a country's decision regarding how much money to print. In the United States, the decision of how much money to print falls primarily on the Federal Reserve Bank (FED). The law of supply and demand applies to money, so if a country prints more money, the value of its currency declines—a process called monetary inflation. If a country prints less money, or more specifically, if the money supply grows at a rate that is lower than the growth rate of the economy, the result is deflation. As the value of a country's currency declines, its people become poorer but its businesses become more competitive globally. Businesses that are more competitive mean more jobs. Policy makers at the FED are always trying to balance the preservation of wealth of the country's citizens with the competitive needs of domestic companies.

- The term "fiscal policy" refers to a country's decision regarding whether to run a budget deficit or a surplus. In the United States, fiscal policy is determined by Congress. A budget deficit will cause the value of the dollar to decline because budget deficits often lead to monetary inflation. A budget surplus will usually cause the value of a dollar to strengthen.

- Most countries attempt to reduce any short-term fluctuations in the value of their currencies by directly intervening in the currency market. If the country's currency is being sold, they will buy; if it is too strong, they will sell. Short-term fluctuations can have negative effects on business and global trade.

ROLE OF SPECULATORS

The most powerful factor on exchange rates over the short term is speculators. Speculators have tremendous amounts of capital that they can use to either buy or sell any currency. Their actions can cause the value of any currency to fluctuate, sometimes sharply. George Soros led the most famous speculative assault against a currency. He led an effort to sell the British pound that ultimately forced the British government to devalue the pound. By selling pounds before the devaluation and buying them after the devaluation, Soros made the investors in his "Quantum Fund" a profit of more than one billion dollars in a single month.

United States Investors and Non-dollar Investments

There are many ways United States investors can use non-dollar investments to improve their portfolios. These include improving the:

- Strategic asset allocation.
- Tactical asset allocation.
- Sector/industry allocation.
- Security selection process.

IMPROVING THE STRATEGIC ASSET ALLOCATION

Adding non-dollar investments to a portfolio composed exclusively of United States securities improves the portfolio by decreasing the risk-to-reward ratio. The prices of United States securities and non-dollar securities often move in opposite directions. Therefore, they somewhat offset each other's volatility. Because the risk of the dollar and non-dollar securities partially offset each other, the overall volatility of a portfolio that is the combination of the two types of securities is lower than the risk of each type of security alone. Combining different asset classes in order to improve a portfolio is referred to as strategic asset allocation. It is often the first step in creating well-designed portfolios. (See Figure 21-4.)

Figure 21-4
Well-designed Portfolio

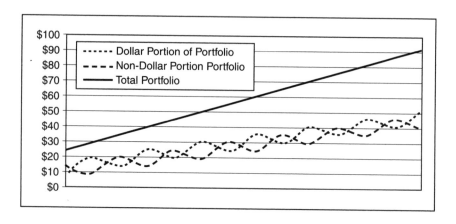

IMPROVING THE TACTICAL ASSET ALLOCATION

Many investors shift money back and forth between dollar and non-dollar investments, based upon whether they expect dollar or non-dollar investments to outperform over the short term. If investors expect the dollar to strengthen, they will shift some money out of non-dollar investments and into dollar investments. In the jargon of the trade, they will "underweight" non-dollar investments and overweight dollar investments. If the dollar is expected to decline, investors will overweight non-dollar assets.

IMPROVING THE SECTORS/INDUSTRIES

Many investors also shift money into and out of different market sectors or industries depending upon their outlook for the dollar. For example, the United States agricultural industry is heavily dependent upon exports. As the dollar rises, the entire industry suffers. Likewise, the consumer disposable sector of the market tends to do poorly when the dollar rises, since imports become cheap.

IMPROVING STOCK SELECTION

Many United States companies are either net importers, net exporters, have overseas operations, or have overseas competitors. Examining how changes in the value of the dollar might affect a company's earnings is a part of the fundamental analysis process. For example, the price "in dollars" of a non-dollar stock is equal to:

$$Price = Earnings \times Multiple \times Exchange\ Rate$$

Investors who buy non-dollar stocks always have to be concerned that the currency in which their non-dollar investments are denominated will get weaker relative to the United States dollar. If the currency does weaken, when it is converted back into dollars, the currency will buy fewer dollars. Consider the following illustrative example:

While looking for attractive investment opportunities, a United States investor discovers a British company currently earning £1 per share per year that is trading at £15, or 15 times earnings. After doing some analysis, the investor believes that over the next year, the earnings will increase to £1.20 and that the multiple will expand to 17 times earnings. This would make the projected price in pounds in one year equal to:

$$Price\ in\ One\ Year = £1.20 \times 17 = £20.40$$

This would result in an annualized return, in pounds, of:

$$(£20.40 - £15) / £15 = 36\%$$

Of course, in order to determine the return in dollar terms, a United States investor also has to take the change in the FX rate over the investment period into account. Suppose when the investment is made, the $/£ exchange rate is 2.0000. In the standard jargon of the industry, the exchange rate would be expressed as:

$$USD/GBP = 2.0000$$

This expression is read as "the number of dollars that can be purchased for a pound is 2.0000." Conversely, the reciprocal expression is:

$$GBP/USD = .5000$$

This is read as "the number of pounds that can be purchased for a dollar is .5000."

Given this exchange rate, 1,000 shares of the British stock would initially cost the United States investor $30,000. The investor can exchange $30,000 for £15,000. The £15,000 can be used to buy 1,000 shares of the British stock. However, if over the next year the pound weakens against the dollar so that in one year the $/£ exchange rate is 1.6000, the return in dollar terms would be:

Price = Earnings × Multiple × Exchange Rate
Initial Price = £1.0000 × 15.00 × 2.0000 = $30.00
Final Price = £1.2000 × 17.00 × 1.6000 = $32.64
Therefore, the dollar return is: ($32.64 − $30.00) / $30.00 = 8.80%

Thus, the decline in the value of the dollar dropped the annualized return from 36% to 8.80%, seriously reducing the attractiveness of the investment.

Ideally, a United States investor wants to invest in non-dollar instruments denominated in currencies that will strengthen against the United States dollar. Consider another example. Suppose the current yen/dollar exchange rate is ¥/$ = 120, meaning that $1 buys ¥120. Conversely, one yen buys .008333 dollars. A United States investor finds a Japanese stock he believes to be attractive. The stock is currently earning ¥100 per share and is selling at 14.4 times earnings. The United States investor buys the stock for:

Price per share ($) = ¥100 × 14.4 × .00833333 = $12.00

If, one year later, the earnings are ¥115, the multiple is 18.55, and the exchange rate is $/¥ = .01000000, the stock's value in dollars would be:

Price per share ($) = ¥115 × 18.55 × .01000000 = $21.33

In this example, the return in dollars would be:

($21.33 − $12.00) / 12.00 = 77.77%

In this example, the yen got stronger, increasing the return in dollar terms. Thus, with every non-dollar investment, the currency risk is a two-edged sword and needs to be taken into account when the investment's potential is being assessed.

Influence of the Euro

In May 1998, eleven European countries agreed to adopt a single European currency called the Euro. On January 1, 1999, the exchange rate at which each of these eleven countries' currencies would be converted in Euros was fixed. After a transition period, the various country's individual currencies will be phased out completely. By July 1, 2002, there will be no more French francs, German marks, Dutch guilders, and so on, and all financial transactions in these nations will be done in the Euro. (See Figure 21-5.)

Figure 21-5
Fixed FX Rates to Euro

Euro Countries and Exchange Rate			
Austria	13.7603	Luxembourg	40.3399
Belgium	40.3399	Netherlands	2.20371
Finland	5.94573	Portugal	200.482
France	6.55957	Spain	166.386
Germany	1.95583	Denmark	TBA
Ireland	.787564	Greece	TBA
Italy	1936.27	England	TBA

These countries agreed to adopt a single European currency in order to accomplish several objectives:

- Create one large market instead of many small markets. In this respect, Europe wanted to create a common market that mirrors the way goods flow freely from state to state in the United States.

- Lower the cost of living. The inefficiencies introduced by the trade barriers, currency conversions, multiple labeling requirements, and import restrictions all serve to raise the price of goods and services for European consumers.

- Lower regulation in order to make European industry more competitive. By lowering their costs of production and distribution, European companies hope that their goods become more competitive not only domestically, but also globally.

- Improve political climate. People who share a common market and a common currency are less likely to go to war with each other—at least according to the politicians.

As of this writing, Britain, Scandinavia, and Switzerland were considering adopting the Euro, although local political resistance is still high. The advent of the Euro will result in dramatic change across Europe, and change always creates opportunities for investors. Specifically, the creation of the Euro is expected to generate a wave of mergers and acquisitions throughout Europe.

Alternative Ways of Investing in Non-dollar Equities

United States investors have several alternative ways to invest in non-dollar equities other than simply investing directly in the non-dollar equity.

AMERICAN DEPOSITORY RECEIPTS

While many United States investors find investing in non-dollar stocks to be attractive, they are reluctant to buy individual shares in non-dollar markets for three reasons.

1. Buying and selling non-dollar stocks in some markets creates some operational problems. Settling the trade and arranging for the delivery of the stock certificate can be an expensive process. While in the United States this process is highly efficient and automated, in some emerging markets, this process is slow, paper intensive, and prone to error.

2. Many United States citizens are, understandably, uncomfortable having their money outside of the legal jurisdiction of the United States. Despite all its faults, the United States legal system is very consumer friendly and reasonably quick at resolving problems, unlike the systems in many other parts of the world.

3. Direct investment in overseas securities can create tax problems.

One solution to these problems is an American Depository Receipt (ADR). An ADR is a security that represents ownership of a foreign security held in trust within the legal jurisdiction of the United States, usually at a United States trust company. For example, a United States bank might buy 1,000,000 shares of a non-dollar stock, put the stock into a trust account, and issue 500,000 ADRs against the stock in the trust account. Each ADR represents ownership of two of the underlying shares. As the price of the non-dollar shares rises and falls in dollar terms, so will the price of the ADR. Owners of ADRs usually can exchange them for the underlying shares in order to ensure that the prices of the ADRs and the underlying shares remain equal.

Equity-linked Notes

Equity-linked notes are debt instruments that do not have a traditional coupon. Instead of paying a stated return, their return is tied to the return of a specific equity market. A specific note might pay a return equal to 70 percent of the return of the British Equity Market as measured by the Financial Times-Stock Exchange Index or FT-SE (pronounced "foot-see") or some other widely known non-dollar market index. (See Figure 21-6.)

Figure 21-6
Composition of Company Dollar Index

Country	Index	Composition
Britain	FT-SE 100	Index of the stocks of the 100 largest companies listed on the London Exchange
Germany	DAX-30	Index of the stocks of the 30 largest companies listed on the German Exchange
Japan	Nikkei-225	Index of the stocks of the 225 largest companies listed on the Tokyo Exchange

The way the "coupon" is defined varies widely among different issues of index-linked notes. A typical deal structure would pay the note buyer a return equal to 70 to 80 percent of however much the underlying index appreciates. Thus, if the index appreciated 10 percent over a year, the investor would receive a payment equal to 7 or 8 percent of the note's face value. If the index declines, the investor typically receives no return. Note that for some index-linked notes, the coupon payment is made in a non-dollar currency, while in others, the return is first converted into dollars before it is paid out.

World Equity Benchmark Securities

One of the more popular ways for United States investors to invest overseas is via World Equity Benchmark Securities (WEBS™). WEBS™ are United States securities that trade on the American Stock

Exchange. Each WEB™ mirrors the performance of a different country's stock market. Like ADRs, the sponsor actually buys a widely diversified portfolio of securities from the country and holds them in trust. The securities in the trust serve as security for the WEBS™. These trusts are passive in that the manager simply tries to build a portfolio that mirrors the country's performance, not exceeds it.

Investors can buy and sell WEBS™ from each other on the American Exchange, or if the supply and demand get significantly out of alignment, the sponsor can buy more securities for the trust or sell securities from the trust. Dividends and capital gains are paid in dollars. WEBS™ are currently available for the countries listed in Figure 21-7. The figure also illustrates the 10-year average return for the WEBS™.

Figure 21-7
10-year Return for WEBS™

Country	Return	Country	Return
Belgium	13.31%	Australia	8.62%
Italy	7.78%	Austria	4.52%
Spain	12.97%	Canada	7.44%
France	13.38%	Japan	−2.38%
Germany	13.84%	United Kingdom	15.04%
Switzerland	17.70%	Netherlands	17.73%
Hong Kong	20.93%	Sweden	14.83%

Many investors use WEBS™ to execute tactical asset allocation work and as a low-cost passive investment alternative. Additional information about WEBS™ can be found at:

http://websontheweb.com

Mutual Funds

Just as there are thousands of mutual funds that invest in United States securities, there are also thousands of funds that invest in non-United States securities. Investors considering non-dollar equity funds have two special issues to consider, in addition to all of the issues discussed in Chapter 20.

1. Some non-dollar funds are managed to maximize their return in United States dollars, while others are managed to maximize their return in another currency. Whatever currency the fund manager is using to measure return is referred to as the "reference currency." Consider two managers who manage two global non-dollar funds. Manager A's reference currency is the pound and Manager B's reference currency is the United States dollar. Both managers think that a particular British stock will rise and that the United States dollar will strengthen against the British pound. Given this, Manager A would buy the stock, while Manager B would seek opportunities in other countries.

2. Some non-dollar funds try to hedge the currency risk, while others make no effort to hedge the FX risk. Funds that hedge the FX have less risk and less potential reward.

Investing in Non-dollar Fixed Income

In addition to investing in non-dollar stocks, many United States investors also invest in non-dollar fixed income. While many non-United States companies issue debt, most United States investors prefer to stick with the debt issued by the governments of other countries. Debt issued by national governments is referred to as "Sovereign Debt," because the nations that issue it have sovereign powers. Without exception, these debt instruments are backed by the full faith and credit of the countries that issue them.

British bonds are referred as "gilts," a name stemming back to the time when the British Empire was vast and the British bonds were considered to be gilt edged—or the world's safest investment. Bonds issued by the German government are referred to as "bunds," while bonds issued by the Japanese government are referred to as "JGBs" (pronounced "jay-gee-bees").

ABOUT THE AUTHOR

Stuart R. Veale is Senior Vice President, Portfolio Strategy and Design, for the National Sales Department of Prudential Securities, Inc. He is responsible for providing portfolio design and strategy support to the firm's financial advisors.

Mr. Veale has published numerous books on investment strategy, tactics, and products, including, *The Handbook of the US Capital Markets, The Essential Guide to Asset Allocation, Tapping the Small Business Market, The Essential Guide to Investment Math, The Essential Guide to Mortgage Backed Securities*, and *The Corporate Officers Guide to Investing Surplus Cash*. He has also written numerous articles on investment-related topics for *Medical Economics, Cashflow Magazine* and *Registered Representative*. Mr. Veale is currently writing *The Prudential Securities Guide to Portfolio Management*.

Prior to joining Prudential, Mr. Veale held the positions of Senior Vice President, Advanced Broker Development, at PaineWebber, Inc.; Founder and President of the International Financial Training & Technology, Inc.; President of the Financial Services Institute; and Vice President of Marketing/Training for the New York Institute of Finance.

INDEX